BED & BREAKFAST
HOMES
BEST
OF THE
WEST COAST

9th Edition

by

George Winsley
Diane Knight
Jane McAllister

KNIGHTIME PUBLICATIONS

Copyright © 1981, 1982, 1984, 1986, 1988, 1990, 1992, 1994 by Diane Knight

Copyright © 1996 by George Winsley

Knighttime Publications
PO Box 128
Jacksonville, OR 97530

All rights reserved. No part of this publication may be reproduced, stored in a retrieval system, or transmitted, in any form or by any means, electronic, mechanical, photocopying, recording or otherwise, without the prior written permission of the publisher.

Edited by Stephanie Keenan
Page graphics and layout by Barbara Whalen & others
Cover design by Alicia Griffith, Griffith Graphics
Front cover photo Copyright © by Don Best/Best Impressions Picture Co., Rockaway Beach, OR
Back cover photo by George Winsley
Maps by Eureka Cartography, Berkeley, California
Desktop publishing by George Winsley
Printed and bound in the USA by Griffin Printing, Sacramento, California

Distributed in the USA by Publishers Group West
4065 Hollis Street, Emeryville, CA 94608

Distributed in Canada by Whitecap Books Ltd.,
351 Lynn Avenue, North Vancouver, British Columbia V7J 2C4

ISBN 0-942902-10-2

ISSN 1086-9964

CONTENTS

INTRODUCTION iv

CHANGES IN THE 9th EDITION vi

NOTES FROM THE AUTHOR vii

ABOUT DINING HIGHLIGHTS ix

ABOUT B&B IN PRIVATE HOMES x

HOW TO USE THIS DIRECTORY xii

HOW TO ARRANGE A B&B VISIT xiv

B&B LISTINGS BY STATE AND PROVINCE

CALIFORNIA
Northern California Map 16
Southern California Map 17
Bed & Breakfast Listings 18
Dining Highlights 78

OREGON
Oregon Map 96
Bed & Breakfast Listings 97
Dining Highlights 130

WASHINGTON
Washington Map 138
Bed & Breakfast Listings 139
Dining Highlights 168

BRITISH COLUMBIA
British Columbia Map 174
About British Columbia 175
Bed & Breakfast Listings 179
Dining Highlights 243

INDEX OF CITIES AND TOWNS 249

INDEX OF B&Bs BY NAME 251

Forms - Follow the index
B&B Listing Invitation Form
Travelers Report Forms
Order Form for additional books

INTRODUCTION

This book is the 9th in a series of B&B guidebooks published since 1981 by Diane Knight. Over the years, the range of listings has expanded from a directory of mostly California B&Bs to a well balanced guide to B&Bs from San Diego to the inland Rocky Mountain area of British Columbia. The reader can use this guidebook to plan an extended vacation through the West Coast states and province of British Columbia, all the while meeting local folks by staying in private homes that offer B&B accommodations. These homes are located in urban cities, suburbs, small towns, rural countryside, and spectacular resort areas. Their styles range from contemporary structures in grand settings to suburban mansions, farms, historic Victorian homes, private romantic cottages, boats, beach and mountain cottages, apartments, and a few inns.

Briefly, the book is organized by state: California, Oregon, Washington, and British Columbia are independent sections, each is introduced by a map. The maps locate and identify the cities and towns that have listed B&Bs. These selected towns are listed alphabetically within each state section. B&Bs are listed alphabetically within each town. Restaurant suggestions are listed by city in a separate Dining Highlights section that follows the B&B descriptions for the state.

There is always controversy over the issue of guidebook authors charging B&B owners to be listed. Knighttime Publications *does* charge a listing fee of two times the average double rate of the B&B. In our era of consumerism this may seem to be a questionable policy, but we always keep in mind that we owe allegiance and must be fair to the readers who use this book to plan their B&B vacations.

Every effort is made to include only those B&Bs that meet our criteria of cleanliness, comfort, hospitality, and value. This book is one of the very few where the author of the B&B description has personally visited the B&B, describing it from firsthand experience. The listing fee is accepted only *after* the B&B is visited and approved. Any B&B judged unsatisfactory in an above-mentioned area is not included. Not every visited B&B is listed. We do not list any B&B that we would not personally be pleased to stay in.

In addition to the expense of visiting every new B&B and occasionally revisiting old ones, there are substantial expenses to publish *BED & BREAKFAST HOMES - BEST OF THE WEST COAST*, and given the discount policies and distribution expenses of the book business, it would not be possible to produce the book without the income derived from the listing fees.

B&B guests, be assured that you are our foremost concern. It is the publisher's goal to keep the integrity of this book at the highest level so that you will continue to buy and use it, and so we can continue to do the work we love.

B&B hosts have agreed to honor published rates for our readers at least until the end of 1996. For these rates to be honored, be sure to tell the host you found their B&B in this current 9th edition. Some hosts offer a special discount to readers, as noted; you must have a copy of this edition to obtain the reader discounts.

Feedback regarding your experiences while using this book is strongly encouraged. Comments and suggestions should be addressed to: Knighttime Publications, PO Box 128, Jacksonville, OR 97530. Forms for comments are located in the back of the book.

The information contained in these listings has been prepared with great care, but Knighttime Publications does not guarantee it is complete or in all cases correct. It is the user's responsibility to verify information when making arrangements. Knighttime Publications may not be held liable for any damages or inconvenience suffered as a result of relying on, or using, the information provided herein nor for the actions or negligence of the host and/or staff of the accommodations or restaurants listed herein.

CHANGES IN THE 9th EDITION

This 9th edition brings several changes to the publication of this book. Diane Knight, publisher of the book since 1981, sold Knighttime Publications to George Winsley in 1994. George, co-owner of *Reames House 1868* in Jacksonville, Oregon, thoroughly subscribes to the philosophy adopted by Diane when she first created the book. That philosophy: The book is a means of publicizing accommodations in B&B **HOMES** along the West Coast. Every home listed will be personally visited; every description will be personally written (a review and minor editing by the host(s) is allowed); only facilities we would personally be pleased to stay in will be listed. With few exceptions, the owner of the home will be the host during your stay. A few listed homes have evolved into more commercial inn-type accommodations over the years they have been listed. Such inns are still listed due to their long connection with this book and their continued emphasis on reasonably priced, homey accommodations and personal service.

The new ownership brings other changes, one being the new title: Formerly *BED AND BREAKFAST HOMES DIRECTORY - WEST COAST*, we think our new title, *BED & BREAKFAST HOMES - BEST OF THE WEST COAST*, better describes the homes we list in this edition. We believe these homes are "The Best" from our personal visits and personal contact with the host-owners. You may find fancier homes, more elaborate structures and amenities, but you won't find more friendliness, hospitality, or value than is offered by the homes listed and described in this book. Oh, if you do find other "best homes," please let us know so they can be contacted for possible inclusion in our next book.

George Winsley visited and wrote about the newly listed homes in California, Oregon, and Washington. Jane McAllister, owner of *The Carriage Stop* in Victoria, British Columbia, visited and wrote about the new homes listed in British Columbia and also authored the introductory section on traveling in BC. Descriptions written by Diane Knight for earlier editions are used to describe homes that have maintained their prior listings. Host names have been added to each listing as a way to further personalize the listing and to recognize the people who work so hard to create and maintain the ambiance of their B&B home. Lastly, hosts have been encouraged to suggest little-known points of interest and activities in the vicinity of their home. You will find many such "secrets" scattered throughout the book. Follow up on them to enjoy some special activities and events and locate great places to visit during your travels.

NOTES FROM THE AUTHOR

My experiences visiting and writing about the new B&Bs listed in this book have been wonderful. Hosts have been warm, pleasant, and accommodating. But beyond that, I have had an opportunity to visit and sample the wide range of accommodations provided under the generic term "Bed and Breakfast" The term was used to describe home-stay accommodations in Britain and Europe for many years. In the 1970s and early 1980s, these home-style accommodations became more and more prevalent in the United States and finally developed into an industry of their own in the 90s. Some motels now call themselves "Bed and Breakfasts" assuming they can use the term because they serve coffee and store-bought pastries wrapped in sanitary cellophane for early-morning risers.

But the B&Bs listed in this book are much more. They give you a chance to meet their hosts on their home turf. They give you a chance to meet other travelers in a casual, friendly atmosphere, and exchange ideas on a variety of subjects in a manner rarely available in our culture. Where else can you say, "Hi, I'm George, it's nice to meet you. Where did you drive in from today? Where are you going tomorrow?" And then start on into talk other interests as the conversation develops; perhaps other folks come to the table, join in, and you discover mutual interests. As a B&B owner and host, the most enjoyable part of hosting is our family-style breakfast service, watching and hearing these breakfast conversations develop and grow to cover a wide range of subjects and concerns explored in open and enjoyable information exchanges.

Television doesn't encourage conversation. The rapid pace of our hurried lives doesn't encourage conversation. The isolation of the private automobile doesn't encourage conversation nor personal contact. Nor do work situations encourage conversation other than about the latest layoff or crisis in the workplace. Perhaps such conversations can be carried on over computer e:mail and data service forums, but it's just letters and pictures on a screen, not the person-to-person give and take that can happen at the breakfast table or over cheese, wine, tea, and cookies at a late afternoon gathering of guests.

I've had people say: "My husband likes his privacy," or, "I'm not a morning person." Well, don't give up on B&B accommodations. With the wide range of alternative B&B accommodations available today, everyone can find something to suit them. There are, of course, the "normal" guest rooms with either ensuite bath or bath across the hall. But there are also studio apartment units, separate cottages, basement suites, 3rd floor suites with magnificent views, middle-class homes, mansions, and oceanfront villas you'd die for—homes, hideaways and special places you wouldn't see, much less visit, any other way! And these are available to you at really modest rates from folks who enjoy meeting you, and acquainting you with the special places they have discovered near their B&Bs.

Toward this end of finding your "special place," consider carefully the difference between B&Bs where all guests use the main entrance and B&Bs with separate entrances. The B&B where everyone comes in through the front door and dines together at breakfast is going to be a B&B where isolation takes second seat to community. The B&B unit with a separate entrance allows you to come and go without seeing, or much less exchanging hellos, with other guests. You might see your host when you check in and out. But the host will be close in the event you want help or ideas on sights to see and places to visit. It's a totally different feel than you get sharing a home with your hosts and other guests and each has its place. At different times, each may appeal to you on a trip. But it is the most defining part of the B&B experience.

Wherever you go, go with a sense of adventure, an open mind, and anticipation of the new and exciting experiences you will surely encounter. When you return, may you enjoy the memories for years to come.

George Winsley

ABOUT DINING HIGHLIGHTS

Continued in this edition is a listing of recommended restaurants for each state and province covered. This is not intended to be a comprehensive listing of good restaurants, nor does it contain extensive information about each listing. It merely offers some assistance in finding suitable places for lunch or dinner as you travel through unfamiliar territory. Call or drop by the establishment you're considering to find out more about it.

Restaurants have been selected both from the authors' own dining experiences and from suggestions made by hosts. Part of the motivation in compiling the listings is the marvelous convenience of having the names, addresses, and phone numbers of an excellent assortment of wonderful restaurants spanning the U.S. and Canadian west coasts. When we update each listing, hosts are asked to identify restaurants in their town they can recommend without hesitation. Restaurants range from a simple taco stand in Santa Barbara to a world-class restaurant in Sooke, B.C., and prices vary accordingly. Restaurants are not charged for their listing.

Criteria for selection are good-quality ingredients, careful preparation, a pleasant atmosphere, and superior value. The majority of restaurants included are gems—really wonderful little places that tourists would be unlikely to discover on their own. While most offer good food at reasonable prices, some "splurge" restaurants are included—and judged to be well worth the cost.

Although most of the restaurants have proven track records, no guarantees are possible. Your feedback on these recommendations is encouraged.

We emphasize that the number of restaurants listed for any given town is simply a product of information available to us.

ABOUT B&B IN PRIVATE HOMES

Most B&Bs in this directory are strictly private homes, not commercial establishments. While some small, owner-occupied inns are also included, they are still the *homes* of the people who operate them. As a guest, remember to act with the same courtesy and consideration that you would expect of a guest in your own home.

The trend in B&B hosting today is to be more "professional." However many home B&B hosts don't consider themselves innkeepers—they do not consider sharing their home a business—and therein lies some of the appeal: being treated "like family." There may be times when hosts can't accommodate you because they're on vacation, or because Great Aunt Martha from Omaha will be using the guest room.

In a few cases, daily maid service may not be provided. Room service is usually not provided, but snacks and beverages may be served or be available for you to help yourself. This varies a great deal from one B&B to the next. But generally, the smaller and less expensive accommodations do not offer such services. However, it is at this type of B&B that you are likely to encounter the spontaneous personal favor at just the right moment.

A number of B&B hosts accept only cash or traveler's checks in payment for accommodations. But more and more hosts will take credit cards. Credit card information is now included in the second paragraph of each description. Be sure to verify which forms of payment will be accepted *before* your visit.

When reserving accommodations in B&B homes, it is very important to advise your host about your expected time of arrival. There is always some flexibility, but arrival time should be discussed. If it appears that you will be later than planned, it is only considerate (and most appreciated) that you call and let your host know.

Room rates include at least a Continental breakfast. In many cases, the rate includes a full breakfast. In a few situations, there may be an extra charge (as noted) for a full breakfast. If anything more than a Continental breakfast is served, it is so stated in the listing.

Many hosts look forward to having guests join them for a family-style breakfast. In some cases—if the guest unit is totally separate and has cooking facilities—the host will simply leave the ingredients for breakfast so that you may prepare it at your leisure. Some hosts will be glad to serve you breakfast in your room, or even in bed. Morning may find you at a table of your own, or perhaps you'll be served at a large table with other B&B guests. As in many aspects of B&B travel, the accent is on *variety*.

And what about tipping? As noted above, most hosts do not consider themselves innkeepers and are in the business because they enjoy sharing their home and meeting people. The relationship of host and guest is more personal than most other service relationships. (What other service providers invite you into their home?) On the other hand, being "up" and ensuring that their home is ready for you is hard work. Like the rest of us, hosts really do appreciate it when the quality of their service is recognized and personally rewarded. So if you feel that you've been well provided for during your stay, a cash gratuity is a nice way to say "Thanks." Required? No. Appreciated? You better believe it!

HOW TO USE THIS DIRECTORY

For each listing:

The first line is the name of the B&B and the phone number to call for reservations.

The second line is the host name and an alternative phone number or FAX number.

The third line provides a mailing address for the B&B to use if you're writing for reservations or sending a deposit. Sometimes an e:mail address will be listed for an alternate contact address.

The fourth line gives the general location of the B&B. You should get specific directions to the home from your host.

Next, you'll find a descriptive paragraph about the B&B. It often tells something about the unique qualities of the home itself, the setting, the host, and points of interest in the area.

The second paragraph indicates whether there are indoor pets and gives host preferences and policies, such as "no smoking" or "children welcome." They are given only if the host has indicated a specific policy on the subject. The paragraph also lists facilities or features available to guests, such as "laundry" or "hot tub".

Available transportation is sometimes indicated, as well as the hosts willingness to pick up guests at a nearby airport (largely for the benefit of private pilots).

The following code refers to the headings at the end of each description:

ROOM — Refers to a guest unit. The unit may be a room in the B&B home, an adjoining apartment, or a separate cottage near the home. The units are identified by letters (A, B,), numbers (1, 2,), or names. Each designates one guest unit, whether it has one, two, or more rooms.

BED — The number and size of the beds in each guest unit. **T** = twin, **D** = double, **Q** = queen, **K** = king

BATH — **Shd** means you'll share a bath with the host or other guests, if present. (You may have it all to yourself, especially midweek or off-season.) **Pvt** means the bath goes with the guest unit and is shared by no one else. The bath may be across the hall, but it is all yours.

ENTRANCE	**Main** indicates you'll use the main entrance of the home. **Sep** means there is a separate entrance for guests.
FLOOR	The floor of each guest unit is indicated by a number. **LL** means lower level, usually with steps down. **1G** means a ground level room, with no steps.
DAILY RATES	**S** refers to a single (one person); **D** refers to a double (two persons); **EP** refers to the rate charged for an extra person (above two) traveling with your party (generally, when there is an extra bed in the guest unit). Most of the rates quoted have local tax added. When this is the case, a plus sign + is used by the **EP** rate. Some stated rates **include** the tax.

Example:

ROOM	BED	BATH	ENTRANCE	FLOOR	DAILY RATES		
					S	D	EP+
A	1K	Pvt	Main	2	$70	$80	$10

Room (or unit) A has one king-sized bed, a private bath, uses the main entrance to the home and is on the second floor. One person will pay $70; two persons will pay $80; an extra person will pay $10. A local tax will be added.

A NOTE FOR US TRAVELERS IN CANADA: Some Canadian B&Bs must charge a Goods and Services Tax (**G.S.T.**), which is fully refundable to travelers upon leaving Canada. Hosts will assist with procedure. Some must charge a municipality tourist tax which is not refundable.

Abbreviations used:

AC	=	Air Conditioning
TV	=	Television
VCR	=	Video Cassette Recorder
AMEX	=	American Express Card
DS	=	Discover Card
MC	=	Master Card
V	=	VISA Card

HOW TO ARRANGE A B&B VISIT

1. Try to plan your visit as far ahead as possible. This helps to ensure you'll get to stay at the B&B of your choice, in the room of your choice. Call or write for brochures from each B&B you are considering. When your visit will be at peak season or during special events, be sure to write for information well in advance. Often, by the time you receive all the brochures, many B&Bs will already be booked.

2. Call your host for reservations between 10 a.m. and 9 p.m. (after breakfast activity). Be sure to allow for the time difference if you're not on Pacific Time.

3. Carefully check details about the B&B you're considering before calling or writing. Confirm with your host anything that's not clear to you. Ask pertinent questions! Your host will be glad to give information to avoid later misunderstandings. The person on the phone will probably be the person hosting you during your stay and will want to have a pleasant and enjoyable visit with you, just as you want a relaxing and comfortable stay at the B&B.

4. One the most important questions to ask your B&B host is the details of their **Cancellation Policy**. Notification requirements for cancellation and refunds vary widely, and you must comply with terms in order not to lose your deposit or have your credit card charged.

5. Check what form of payment your host will accept. Ask if a deposit is required, and when it must be paid.

6. Agree on time of arrival.

7. Immediately notify your host of any change in plans!

Hosts listed in *BED & BREAKFAST HOMES* have agreed to honor rates stated in the directory until the end of 1996.

The information contained in these listings has been prepared with great care, but Knighttime Publications does not guarantee that it is complete or in all cases correct. It is the user's responsibility to verify important information when making arrangements. Knighttime Publications may not be held liable for any damages or inconvenience suffered as a result of relying on, or using, the information provided herein nor for the actions or negligence of the host and/or staff of the accommodations or restaurants listed herein.

CALIFORNIA

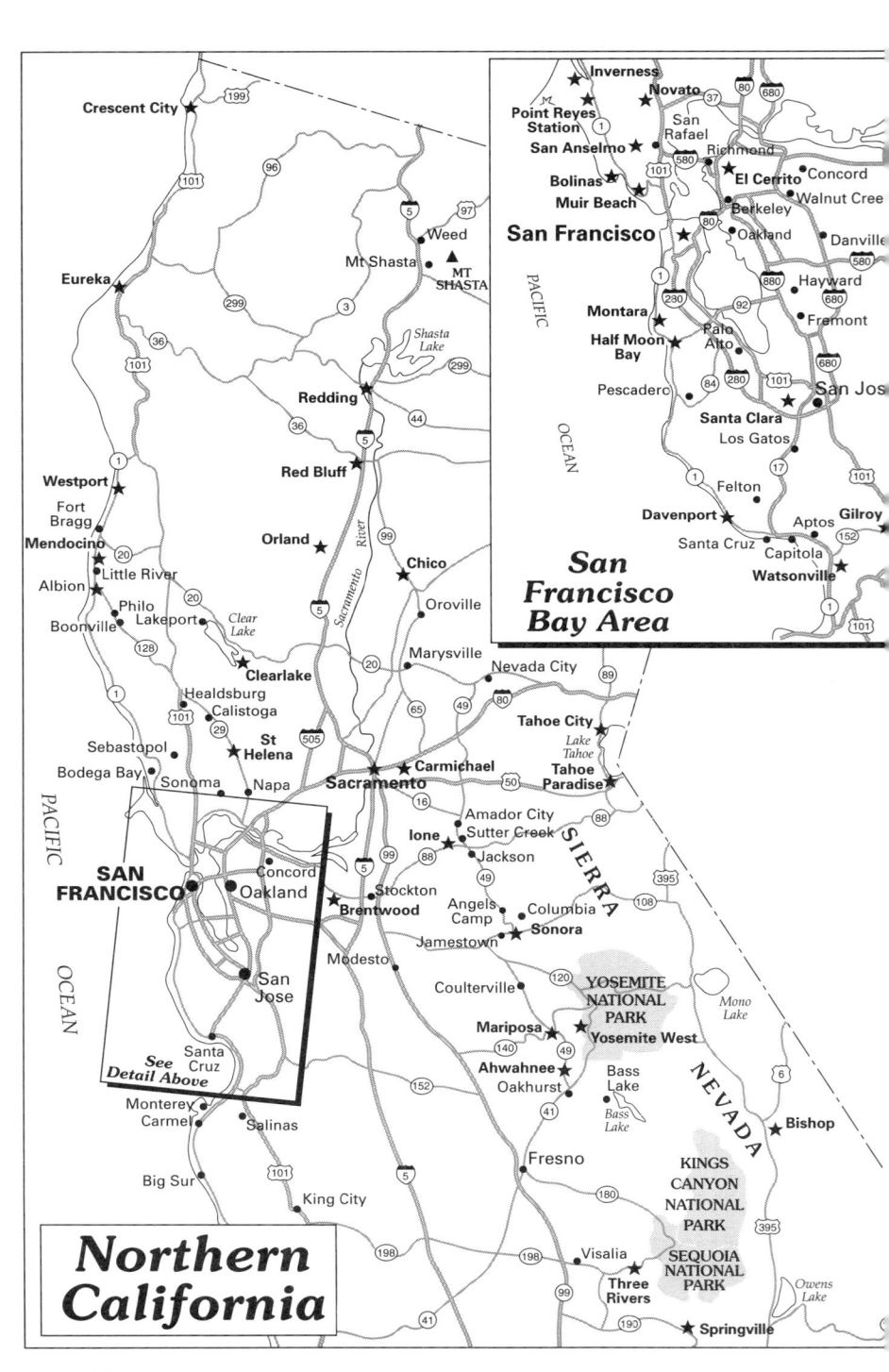

Northern California

San Francisco Bay Area

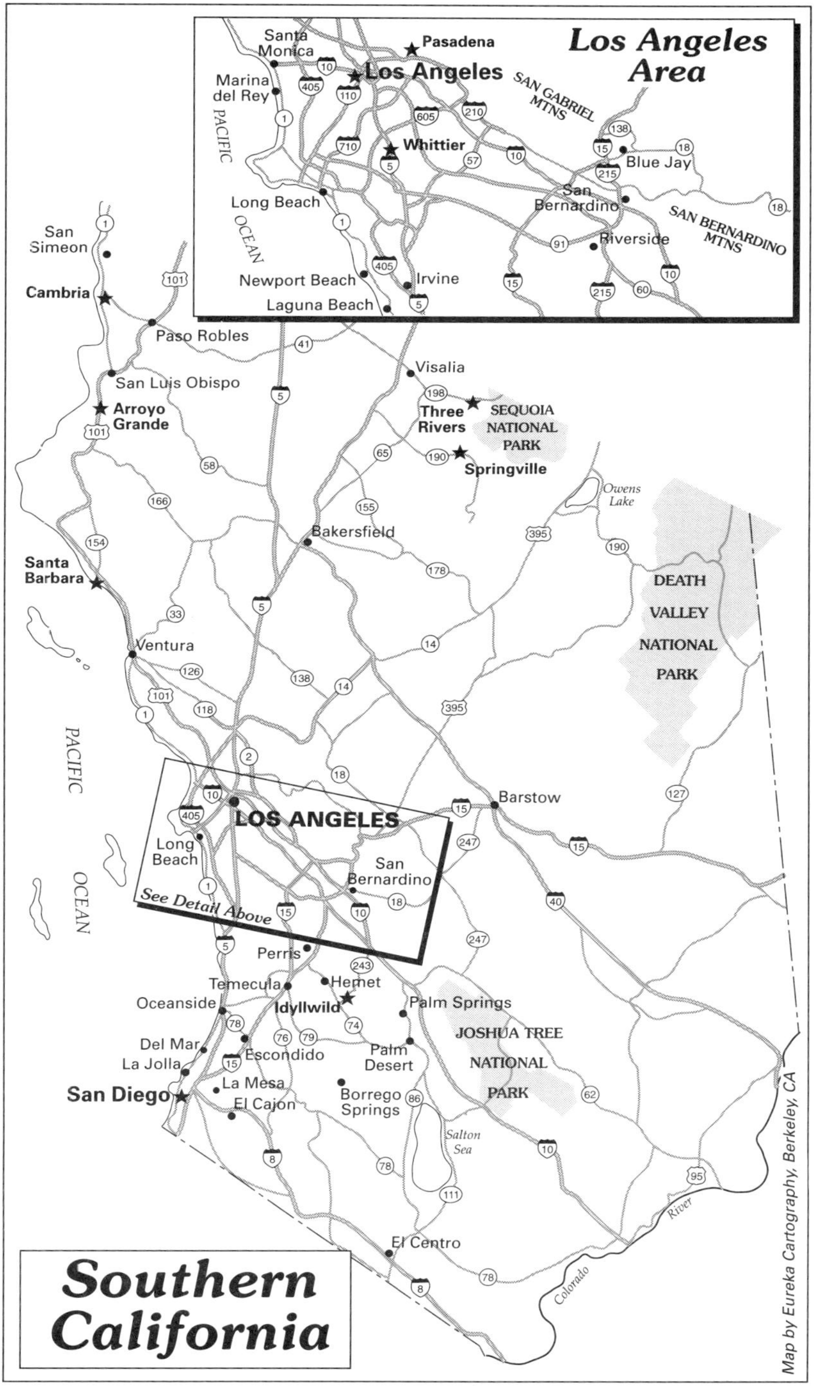
Los Angeles Area
Santa Monica
Pasadena
Los Angeles
Marina del Rey
SAN GABRIEL MTNS
PACIFIC
OCEAN
Whittier
Blue Jay
Long Beach
San Bernardino
Riverside
SAN BERNARDINO MTNS
Newport Beach
Irvine
Laguna Beach
San Simeon
Cambria
Paso Robles
San Luis Obispo
Arroyo Grande
Visalia
Three Rivers
SEQUOIA NATIONAL PARK
Springville
Owens Lake
Bakersfield
Santa Barbara
DEATH VALLEY NATIONAL PARK
Ventura
LOS ANGELES
Barstow
Long Beach
San Bernardino
See Detail Above
Perris
Hemet
Temecula
Oceanside
Idyllwild
Palm Springs
JOSHUA TREE NATIONAL PARK
Del Mar
Escondido
Palm Desert
La Jolla
La Mesa
San Diego
El Cajon
Borrego Springs
Salton Sea
El Centro
Colorado
River
Southern California
Map by Eureka Cartography, Berkeley, CA

AHWAHNEE

Silver Spur Bed & Breakfast (209) 683-2896
Hosts: Patty and Bryan Hays
44625 Silver Spur Trail, Ahwahnee, CA 93601
On Highway 49, 8 miles north of Oakhurst or 18 miles south of Mariposa.

You can admire Patty and Bryan's impressive log home with high peaked ceilings and massive beams while taking your morning meal on the deck above the Oakhurst Valley. Patty generally uses eggs from her own chickens in her breakfast breads and pastries. The continental breakfast includes hot drinks and a luscious plate of fresh fruit. Both guest rooms are Western-themed: *Cowboy* highlights the cowboy's role in the West, while *Indian's* borders use Native American designs. Both showcase unique local barbed-wire art (and it's for sale, too). The quiet rooms front a sheltered and fenced yard with chairs and picnic tables—great for evening barbecues. Patty and Bryan have many activities to suggest to their guests including winter snow skiing at Yosemite, or summer water skiing at Bass Lake. Also good golfing can be found nearby at several golf courses in Ahwahnee and Oakhurst. Ahwahnee is just south of the Wawona entrance to Yosemite National Park and on California's scenic historic Gold Chain Route, State Highway 49. So linger awhile and enjoy the area, the scenery, the restaurants, and the many activities found here.

Dog, cat and chickens; pets with prior arrangement; smoking outside only; children welcome; extended continental breakfast; AC; off street parking; reduced off-season and midweek rates; credit cards (MC,V,DS).

ROOM	BED	BATH	ENTRANCE	FLOOR	DAILY RATES S	D	EP
Cowboy Room	1Q	Pvt	Sep	1G		$60	
Indian Room	1Q	Pvt	Sep	1G		$60	

AHWAHNEE

Yosemite's Apple Blossom Inn Bed & Breakfast (209) 642-2001
Hosts: Lynn, Jenny and Lance Hays
44606 Silver Spur Trail, Ahwahnee, CA 93601
On Highway 49, 8 miles north of Oakhurst or 18 miles south of Mariposa.

Lynn, Jenny, and Lance's Apple Blossom Inn is entirely given over to guests. It is near their home south of Yosemite National Park. They're careful to make everyone comfortable in the cute, inviting inn. Sited just below the apple orchard, the inn provides a view of Oakhurst Valley and the Sierra Nevada Mountains. Rooms are spotless and inviting, with private baths, and access to the ground-floor kitchen, and deck with spa. *Red Delicious* has its own TV/VCR and two double beds. *Granny Smith* features a spacious tub shower and private balcony. Stuffed furniture, games, and video library brighten the living room, and there's a fully-equipped kitchen, too. Greeting you with tea and cookies, Lynn and Jenny are glad to suggest local attractions such as Yosemite National Park or Bass Lake, plus hiking, mountain biking, horseback riding, and 9-hole and 18-hole golf courses. And then there's the Oakhurst Peddler's Fair held on both Memorial Day and Labor Day weekends. It's where you can admire and acquire various crafts, antiques, and collectibles.

No pets; smoking outside only; children welcome; full breakfast; AC; TV/VCR; video tape library; wood stove; games; hot tub; kitchen available; off street parking; credit cards (MC,V,AMEX).

ROOM	BED	BATH	ENTRANCE	FLOOR	DAILY RATES S	D	EP+
Red Delicious Room	2D	Pvt	Sep	1	$70	$85	$15
Granny Smith Room	1Q	Pvt	Sep	2	$65	$80	$15
Blossom Room	1D	Pvt	Sep	2	$55	$70	$15

ALBION

The Wool Loft (707) 937-0377
Hosts: Jan Tarr and Sid Spring
32751 Navarro Ridge Road, Albion, CA 95410
Ten miles south of Mendocino.

The Wool Loft's setting overlooking the sea reminds me of some B&Bs in Ireland or Scotland. Sheep graze in nearby fields; the family garden and henhouse contribute food to the table. Jan and Sid offer three cheery guest rooms with private baths in the main house to guests who prefer traditional bed and breakfast; one of these *Eweview* is a newer room with wonderful river and ocean views. The *Wool Loft* itself is a separate accommodation. It's a spacious studio apartment with queen-sized bed, fully equipped kitchen, bath, wood-burning stove, and huge windows that afford magnificent vistas. Get into the outdoors on some of the hiking trails in the area or just beach-walk. There is the Mendocino Music Festival in July and Wine Tasting Festival in September. Otherwise, quiet and cozy seclusion on the famous Mendocino coast is yours if you choose The Wool Loft.

No pets, children, or smoking; gather eggs for breakfast if desired; large sun room, deck, and fireplace in main house; firewood provided in *Wool Loft*; off-street parking; two-night minimum; three-night minimum on holiday weekends; special weekly rate for the *Wool Loft*, $600; no breakfast served during week. Open weekends for B&B (Friday-Sunday only).

ROOM	BED	BATH	ENTRANCE	FLOOR	DAILY RATES S	D	EP+
Wool Loft	1Q	Pvt	Sep	2		$100	$20
Eweview	1Q	Pvt	Main	1		$85	
Quail Nest	1Q	Pvt	Main	1		$65	
Beehive	1Q	Pvt	Main	1		$65	

ARROYO GRANDE

The Guest House   **(805) 481-9304**
Hosts: Mark Miller and James Cunningham
120 Hart Lane, Arroyo Grande, CA 93420
Off U.S. 101, seventeen miles south of San Luis Obispo.

Homesick New Englanders, look no further than The Guest House at Arroyo Grande. It was built in the 1850s by a sea captain from the east and bears an unmistakable resemblance to the homes he left behind. Mark and James, have kept the flavor of old New England alive in the house. Stenciled wall designs, American primitives, Oriental rugs, and family heirlooms add to the mellow, inviting atmosphere. A crackling fire in the hearth and comfortable places to sit make the living room a haven for easy conversation. The afternoon social hour often takes place in the bay-windowed sun room with French doors that lead out to the garden. Breakfast is appropriately hearty fare, served in the sun room or out in the garden. For traditional Yankee hospitality at the sign of the pineapple, The Guest House is a classic.

Cat in residence; no pet or children; full breakfast; afternoon refreshments; city park in turn-of-the-century village of Arroyo Grande; many antique shops in town and wineries in surrounding countryside; off-street parking.

ROOM	BED	BATH	ENTRANCE	FLOOR	DAILY RATES S D	EP+
A	1Q	Shd	Main	2	$47.50 $65	$10
B	1D	Shd	Main	2	$47.50 $65	$10

BISHOP

The Matlick House   (619) 873-3133
Hosts: Barbara and Ray Showalter
PO Box 744, Bishop, CA 93514
1313 Rowan Lane in Bishop.

Pioneer Alan Matlick moved to Owens Valley in the late 1800's, building a home in Bishop in 1906, where he and his family ran a dairy, creamery, and apple orchard. For the Showalters, the warm, old-fashioned Matlick house is your home-away-from-home—you're just one of the family, and outgoing Barbara soon involves you in her crafts. Rooms feel very turn-of-the-century with antique bed headboards, beveled glass doors on the armoires, lace curtains, and handmade quilts. *Jenny's Suite* and *Tillie's Suite*, both named for Matlick family members, boast dramatic views of the 13,000-foot Sierra Nevada mountains. Spacious *Mabel's Suite* opens onto the second-floor porch. Barbara serves a full country breakfast, and for a modest charge, she'll pack a picnic meal, too. Ray and Barbara suggest hiking, camping, backpacking, trout fishing, or winter skiing at Mammoth Lakes. And don't miss the visiting the White Mountains, joining the Mules Day celebration, or attending the Lone Pine film festival if you are in the area.

Cat in residence; no pets; smoking outside only; children over 12 welcome; full breakfast; AC; TV/VCR; fireplace; off street parking; senior discount; credit cards (MC,V,AMEX).

ROOM	BED	BATH	ENTRANCE	FLOOR	DAILY RATES S	D	EP+
Minnies & Al's	1Q	Pvt	Main	1		$79	
Mabel's Suite	2T	Pvt	Main	2		$89	
Lenna's Suite	1Q	Pvt	Main	2		$89	
Jenny's Suite	1Q	Pvt	Main	2		$79	
Tillie's Suite	1Q	Pvt	Main	2		$79	

BOLINAS

Thomas' White House Inn   **(415) 868-0279**
Host: Jackie Thomas
PO Box 132, Bolinas, CA 94924
Between Stinson Beach and Point Reyes National Seashore.

The magic and mystery of Bolinas lies in its refusal to go the way of so many other seaside communities that nurture tourism at the expense of the natural environment. Bolinas is not easy to find; it's been said that if you want to find it, you will. Its startling beauty is nowhere more apparent than at this marvelous bluffside inn overlooking the Pacific. Just to breathe the fresh air here, to savor the panorama of blue sea, Stinson Beach, the foothills, and Mount Tamalpais, feels like a privilege. The New England-style home of Jackie Thomas is a crisp white with red trim. It has two stories and, at the top, an observation deck. Two large, artfully appointed bedrooms and a half-bath comprise the second floor. The first floor offers a full bath with an aviary for zebra finches, a living room with a fireplace accented by Mediterranean blue tile, a sun porch, and an open country kitchen with dried flowers hanging from the beams. Bolinas is surrounded by the Golden Gate National Recreation Area and from bedrooms, common rooms, and from the beautifully cultivated grounds, the view is omnipresent—just as it should be.

No pets; no smoking on second floor; expanded Continental breakfast; off-street parking.

ROOM	BED	BATH	ENTRANCE	FLOOR	DAILY RATES S	D	EP+
Q	1Q	Shd	Main	2		$95	$10
D	1D	Shd	Main	2		$85	$10

BRENTWOOD

Diablo Vista (510) 634-2396
Hosts: Myra and Dick Hackett
2191 Empire Avenue, Brentwood, CA 94513
Just east of Antioch, off Lone Tree Way.

This elegant ranch-style home is set on two acres of fruit and nut trees, with a view of Mount Diablo in the distance. It's an hour from San Francisco and ten minutes from the Sacramento River Delta. For hikers and cyclists, Black Diamond Regional Park, with its many trails and historic sites, is only four miles away, as is Contra Loma Lake for swimming, windsurfing, and fishing. Brentwood is famous for its many "U-Pick" fruit and vegetable farms, and maps are available from hosts Dick and Myra Hackett. Their main guest room (A) is located at one far end of the house. This huge room has its own entrance, bath, kitchenette, small library, TV, stereo system, and AC/heating units. Subtle colors, Oriental rugs, custom-made window cushions, and American antiques create a harmonious, soothing effect. Room (B) is a cozy room with twin beds; the bath is a few steps down the hall. Guests in this room, or the other two (C and D), enjoy reading or relaxing in the sitting room of the main residence. Take a swim in the pool, soak in the hot tub, sip a drink in one of the two gazebos, or relax in the lovely garden. Hosts have thoroughly searched out the best restaurants in the area, a boon to those of us who take our dining seriously.

No pets; children over eight (swimmers) welcome; smoking outside only; TV; stereo; swimming pool; hot tub; jogging and biking trails surround property; ample parking; some Spanish spoken.

ROOM	BED	BATH	ENTRANCE	FLOOR	S	D	EP
A	1Q	Pvt	Sep	1G		$75	$10
B	2T	Shd	Main	1G		$60	$10
C	1D	Shd	Main	1G		$60	$10
D	1T	Shd	Main	1G	$50		

CAMBRIA

PineStone Bed & Breakfast By The Sea (805) 927-3494
Hosts: Frank and Barbara Banner
221 Weymouth Street, Cambria, CA 93428
Overlooking Moonstone Beach.

From this Victorian-style inn you can watch the sunset and moonrise, hear the sounds of the surf, or take a walk on the beach. The lower floor is just for guests. The foyer is carpeted in mauve and attractively painted light green using a stippling technique. The carpeting and stippling are carried into one rose guest room and another that is blue. Each has a full private bath, a gas fireplace, cable TV, and a sliding glass door to an individual garden patio. The quiet, relaxing rooms are as pretty as can be. On the second floor, there is another room for guests with a small private deck. Frank and Barbara welcome people to enjoy the wide view from the lounge by the large stone fireplace, in the breakfast area, or on the front deck. Their warm hospitality includes a welcome tray on arrival, generous buffet breakfasts, and anytime-coffee, tea, or chocolate. A sterling location plus all the comforts of home make staying at PineStone Inn By The Sea a total pleasure. Cambria is close to the Hearst Castle at San Simeon, has many high quality art shows and shops, and is headquarters of the California Carvers Guild (museum).

No pets, children, or smoking; walking distance to Cambria village shops and restaurants; off-street parking; credit cards (V,MC); for conversion to twin beds in Room B, $10 extra, first night only.

ROOM	BED	BATH	ENTRANCE	FLOOR	DAILY RATES S	D	EP+
A	1Q	Pvt	Main	1		$85	
B	1K	Pvt	Main	1		$85	
C	1Q	Pvt	Main	2		$85	

CAMBRIA

Seaview Through the Pines (805) 927-3089
Hosts: Audrey and Bill Mankey
570 Croyden Lane, Cambria, CA 93428
East of Highway One, in the pines overlooking the coast.

The large, contemporary, cedar home of Audrey and Bill Mankey is perched on a hillside in the pines with a broad-range view to the sea. The entire lower level is a guest accommodation—a clean, inviting place to unwind and settle into. The apartment has a full, well-stocked kitchen; a living room with a sitting area, cable TV and VCR, a fireplace, and a table for dining; a full bathroom; and a bedroom with an ocean view through the open doorway. A door from the kitchen leads to a private deck with a hot tub, a hammock, chairs, and view. Guests find refreshments upon arrival, plus a host of helpful information and a menu describing the wonderful breakfast choices. Neutral tones add to the tranquil environment, and it's obvious that everything, from bed to sofas to chairs, was built for comfort. Nestle into a beautiful world all your own at Seaview Through the Pines.

No pets; infants and children over thirteen welcome; no smoking; full breakfast; off-street parking.

ROOM	BED	BATH	ENTRANCE	FLOOR	DAILY RATES S	D	EP
A	1Q	Pvt	Sep	LL		$95	$15

CAMBRIA

Whispering Pines   **(805) 927-4613**
Hosts: Ginny and Jack Anderson
P.O. Box 326, Cambria, CA 93428
At 1605 London Lane, off Ardath.

California

For many, discovering Cambria is an added bonus to visiting the magical Hearst Castle at San Simeon. The quaint coastal town retains its homespun charm even though it becomes more arty and sophisticated each year. In a lovely, tranquil area just a short drive from the old Cambria village is Jack and Ginny Anderson's multi-level contemporary home with views of rolling hills and pines—Whispering Pines, that is. Guests may retreat to the total privacy of a deluxe, tri-level apartment with its own entrance, and a flagstone patio and hot tub just outside. Light, immaculate, and tastefully decorated, the unit consists of a living room with fireplace, TV/VCR, dining area, kitchenette, full bath, and large loft bedroom. A tantalizing choice of breakfast entrees is offered, along with the luxury of delivery to your quarters, or perhaps the patio. Simply put, Whispering Pines is a great little hideaway on the central coast.

No pets; smoking outside only; full breakfast; off-street parking. The Andersons also operate Bed & Breakfast Homestay, a reservation service listing $65-$95 rooms and apartments in the area. **KNIGHTTIME PUBLICATIONS SPECIAL RATE: 10% discount with this book.

ROOM	BED	BATH	ENTRANCE	FLOOR	DAILY RATES S / D / EP+
A	1K or 2T	Pvt	Sep	2 & 3	$95

CHICO

The Esplanade Bed & Breakfast   (916) 345-8084
Host: Lois I. Kloss
620 The Esplanade, Chico, CA 95926
Two short blocks from downtown Chico and across from the Bidwell Mansion.

When your travels take you to Chico, the most convenient lodging accommodations you will find are at The Esplanade Bed & Breakfast. The house, built in 1913 as an executive home for Diamond Match Company, is right across the street from the historic Bidwell Mansion and is steps from California State University Chico. Lois has restored the home with care and sensitivity retaining the look of the early 1900's with both exterior and interior decor. Five of the six guest rooms are named after Lois's grandchildren who each picked the room which bears their name and contains their picture. Every room has a TV nicely hidden in the room's armoire. Kelsey's room is a lush indoor garden with wrap-around windows that overlook the neighborhood. Kelsey's room and Twila's room each have a private lavatory and toilet, share a tub shower. Breakfast's are served at your convenience in the dining room or on the tree shaded porch. You will arrive at The Esplanade as a stranger and leave with hugs. The home grows on you as you enjoy the small-town ambiance of Chico. Lois suggests you visit the historic Bidwell Mansion and enjoy the hiking and biking in Chico's Bidwell Park (2200+ acres) which extends from the city center to the Sierra foothills.

Pets accepted with damage deposit; smoking outside only; children by prior arrangement; full breakfast; AC; TV in each room; fireplace; airport pickup at Chico airport; credit cards (MC,V).

ROOM	BED	BATH	ENTRANCE	FLOOR	DAILY RATES S / D / EP+
Natalie's Room	1Q	Pvt	Main	G	$65
Nick's Room	2T	Shd	Main	G	$55
Susan's Room	1Q	Pvt	Main	2	$55
Katie's Room	1Q	Pvt	Main	2	$55
Kelsey's Room	1Q	Shd	Main	2	$55
Twila's Room	1D	Shd	Main	2	$45

CLEARLAKE

Big Canyon Bed & Breakfast　　　　　　**(707) 928-5631**
Hosts: John and Helen Wiegand　　　　　　**(707) 928-4892**
P.O. Box 1311, Lower Lake, CA 95457
Seigler Springs, at the foot of Cobb Mountain.

California

    The remote and woodsy mountain setting makes Big Canyon Bed & Breakfast a perfect place to escape to the quiet, natural world that inspires true relaxation. The Cape Cod-style home of John and Helen Wiegand has two spacious rooms for guests on its upper floor. One (A) has its own entrance, wood stove, skylight, and kitchenette, while the other (B) has a cozy alcove window seat. The entire floor makes an ideal family or group accommodation. In the immediate surroundings you may enjoy identifying spring wildflowers, gazing at bright stars, and finding Lake County diamonds. There are glider rides at the glider port in Middletown or take a twenty-minute drive to Clear Lake and get into the swim of things. The casual country atmosphere of Big Canyon is conducive to doing simply whatever you please.
    Smoking outside only; AC; (main) kitchen privileges; barbecue pit; bring mountain bikes; golf courses and award winning wineries with tasting rooms nearby; double sofa bed in Room A (no charge for use); off-street parking. ****KNIGHTTIME PUBLICATIONS SPECIAL RATE: Two nights for the price of one Sunday-Thursday with this book.**

ROOM	BED	BATH	ENTRANCE	FLOOR	DAILY RATES S	D	EP+
A	1Q	Pvt	Sep	2		$65	
B	1Q	Pvt	Main	2		$65	

CLEARLAKE

Muktip Manor   (707) 994-9571
Hosts: Jerry and Nadine Schiffman
12540 Lakeshore Drive, Clearlake, CA 95422
South shore of Clear Lake.

    The home of Jerry and Nadine Schiffman (affectionately known as Muktip Manor) has an Early California charm all its own. The living quarters are all on the second floor, with doors opening onto a wrap-around verandah. Located opposite the lake, it affords good views and a small, private beach. The guest unit consists of a bedroom, living room, kitchen, and bath. While not luxurious, the decor is delightfully country. Jerry is a former actor. (Look for him on reruns of Streets of San Francisco; he always played a cop or a corpse.) Occasionally he enjoys an evening sail in his catamaran with guests who so choose. Whatever your particular pleasure might be, there's a host of activities to choose from: boating, wind surfing, swimming, canoeing, fishing, rock-hunting, and wine-tasting at Lake County wineries. The lifestyle at Muktip Manor is casual, unpretentious, and laced with humor—a thoroughly engaging combination.
    Cats in residence; no children; pets welcome ($5 extra); full breakfast; TV; kitchen; large deck; canoe available; launch ramp and public fishing piers nearby; ample street parking; animal lovers preferred.

ROOM	BED	BATH	ENTRANCE	FLOOR	DAILY RATES S D EP
A	1D	Pvt	Sep	2	$65

CRESCENT CITY

Pebble Beach Bed & Breakfast (707) 464-9086
Hosts: Cliff and Margaret Lewis (800) 821-9816
1650 Macken Avenue, Crescent City, CA 95531
Across from a state beach.

Experience an out-of-the-way surprise at this lovely home situated near a beautiful stretch of coastline you might not otherwise discover. Pebble Beach Bed & Breakfast is a quiet and gracious place. Watch sunsets from your room, relax in the guest lounge area, or go for a walk on the beach. The entire second floor is a suite for guests, with king bed, private bath and lounge area. For extra guests in the same party, there are more bedrooms. Outside, it's only steps to that gorgeous beach. The heart of the Redwood National Park is only minutes away. Whatever brings you to this northwest corner of California, you'll remember it fondly after a stay at Pebble Beach Bed & Breakfast.

No pets; children by special arrangement; smoking on the patio only; full breakfast; lounge with telephone, desk, and refrigerator; cable TV/VCR; stereo system; CD library; VCR movie library; off-street parking; rate for four people, two bedrooms $150.

ROOM	BED	BATH	ENTRANCE	FLOOR	DAILY RATES S / D / EP+
King Room	1K	Pvt	Main	2	$80
Additional bedroom for one guest in the same party					$35

DAVENPORT

New Davenport Bed & Breakfast (408) 425-1818
Hosts: Marcia and Bruce McDougal (800) 870-1817
PO Box J, Davenport, CA 95017 FAX: (408) 423 1160
Nine miles north of Santa Cruz.

    The New Davenport Bed & Breakfast was first located in one of Davenport's original old buildings, just across the Coast Highway from the ocean. Four rooms (listed below) are located at the Inn House next to the restaurant. Eight additional rooms have been added above the adjoining New Davenport Cash Store and Restaurant. Rooms are bright and comfortable, furnished with antiques, crafts and ethnic treasures. Delicious breakfasts are served in the sitting room or in the very popular restaurant which is open for breakfast, lunch, and dinner throughout the week. Weekend festivities often include live music and a lively crowd. The Cash Store offers an interesting mixture of crafts, jewelry, and handcrafted wares from around the world. The New Davenport is an ideal getaway from the Bay Area. Realize it is larger and less "homey" than most of the other listings in this book. However, the trip is short, and there's a wonderfully remote feeling about the place. When you don't have to spend hours driving, there's much more time for fun.

    No pets; smoking outside only; off-street parking; bus service from Santa Cruz; most rooms have ocean views; some family rooms; credit cards (V,MC,AMEX).

ROOM	BED	BATH	ENTRANCE	FLOOR	DAILY RATES S D EP+
A	1D	Pvt	Main	1G	$70
B	1D	Pvt	Main	1G	$70
C	1Q	Pvt	Main	1G	$75
D	1D	Pvt	Main	1G	$70

EUREKA

Old Town Bed & Breakfast Inn   (707) 445-3951
Hosts: Leigh and Diane Benson   (800) 331-5098
1521 Third Street, Eureka, CA 95501   FAX: (707) 445-8346
Third near P, east end of the Old Town district.

Built in 1871, this historic home is one of the few remaining Greek Revival Victorians in the area. It was the original home of the local lumber baron until he built the Carson Mansion. Then it was moved to its present location, just a block and a half from the Mansion. Leigh and Diane have kept the spirit of the past alive by furnishing the inn with antiques of the period. They've added their own whimsical touches, such as a teddy bear on each bed and rubber ducks and bubble bath for the clawfoot tubs. The result of their labors is the quintessential bed and breakfast inn. After a stroll around Old Town, relax by the fireplace in the Raspberry Parlor. Complimentary afternoon teas, fresh fruit, and Diane's homemade cookies await you. In the morning, sample one of Diane's country breakfast creations such as Eggs Derelict or Lumber Camp Breakfast Pie and homemade biscuits and award winning jams. Old Town Bed & Breakfast Inn's warm atmosphere and convenient location will make your stay in Eureka a memorable experience. Almost as memorable are the local artist's murals on many Eureka buildings. Also, the World Championship Kinetic Sculpture Race is held annually.

Cats in residence; no pets; children over ten welcome; full breakfast; afternoon refreshments; outdoor hot tub on private patio; off-street parking; all major credit cards; extended stay and business traveler discounts. The Inn was totally renovated in 1995 and the new guest wing features a deluxe accommodation with private bath, clawfoot tub and shower.

ROOM	BED	BATH	ENTRANCE	FLOOR	S	D	EP+
Gerri's Room	1K or 2T	Pvt	Main	2	$80	$100	$20
Rose Parfait	1Q	Shd	Main	2	$60	$75	$20
Maxfield Parrish	1Q	Shd	Main	2	$60	$75	$20
Sumners Room	1D	Pvt	Main	2	$60	$75	$20
Wm. Carson Room	1Q	Pvt	Main	1	$100	$120	$20
Carlotta Carsons Room	1K	Pvt	Main	2	$125	$150	$20

GILROY

Country Rose Inn Bed and Breakfast (408) 842-0441
Host: Rose Hernandez
PO Box 2500, Gilroy, CA 95021
A mile off Highway 101, Masten exit between Gilroy and Morgan Hill at 455 Fitzgerald Avenue #E.

Down the quiet back lane, past the truck crops of cauliflower or peppers, you'll turn into a grove of immense old valley oak trees to find Country Rose Inn, a dignified Dutch Colonial manor with flower gardens, antique farm tools, and a warm, gracious proprietress, Rose Hernandez. Rose, an area native, has fashioned her stately B&B with lace curtains, armoires, wonderful antique headboards, and fully modern private baths. The *Garden Room* boasts a high, elaborately carved "pineapple-style" headboard, and personal touches: her parents' wedding picture above the marble fireplace, her mother's wedding gown in the armoire. The *Rambling Rose Suite* with separate entrance has a free-standing wood stove, sofa and writing desk, huge king bed, and spacious bathroom with large mirror, steam shower, and jetted two-person tub—wonderful for romantic retreats! Rose serves a full breakfast before you head off to explore nearby Monterey or Santa Cruz. Whether you're just passing through or seeking a relaxing, quiet, and nearby retreat to refresh your spirit, Country Rose Inn is a fine bed and breakfast destination.

Cat in residence; smoking outside only; full breakfast; AC; TV/VCR; guest phone; fireplace; credit cards (MC,V).

ROOM	BED	BATH	ENTRANCE	FLOOR	S	D	EP+
Garden Room	1D	Pvt	Main	1		$119	
Double Delight	1K or 2T	Pvt	Main	2		$79	$30
Imperial Rose	1Q	Pvt	Main	2		$99	
Sterling Rose	1Q	Pvt	Main	2		$109	
Rambling Rose Suite	1K	Pvt	Sep	2		$169	

HALF MOON BAY

The Goose & Turrets Bed & Breakfast   (415) 728-5451
Hosts: Raymond and Emily Hoche-Mong
P.O. Box 370937, Montara, CA 94037-0937
Twenty-five miles south of San Francisco; a half mile from beach.

Proximity to the Bay Area, a colorful history, and natural beauty that hasn't been overtaken by development make the coastal hamlet of Montara, 8 miles north of the town of Half Moon Bay, an ideal country escape. Raymond and Emily Hoche-Mong welcome guests to The Goose & Turrets, built around 1908 in the Northern Italian villa style. It is an historic, earth-friendly inn catering to readers, nature lovers, pilots, and enthusiastic eaters! Step out back to the old-fashioned gardens and "chat" with the resident mascot geese, watch the hummingbirds in the fuschias, smell the bread baking in the oven, play bocce ball, hike down to beaches and rocky coves, or just lounge about. You can lose yourself in a good book or practice the art of doing absolutely nothing while the surf and perhaps the fog horns sound in the distance.

No pets; smoking outside only; four-course breakfast; afternoon tea; common room with woodstove, piano, game table, tape deck, and eclectic library; *Hummingbird Room* has sitting area with woodstove; *Lascaux* has an ecologically correct fireplace; major credit cards; French spoken; airport pickup by host/pilots (Half Moon Bay, San Carlos, Palo Alto) by prior arrangement; also, pickup for sailors at Pillar Point Harbor at Princeton; twenty minutes from San Francisco International Airport.

ROOM	BED	BATH	ENTRANCE	FLOOR	DAILY RATES S D EP+
Hummingbird Room	1Q	Pvt	Main	1	$110
Goose Room	1Q	Pvt	Main	1	$90
Whale Room	1Q or 2T	Pvt	Main	1	$95
Clipper Room	1K	Pvt	Main	1	$95
Lascaux Room	1D	Pvt	Main	1	$85

IDYLLWILD

Wilkum Inn   (909) 659-4087
Hosts: Annamae Chambers and Barbara Jones   (800) 659-4086
P.O. Box 1115, Idyllwild, CA 92549
In the mountains above Palm Springs at 26770 Highway 243.

That at-home feeling greets you as you enter Wilkum Inn. The warmth of pine, lace curtains, quilts, an organ, a large river rock fireplace, and cozy places to sit makes you want to don a bathrobe and curl up with a good book. The guest rooms are comfy and full of personality, too. *Garden* is on the main floor; others on the second floor include the *Eaves*, a two-room suite. Need a totally separate space where you can hole up in wooded seclusion? Try the inn's most private quarters: the self-catering *Loft* with its own entrance, kitchen, and loft bedroom. Wherever you stay, you'll be surrounded by trees and mountain vistas. And for your culinary pleasure, Annamae and Barbara serve an expanded Continental breakfast that might include crepes, Dutch babies, cheese-stuffed French toast, or *aebleskivers*.

No pets or smoking; robes provided; complimentary beverages and snacks; hiking trails, a rock climbing school, Idyllwild Arts Academy; unique shops and good restaurants nearby; off-street parking; two-night minimum for *Loft*; discounts for two or more nights and for single travelers.

ROOM	BED	BATH	ENTRANCE	FLOOR	DAILY RATES S	D	EP+
Garden	1D	Pvt	Main	1		$80	
Eaves	1Q	Pvt	Main	2		$85	
Garret	1Q	Shd	Main	2		$75	
Toll Gate	1K or 2T	Shd	Main	2		$80	
Loft	1Q	Pvt	Sep	2		$95	

INVERNESS

Terri's Homestay (415) 663-1289
Hosts: Theresa "Terri" Elaine and Maya Cavelti (800) 969-1289
P.O. Box 113, Point Reyes Station, CA 94956
83 Sunnyside Drive, Inverness Park.

High atop Inverness Ridge in a remote, "above it all" location adjoining Point Reyes National Seashore is Terri Elaine's comfortable redwood home. Here guests have plenty of space and privacy in quarters that include a large bedroom with a sitting area, a private bath, separate entrance, wood-burning stove, deck access, and an amazing view over ridges of Bishop pine toward the sea. Guatemalan artwork and fabrics add zest to the natural environment. Feel like exploring? Take a hike to the top of Mount Vision for a rewarding panorama; spend some time on secluded, bluff-lined beaches; see how many different species of wildlife you can spot; springtime wildflowers are spectacular on the rolling hills. In the evening, enjoy a soak in the ozone-purified outdoor spa. To round out a thoroughly relaxing holiday, schedule a massage by Terri who practices a variety of disciplines including "Watsu" water therapy in 97 degree water. This quiet, sunny spot offers an array of pleasures you won't soon forget.

Dogs on premises; children and outdoor dogs welcome; no smoking; expanded Continental breakfast; hammock, CD player, and extra futon in room; massage by appointment for one or two at a time (masseur also on hand); ample street parking; inquire about midweek, off-season, and extended stay rates.

ROOM	BED	BATH	ENTRANCE	FLOOR	DAILY RATES S	D	EP+
Chili	1Q & 1D	Pvt	Sep	1	$95	$115	$15
Huichol	1Q & 1D	Pvt	Sep	1	$95	$115	

IONE

The Heirloom Bed & Breakfast Inn (209) 274-4468
Hosts: Melisande Hubbs and Patricia Cross
PO Box 322, Ione, CA 95640
214 Shakeley Lane in Ione.

Magnolia, Walnut, Myrtle, Cedar, and Loquat shield The Heirloom from view until you turn down Shakeley Lane driveway. It's then that you'll see this stately brick home with its classical columns reminiscent of the South, the brick and balconies reminiscent of early-California. Inside, you're back in time with antiques such as the 400-year-old family table; a piano played by the late Lola Montez; the Empire headboards of the *Spring* and *Summer* rooms; and *Autumn's* authentic brass bed. *Early America* and *Early California* close by the main house are made of traditional rammed earth and feature hand-thrown sinks and large, tiled showers. Wood stoves and heavy beams suggest adobe, yet with all the amenities. The surrounding English Romantic gardens, complete with gazing ball, make a lovely setting for private events. For local visits, Melisande and Patricia mention the many wineries of Amador County, and the 18-hole golf course five blocks away. Ione is halfway between Yosemite and Lake Tahoe and an hour from skiing and smack in the middle of California gold country. A full French country breakfast is served to get you started on your day.

No pets; smoking outside only; children over ten welcome; full breakfast; fireplaces; fireplace in *Winter's Room*; off street parking; credit cards (MC,V,AMEX).

ROOM	BED	BATH	ENTRANCE	FLOOR	DAILY RATES S	D	EP+
Springtime	1K	Shd	Main	2		$85	
Summer	1T & 1D	Pvt	Main	2		$75	$15
Autumn	1D	Shd	Main	2		$60	
Winter's	1Q	Pvt	Main	2		$92	
Early American	1T & 1Q	Pvt	Sep	1G		$85	$15
Early California	1Q	Pvt	Sep	1G		$85	

LOS ANGELES

Norja Bed & Breakfast Inn   (213) 933-3652
Host: Norja Bercy   Msg: (213) 935-3521
1139 South Tremaine Avenue, Los Angeles, CA 90019
Centrally located near the Santa Monica Freeway.

Norja Bed and Breakfast Inn provides a unique L.A. experience in this city of contrasts. On the outside, Norja is a huge, peach-colored Spanish/Mediterranean/Art Nouveau house, built in 1929. On the inside, you glimpse the elegance and romance of California's past. High ceilings, hardwood floors, chandeliers, antique lamps, couches, and chairs—that's Norja. A stone staircase with wrought-iron banisters leads you to the second-floor rooms with etched and beveled mirrors, antique furniture, king beds, thick comforters, and more. Norja herself likes green, and rooms reflect this in name and decor: the large *Jade Room*, with a floor-to-ceiling lace canopy bed, the downstairs *Garden Room*, with deep green walls and private garden access (and a TV, too), the green *Fern Room*. Norja Bed & Breakfast is in a quiet residential neighborhood, and you can easily reach Beverly Hills, Century City, the La Brea Tar Pits, Farmer's Market, Hollywood, and downtown Los Angeles. It's truly a "LA" experience.

Dog and cat in residence; no pets or smoking; children over nine welcome; full breakfast; TV; robes provided; major credit cards; long-term rates available.

ROOM	BED	BATH	ENTRANCE	FLOOR	DAILY RATES S	D	EP+
Fern Room	1K	Shd	Main	1		$75	$20
Garden Room	1K	Shd	Main	1		$85	$20
Emerald Room	1D	Pvt	Main	2		$75	$20
Mint Room	1K	Pvt	Main	2		$110	$20
Jade Room	1K	Pvt	Main	2		$125	$20

LOS ANGELES

Salisbury House (213) 737-7817
Hosts: Sue and Jay German (800) 373-1778
2273 West 20th Street, Los Angeles, CA 90018
Near Santa Monica Freeway and Western Avenue.

Experience a cozy kind of luxury at Salisbury House, located in the historic West Adams district of Los Angeles. Here you'll find all the amenities of a manor house in the country, yet you'll be only minutes from downtown and major freeways. This turn-of-the-century California Craftsman home is large and sturdy. An expert restoration job has left its original integrity intact. Graciously proportioned rooms are exquisitely furnished with antiques and collectibles. Colors, fabrics, and nostalgia pieces are imaginatively combined to give each room a distinct personality. The total effect is enchanting. *Attic Suite* provides a spacious 600 square foot accommodations. The generous breakfasts served here are superb, the hospitality boundless. Sue and Jay invite you to treat yourself to the many charms of Salisbury House. I can't imagine a more relaxing or romantic in town spot.

No pets; smoking on porch only; full breakfast; sink in *Blue Room*; ample street parking; major credit cards; inquire about weekly and monthly rates.

ROOM	BED	BATH	ENTRANCE	FLOOR	DAILY RATES S	D	EP+
Blue Room	1Q	Pvt	Main	2		$90	
Rose Room	1Q	Shd	Main	2		$75	
Green Room	1Q	Shd	Main	2		$75	
Sun Room Suite	1D & 2T	Pvt	Main	2		$90	$10
Americana Attic Ste.	1K & 1T	Pvt	Main	3		$100	$10

MARIPOSA

Finch Haven Bed & Breakfast   Phone/FAX: **(209) 966-4738**
Hosts: Bruce and Carol Fincham
4605 Triangle Road, Mariposa, CA 95338
1.6 miles off Highway 140 on the way to Yosemite National Park.

   Bruce and Carol Fincham offer two completely private, separate guest accommodations on the lower level of their quiet country home, where panoramic mountain views and visiting wildlife may be admired from one's own private patio or from the large, flower-studded upper deck. Each room—the *Bluebird* and the *Morning Glory*—has a tasteful, pretty, well-put-together decor that features an original work of art. Each also has a nook for drink and snack preparation. Tasty, nutritious breakfasts are served in your own quarters, on the upper deck, or in the upstairs kitchen. The Finchams provide freshly ground coffee from an award-winning local coffee roasting company; guests are invited there for tours and tastings. Bruce, formerly a park ranger in Yosemite, can provide helpful, interesting tips for exploring the area. Ideas to think about include taking a horse drawn carriage ride in Mariposa, attending the annual Story Telling Festival in March, or the County Fair and Rodeo on Labor Day weekend. Just be sure to allow enough time just to sit and stare at the view!
   No pets; smoking outside only; children welcome; extended Continental breakfast; AC; picnic grounds, tennis courts, and community swimming pool at nearby town park; Yosemite Valley, Mariposa Grove of Giant Sequoias, important points of gold rush history, and California State Mining and Mineral Museum in area; ample parking; airport pickup (Mariposa County).

ROOM	BED	BATH	ENTRANCE	FLOOR	DAILY RATES S	D	EP+
Bluebird	2T	Pvt	Sep	1G		$75	$15
Morning Glory	1Q	Pvt	Sep	1G		$75	$15

MARIPOSA

The Pelennor Bed & Breakfast (209) 966-2832
Hosts: Dick and Gwen Foster
3871 Highway 49 S, Mariposa, CA 95338
Five miles south of Mariposa at Bootjack.

Dick and Gwen Foster follow the Scottish tradition of offering simple, low-cost accommodations, which are in a newer building adjacent to their home. They can provide tips on enjoying the area, a bit of hospitality, and even some bagpipe tunes on request. Both are pipers in two central California pipe bands. Music is a large part of life in the mountains and the Fosters suggest attending folk music concerts in the area and summer weekend street concerts in Mariposa. Also the California State Mineral Exhibit is within a few miles of the Pelennor. Each morning the Fosters serve what they term "a solid breakfast." For informal lodgings just off the main route of the Mother Lode and a short hour's drive from Yosemite, The Pelennor makes a welcome stop for the passing traveler.

Hosts have dogs, cat, and cockatiels; other animals roam the property; smoking outside only; lap pool; spa; sauna; kitchen in guest building available on a "you use, you clean" basis; off-street parking; at most, two rooms share one bath; one extra bedroom in main house is available as needed; available for outdoor weddings.

ROOM	BED	BATH	ENTRANCE	FLOOR	DAILY RATES S	D	EP+
MacLeod	1Q	Shd	Sep	2	$35	$45	$10
Stewart	1Q	Shd	Sep	2	$35	$45	$10
Anderson	1D	Shd	Sep	2	$35	$45	$10
Campbell	2T	Shd	Sep	2	$35	$45	$10

MENDOCINO

Mendocino Farmhouse   (707) 937-0241
Hosts: Margie and Bud Kamb   (800) 475-1536
P.O. Box 247, Mendocino, CA 95460
One and one-half miles from Mendocino village.

If you're seeking the quintessential farmhouse in Mendocino for your north coast getaway, look no further. The home of Marge and Bud Kamb provides superb accommodations in the quietest possible setting, so near and yet so far from the busy village scene. Here, there's a permanent warm glow to the interior that feels authentic to the core—not "decorated." Sloped ceilings, pretty fabrics and rugs, and country antiques give the bedrooms an ambient coziness. Two of the rooms are quite spacious; *John's Room* has a fireplace; a slightly smaller *Jim's Room*, with a wood-burning stove, is irresistibly romantic. Newer quarters have been added in the converted barn overlooking the garden. Each has a separate entrance and a charm all its own, as well as such inviting features as stone fireplaces, coffee makers, and small refrigerators. In the morning, savor a sumptuous farmhouse breakfast in the sun room of the main house while taking in the views of redwood forest, beautiful gardens, a pond, and a meadow. The aura of this lovely home makes an indelible impression on those fortunate enough to stay here. Special events mentioned by the Kamb's include the Mendocino Music Festival in July and Christmas Festival and Evergreen Workshop.

Children by arrangement; smoking outside only; full breakfast; off-street parking; credit cards (V,MC). Single/double rates the same.

ROOM	BED	BATH	ENTRANCE	FLOOR	DAILY RATES S	D	EP+
John's Room	1K & 1T	Pvt	Main	2		$95	$15
Karin's Room	1Q	Pvt	Main	2		$85	
Jim's Room	1Q	Pvt	Main	2		$95	
Cedar Room	1Q	Pvt	Sep	1		$110	
Pine Room	1Q	Pvt	Sep	1		$110	

MUIR BEACH

Muir Beach Bed & Breakfast (415) 381-9125
Host: Leba Wine
Star Route Box 1304, Muir Beach, CA 94965
In Muir Beach, 17 miles from the San Francisco City Hall steps.

Views, views, views—Muir Beach to the Marin Headlands, the Presidio and Golden Gate, south along San Francisco's Ocean Beach to Pacifica—you see it all from the Muir Beach Bed & Breakfast. Leba greets you with a tray of goodies and settles you into your room. Go ahead, open the little fridge and sip a soft drink or a glass of wine. Relax and gaze from the picture windows or choose a book from Leba's library and enjoy the tranquility. Your room's high open-beam ceiling and contemporary decor lend spaciousness. Out the driveway and up the hill you'll find trails to Stinson Beach along the coastal ridges of the Golden Gate National Recreation Area or inland to Muir Woods National Monument. Worked up an appetite? Just head back downhill to the popular Pelican Inn on Highway 1. Next morning, savor Leba's full breakfast while watching the grand sweep of the Marin Headlands appear as the curtain of coastal fog lifts above the ocean.

No pets; smoking OK; children welcome; full breakfast; fireplace.

ROOM	BED	BATH	ENTRANCE	FLOOR	DAILY RATES S / D / EP+
A	2T & 1Q	Pvt	Sep	1	$140

NOVATO

Casa Mia Bed & Breakfast (415) 892-0900
Host: Eve Novak
1116 Elm Drive, Novato, CA 94947
Close and convenient to downtown Novato.

Novato is a quiet Marin County bedroom community 28 miles north of San Francisco and the Golden Gate, with more of a Southern California feel than much of the Bay Area. Eve's Ranch-style home was built in the 50's when Novato was a small town. That town has since become a city. The home has a comfortable and homey atmosphere and is located on a tree lined street just three short blocks from downtown. The accommodations are two studio units each with living room. kitchenette, bedroom, and bathroom. The *Front Suite* has a fireplace, the *Pool Suite* is, of course, right by the pool. It is pleasant having your own apartment with a continental breakfast available in the refrigerator to enjoy on your own schedule. Novato is just 32 miles from wine country and 25 miles from the coast. It is also home to the annual late-summer Renaissance Faire, six weekends of knights, troubadours, and costumed pageantry. Casa Mia is one block from public transportation and the airporter. Two small-aircraft airfields are nearby and transportation can be arranged with your host.

Dog in residence; smoking outside only; children by arrangement; continental breakfast; cable TV in each room; kitchenette; pool and Amish gazebo; patio; barbecue area; winter rates available.

ROOM	BED	BATH	ENTRANCE	FLOOR	DAILY RATES S	D	EP
Pool Suite	1Q	Pvt	Sep	1	$65	$70	
Front Suite	1Q	Pvt	Sep	1	$65	$70	

ORLAND

The Inn at Shallow Creek Farm **(916) 865-4093**
Hosts: Mary and Kurt Glaeseman **(800) 865-4093**
4712 Road DD, Orland, CA 95963
Northern Sacramento River Valley; two and 1/2 miles west of I-5.

Who'd ever guess that just two miles away—and worlds apart—from I-5 you'd find a haven like The Inn at Shallow Creek Farm? The ivy-covered turn-of-the-century farmhouse is the centerpiece of this 3.5-acre citrus orchard where chickens, ducks, geese, and guinea fowl roam freely. It was revived in the early eighties by Kurt and Mary. The house and the hospitality have a genuine old-fashioned quality. Common rooms solely for guests' use include a large living room with a fireplace, a sitting room overlooking the orchard, and a cheery dining room. A large, airy suite on the first floor offers space and privacy; two nostalgic rooms on the second floor are perfect for two couples. A separate four-room cottage offers extra privacy. It has a wood-burning stove, a sun porch, and a full kitchen. In every season, The Inn at Shallow Creek Farm delights city-weary folks who relish its quiet rural atmosphere. The Glaesmans suggest nearby Black Butte Lake for boating, fishing, hiking swimming, and picnic sites. The area has great bicycling too.

No pets; smoking outside only; full breakfast featuring farm fresh eggs and produce; guest refrigerator; excellent area for walking, cycling, exploring, bird watching, stargazing, and photography; poultry, produce, and homemade jams and jellies available for purchase; off-street parking; French, German, and Spanish spoken; credit cards (V,MC); Orland airport pickup.

ROOM	BED	BATH	ENTRANCE	FLOOR	DAILY RATES S	D	EP
Penfield Suite	1Q	Pvt	Main	1		$65	
Heritage Room	1Q	Shd	Main	2		$55	
Brookdale Room	2T	Shd	Main	2		$55	$15
Cottage	1Q	Pvt	Sep	1		$75	$15

PASADENA

The Artists' Inn   **(818) 799-5668**
Innkeeper: Lisa Carroll   FAX: **(818) 799-3678**
1038 Magnolia Street, South Pasadena, CA 91030
Near the historic Mission West District of South Pasadena.

It's always pleasant when a Bed and Breakfast exceeds your expectations, and mine were certainly exceeded by the innkeeper's friendliness and excellent knowledge of the house and the area. The Artists' Inn, a cheery yellow trimmed with white, sits back of profuse rose gardens, with a long porch allowing ample garden views—a soothing place for afternoon tea. The cozy fireplace, white wicker, Victrola, and an antique radio, add to the living room's charm. Owner Janet Marangi decorated the rooms to reflect various artists and art periods. The *18th Century English Room* is the largest room, with an entry hall, king bed, lots of closets, and English antiques. The south-facing *Impressionist Room* has a queen bed, separate tub and shower, fabric-covered walls, and books on Monet and Renoir. Breakfast, either full or continental, is served at individual tables in a first-floor dining room, and roses are everywhere—the dining room, guest rooms, gardens—truly a Pasadena treat in this convenient and comfortable bed and breakfast.

No pets or smoking; children by arrangement; full or continental breakfast; AC; TV; fireplace; library; gardens; off-street parking; credit cards (MC,V,AMEX); business rates; special midweek 2 night package.

ROOM	BED	BATH	ENTRANCE	FLOOR	DAILY RATES S	D	EP+
Impressionist	1Q	Pvt	Main	2		$110	$20
Italian Suite	1Q & 2T	Pvt	Main	2		$110	$20
18th Century English	1K	Pvt	Main	2		$120	$20
Van Gogh	1D	Pvt	Main	2		$100	$20
Fauve	1Q	Pvt	Main	1		$110	$20

POINT REYES STATION

Thirty-nine Cypress (415) 663-1709
Hosts: Julia Bartlett and Barbara Hand
PO Box 176, Point Reyes Station, CA 94956
Near Point Reyes National Seashore.

Thirty-nine Cypress is on 3.5 acres of land a mile north of the village of Point Reyes Station. Drive down the long driveway, park, and walk through a rose-covered arch into a secret garden. The house itself is on a bluff overlooking a 600-acre ranch, the upper reaches of Tomales Bay, and the ridge that is the beginning of the Point Reyes National Seashore. Julia and Barbara have cleverly tucked an inviting spa halfway down the bluff where, while you're soaking, you can watch cattle graze and egrets and herons hunt. The valley is part of a major flyway and, particularly during fall and winter, the site of lots of bird activity. The house is natural and rustic. The redwood walls are hung with original art, and there are shelves of books and a cozy reading corner for rainy days. The antiques and aging Oriental rugs are from Julia's family home in Illinois. Breakfast is served in front of sliding glass doors that are open in fine weather. There is an Indian village at the seashore headquarters, swimming, fishing, kayaking, and horseback rides nearby.

Gardens; patios; spa; off-street parking; credit cards (V,MC,AMEX).

ROOM	BED	BATH	ENTRANCE	FLOOR	DAILY RATES S	D	EP+
A	1Q	Pvt	Main	1G		$130	$20
B	1D	Pvt	Main	1G		$110	$20
C	1Q	Pvt	Main	1G		$110	$20

RED BLUFF

The Faulkner House   (916) 529-0520
Hosts: Harvey and Mary Klingler   (800) 549-6171
1029 Jefferson Street, Red Bluff, CA 96080
North downtown area.

Its setting beside the Sacramento River and the diverse styles of Victorian architecture to be found here make Red Bluff a unique community. It's also the home of the William Ide Adobe, where California's first and only president lived. A great place to stay while soaking up some local history is The Faulkner House, a gracious Queen Anne home on a quiet, shady street where you'll find four inviting guest rooms and a hospitable welcome from Mary and Harvey Klingler. The decor for each room is exactly fitting and the look uncontrived, like an elegant lady aging ever so gracefully. The *Arbor Room* has a European carved bedroom set, while the sunny *Wicker Room* has an iron bed and wicker accessories. The *Tower Room* is small but charming, and the spacious *Rose Room* features a brocade fainting couch. The Klinglers suggest visiting Lassen National Park for hiking or skiing (depending on the season), touring Shasta Caverns, or test your fishing skills in the Sacramento River. A satisfying and relaxing stop is certain to be yours at The Faulkner House.

No pets or children; smoking outside only; AC; fireplace; ample street parking; major credit cards; airport pickup (Red Bluff, Redding).

ROOM	BED	BATH	ENTRANCE	FLOOR	DAILY RATES S	D	EP+
Tower Room	1D	Pvt	Main	2	$60	$65	
Wicker Room	1Q	Pvt	Main	2	$70	$75	
Rose Room	1Q	Pvt	Main	2	$85	$90	
Arbor Room	1Q	Pvt	Main	2	$80	$85	

REDDING

Palisades Paradise Bed & Breakfast (916) 223-5305
Host: Gail Goetz (800) 382-4649
1200 Palisades Avenue, Redding, CA 96003
Central Redding, at edge of Sacramento River.

The name Palisades Paradise isn't an exaggeration. What else would you call a beautiful, newly decorated contemporary home of exceptional comfort with a panoramic view of city lights and river bluff? From the *Sunset Suite*, glass doors open onto a patio with a garden spa where you can watch day turn to evening and soak your cares away. Both the suite and the *Cozy Retreat* are restful indeed, with soft, muted colors and comfortable beds. Gail welcomes business and pleasure travelers, making them feel totally at home in the relaxed atmosphere of her Palisades Paradise. She reminds you to bring binoculars for the excellent bird watching opportunities in the area.

Small dog in residence; children welcome when reserving both rooms; smoking outdoors only; living room with fireplace, wide-screen TV and VCR; cable TV in rooms; AC; spa; off-street parking; credit cards (V,MC,AMEX).

ROOM	BED	BATH	ENTRANCE	FLOOR	DAILY RATES S	D	EP+
Cozy Retreat	1D	Shd	Main	1G		$60	
Sunset Suite	1Q	Shd	Main	1G		$75	$10

SACRAMENTO

Abigail's (916) 441-5007
Host: Susanne Ventura (800) 858-1568
2120 G Street, Sacramento, CA 95816 FAX: (916) 441-0621
Central downtown location.

Besides being at the pulse of California politics and government, Sacramento is a pleasant city in which to live, to vacation, or to do business. Manageable in size and layout, it is also rich in history, culture, and dining opportunities. On a tree-lined street graced with fine old mansions, Abigail's opens its doors to those seeking a refined, home-like atmosphere in a most convenient location. Guests are welcomed into the large, attractive living room of the beautifully maintained 1912 Colonial Revival mansion. A fireplace, comfortable places to sit, and a spirit of friendliness help to put one at ease. A particular charm distinguishes each lovely guest room: *Solarium, Uncle Albert, Aunt Rose, Anne*, and *Margaret*. Delicious breakfasts featuring a different entree each morning are served in the sunny dining room. The neighborhood is great for walking; it's a snap to find your way to the state Capitol and other important attractions. Susanne and Ken Ventura offer an oasis of hospitality in the midst of the bustling city. On summer Thursday nights, enjoy the Farmer's market and music in Old Sacramento.

Two cats in residence; no pets; older children by arrangement; smoking outside only; full breakfast; AC; rollaway bed available; games and piano available; garden patio with hot tub; whirlpool tub in *Aunt Rose* room; public transportation and airport connections; off-street parking; all major credit cards; single midweek rates.

ROOM	BED	BATH	ENTRANCE	FLOOR	DAILY RATES S	D	EP+
Solarium	1Q	Pvt	Main	2	$95		
Uncle Albert	1Q	Pvt	Main	2	$105		
Margaret	1Q	Pvt	Main	2	$135		
Anne	1K	Pvt	Main	2	$145	$35	
Aunt Rose	1Q	Pvt	Main	2	$155	$35	

SACRAMENTO AREA

Mary and Bruce Johnson's Studio (916) 481-1142
Hosts: Mary and Bruce Johnson
PO Box 1574, Carmichael, CA 95609
5346 Kenneth Avenue, in the Sacramento suburb of Carmichael.

Open the wrought iron gate, go a few steps on the walkway alongside the home of Mary Lucile and Bruce Johnson, and you're in for a beautiful surprise. Tucked back from the older, established residential street is a caramel-hued garden hideaway filled with fine art, books, antiques, and soothing comfort. This quiet space, a former music studio, features a sitting area, a unique bathroom that opens out to a hidden patio, a fully-equipped kitchenette, and a queen-sized bed made up with fine linens. Guests also have access to a handsome library, a desk, a phone, and a word processor (by arrangement). Artists or writers in need of a restorative getaway or a tranquil haven in which to work will find a nurturing shelter; business travelers or vacationers will find it an ideal home base while in the Sacramento area. The championship Ancil Hoffman Golf Course which borders the American River with its 26 mile bikeway is close by. Carmichael is convenient for exploring the Gold Country and historic attractions in Sacramento.

No pets; smoking outside only; full breakfast; AC; lots of games and books; 5-minute walk to bus, then light rail into town (50 minutes total); airport pickup by arrangement; two-week maximum stay.

ROOM	BED	BATH	ENTRANCE	FLOOR	DAILY RATES S D EP
A	1Q	Pvt	Sep	1G	$65

SAN ANSELMO

Mario & Suellen Lamorte   (415) 456-0528
45 Entrata Drive, San Anselmo, CA 94960   (415) 485-1971
Walking distance from central San Anselmo. FAX: (415) 454-7179

To stay at the Lamortes' three-story brown-shingled house is to savor the taste of old Marin. It's on a quiet, tree-lined lane that was cut into a hillside long ago; from here, the views of the hilly terrain are a visual feast. The lower floor of the house is a private guest suite that can accommodate up to four people. Natural wood paneling and floors, Oriental rugs, unique paned windows, and a curved redwood sleeping alcove give the interior a warm rustic charm. French doors lead to a private deck where sunlight filters through a canopy of fruit and oak trees. The home is within walking distance of fine restaurants, antique shops, hiking trails, and lakes. San Anselmo, the "Antique Capital of Northern California" is less than an hour from the wine country and Point Reyes National Seashore, yet only fourteen miles from the Golden Gate Bridge. Whether you plan to stroll the "Avenue" or explore the country, the Lamortes' is a good place to start. Should they be booked, don't panic, Suellen's reservation service for Marin County can find you a lovely private homestay or small inn perfect for your needs.

Children welcome ($10 extra for one or two); no smoking; full breakfast; kitchen; TV; phone; rollaway bed available; off-street parking; Italian spoken.

ROOM	BED	BATH	ENTRANCE	FLOOR	DAILY RATES S	D	EP
A	1D & 1T	Pvt	Sep	LL		$70	$10

SAN DIEGO

Bears at the Beach Bed & Breakfast　　　　　**(619) 272-2578**
Host: Doña Denson
1047 Grand Avenue, San Diego, CA 92109
Pacific Beach.

Long-time resident Doña Denson welcomes B&B guests to a small vintage complex of lodgings owned for many years by her Aunt Ruth, who collected bears and other stuffed animals. The furry friends stayed on to serve as the welcoming committee, and they delight visitors almost as much as the superb location, just two blocks from the Pacific Ocean and three from Mission Bay. Guest quarters include two lovely bedrooms, *Bay* and *Beach*, done in soft rose and green with handmade quilts, ceiling fans, cable TV, and other comforting touches. A full bath, a refrigerator, a cozy sitting area, and a private patio complete the accommodations. Baths can be shared or private. Doña is on hand each morning with a different creative, homemade breakfast. To find a place this quiet, clean, attractively decorated, hospitable, and reasonably priced so near the beach and San Diego's many attractions is remarkable, so don't pass up a visit with the Bears at the Beach!

Children by arrangement; smoking outside only; extended Continental breakfast; robes provided; bicycle and skate rentals nearby; restaurants and night life within walking distance; ample street parking.

ROOM	BED	BATH	ENTRANCE	FLOOR	DAILY RATES S	D	EP+
Bay	1D	Shd/Pvt	Main	1G	$75	$88	
Beach	1Q	Shd/Pvt	Main	1G	$75	$88	

SAN DIEGO

Blom House Bed & Breakfast (619) 467-0890
Hosts: John and Bette Blom
1372 Minden Drive, San Diego, CA 92111
In the Mission Heights area.

Its location overlooking Hotel Circle, Fashion Valley Mall, and the intersection of Highways 8 and 163 gives Blom House the advantages of easy access to most any of San Diego's highlights and absolute knockout views from its windows, deck, and hot tub. Only when you step inside this warm, elegant home do you see what a find it is. Enter an invitingly comfortable living and dining area where guests gather for conversation, refreshments, and breakfast; at other times enjoy the expansive deck or hot tub, or spend time ensconced in one of three luxurious suites, tastefully appointed and stocked with every imaginable amenity. For a dreamy, romantic environment, choose the *Honeymoon Suite* facing the deck. A family or two couples may choose the two-bedroom *Family Suite*, while visitors in town for an extended stay might settle happily into the split-level *Lovers' Suite*. Bette loves cooking for and pampering her treasured guests. The Blom's suggest visiting the first weekend of December for the Christmas celebration at the Prado in Balboa Park with free entrance to many musical events, the museum, and zoo. Other wonderful December events are too numerous to mention.

No pets; smoking on deck only; full breakfast; TV/VCR, stocked fridge, and phone in each suite; all rooms AC and individual heaters; fireplace in living room; off-street and street parking; only one to three miles to most attractions. Low season rate: Single $59, Double $69, one bed Sunday-Thursday.

ROOM	BED	BATH	ENTRANCE	FLOOR	S	D	EP+
Honeymoon Suite	1Q	Pvt	Main	1		$75	
Family Suite	1Q & 1K	Pvt	Main	1		$75	$25
Lover's Suite	1Q	Pvt	Main	1		$75	

California

SAN DIEGO

Carole's Bed & Breakfast (619) 280-5258
Hosts: Carole Dugdale and Michael O'Brien
3227 Grim Avenue, San Diego, CA 92104
Near the northeast edge of Balboa Park.

Carole Dugdale is just as keen on preserving her home's history as she is her own. A designated historical site, the 1904 home captures the flavor of the days when San Diego was a "frontier port". Enhanced by a lovely rose garden, the Vernacular Craftsman-style home typically features a gabled dormer roof; leaded glass in some windows; interior wood paneling, ceiling beams, and built-in cabinetry. But it is Carole's appreciation of the past—her home, interesting antiques, and family mementos—that inspired her to create an environment of old-fashioned warmth, comfort, and friendliness. The bedrooms are furnished with queen-sized beds, handmade quilts, and some antiques. Feel free to take a dip in the large swimming pool, play a tune on the piano, or enjoy TV or a movie in the spacious living room. From such a convenient location, you'll explore San Diego with ease.

No pets; ceiling fans; Jacuzzi; walking distance (two blocks) to Balboa Park, zoo, and museums; public transportation; off-street and street parking; Spanish spoken.

ROOM	BED	BATH	ENTRANCE	FLOOR	DAILY RATES S / D / EP+
A	1K	Pvt	Sep	2	$85
B	1Q	Pvt	Sep	1	$85
C	1Q	Shd	Main	2	$65
D	1K	Shd	Main	2	$65

SAN DIEGO

Elsbree House Bed & Breakfast (619) 226-4133
Hosts: Katie and Phil Elsbree FAX: **(619) 223-4133***
5054 Narragansett Avenue, San Diego, CA 92107
In the Ocean Beach area of San Diego.

Just steps from the ocean, Elsbree House, a neatly maintained and attractive Cape Cod, stands out with beautiful grounds. And oh, their Star Jasmine hedge! It's spring blooms have a rich, sweet fragrance that hints of the tropics. Location? You bet: Ocean Beach with its public fishing pier, sea cliffs and tidal pools, surf shops, pubs, antique stores and restaurants—all in walking distance. A short drive takes you to Sea World or the airport; a bit farther, Balboa Park, the famed San Diego Zoo, La Jolla, and Tijuana. Elsbree's rooms have private baths, garden or balcony access, flowered Victorian decor, and wonderful art. Meet fellow guests around the fireplace in the living/dining room, or leaf through the collection of activity books and periodicals. The ample continental breakfast, ready early, gets your day under way, or, if you prefer, eat at your leisure. Phil and Katie particularly suggest exploring the tidal pools at the end of Narragansett Avenue and visiting nearby Sea World Park. In San Diego, if the Star Jasmine isn't in bloom, some of the other garden flowers will be blooming. Whatever the time of year, the sound of the garden fountain will carry away your cares.

Dog in residence; no pets; smoking outside only; well behaved children welcome; extended continental breakfast; TV; fireplace; off street parking; rates listed are for weekend reservations; midweek discount; 6 night discount; surcharge for 1-night stays. *To FAX, first call 226-4133.

ROOM	BED	BATH	ENTRANCE	FLOOR	DAILY RATES S D EP+
B	1Q	Pvt	Sep	1G	$85
C	1Q	Pvt	Sep	1G	$85
D	1K	Pvt	Sep	1G	$85
E	1Q	Pvt	Sep	2	$85
F	1Q	Pvt	Sep	2	$85
Bridal Suite	1Q	Pvt	Sep	1	$130

SAN FRANCISCO

Casa Arguello   **(415) 752-9482**
Hosts: Emma Baires and Marina McKenzie
225 Arguello Boulevard, San Francisco, CA 94118
Presidio Heights, between California and Lake.

Emma Baires makes her B&B guests feel right at home in Casa Arguello, a large, two-floor flat located in a safe residential area. It's within easy walking distance of shops and restaurants on Sacramento Street, Clement Street, and in Laurel Village. Spacious, immaculate rooms feature brass or iron beds with comfortable mattresses. The view from each room and the artwork adorning the walls are constant reminders that you couldn't be anywhere *but* San Francisco. Casa Arguello celebrates its eighteenth year as a B&B home in 1996, and, not surprisingly, it has more return visitors than ever. People appreciate the cheerful, home-like accommodations that Mrs. Baires so graciously provides.

No pets or smoking; TV in each room; large living room for guests; inquire about street parking; Spanish spoken; good public transportation and airport connections; credit cards(V,MC); one-night stays, $5 extra; two-night minimum preferred.

ROOM	BED	BATH	ENTRANCE	FLOOR	DAILY RATES S / D / EP+
A	1D	Shd	Main	3	$55
B	1K	Shd	Main	3	$57
C	1K	Pvt	Main	3	$72
D	1K	Pvt	Main	3	$74
E	1K	Pvt	Main	2	$85

SAN FRANCISCO

The Garden Studio   (415) 753-3574
Hosts: John and Alice Micklewright
1387 Sixth Avenue, San Francisco, CA 94122
Two blocks from Golden Gate Park and U.C. Medical Center.

John and Alice Micklewright are the second owners of this 1910 handsome Edwardian-style home. The Garden Studio is at garden level; it has a separate entrance from the street and a fully carpeted interior. The peach and green color scheme accents the fully equipped kitchen with slate floor and marble counters, and is carried throughout the bath and dressing room. The queen-sized iron bed has a down comforter and a cover with a Marimeko green and white motif. The light and airy apartment opens onto a compact city garden with lawn, flowering border, and a private, serene feeling. Well-traveled guests appreciate the attention to detail hosts have shown in providing many conveniences to enhance their stay in the City. The Garden Studio is located only two blocks from terrific ethnic restaurants. It's also two blocks to Golden Gate Park where you'll find botanical gardens, the Japanese Tea Garden, DeYoung Museum, Steinhart Aquarium, Natural History Museum, children's play ground, and even a Merry-Go-Round.

No pets or smoking; no breakfast provided, but neighborhood cafes nearby; TV/VCR; iron and ironing board; private telephone; rollaway bed; information and maps for neighborhood and City attractions provided; good public transportation and airport connections; inquire about parking; French spoken.

ROOM	BED	BATH	ENTRANCE	FLOOR	DAILY RATES S	D	EP+
Garden Studio	1Q	Pvt	Sep	1G	$65	$70	$10

SAN FRANCISCO

The Herb'n Inn   (415) 553-8542
Hosts: Pam Brennan and Bruce Brennan   FAX: (415) 553-8541
525 Ashbury Street, San Francisco, CA 94117
Haight-Ashbury District.

Brother-sister team Pam and Bruce Brennan are proud of their neighborhood's rock 'n' roll roots. The Haight is still a colorful, lively part of the City, and the hosts can guide you to some of its interesting spots. They are glad to own a handsome Victorian in the midst of it all and are taking pains to restore it to its turn-of-the-century grace while adding modern conveniences, such as a beautiful open kitchen/dining area that overlooks an attractive back yard, complete with garden and decking. Herbs growing in the kitchen window enliven the delicious full breakfasts, and the guest rooms are named for four of them: *Cilantro*, which overlooks the garden; *Coriander*, a front room that serves as a bridal suite; *Rosemary*, which has its own sink; and *Tarragon*, which has a private deck. There are private and shared baths, a variety of bed sizes and decor, and thoughtfully selected quality furnishings. The Brennans' Herb'n Inn is indeed a homey urban retreat. However, don't miss the big events that San Francisco is known for including the Landscape Garden Show in mid April, Bay to Breakers run in May, Lesbian-Gay Parade in June, and Halloween events in October. There's always something happening in the City by the Bay!

No pets; smoking outside only; full breakfast; TV/VCR upon request; good public transportation and airport connections; specialized tours arranged; off-street and street parking.

ROOM	BED	BATH	ENTRANCE	FLOOR	DAILY RATES		
					S	D	EP
Cilantro	1Q	Pvt	Main	2	$70	$75	
Coriander	1Q	Shd	Main	2	$60	$65	
Rosemary	1D	Shd	Main	2	$60	$65	
Tarragon	2T	Shd	Main	2	$60	$65	

SAN FRANCISCO

Marina Gardens (415) 931-2312
Hosts: Deb and Anton Schwarz FAX: (415) 931-2404
3542 Scott Street, San Francisco, CA 94123
In the Marina District near the Presidio.

San Francisco is a city of districts (neighborhoods), each with its own unique flavor, such as Chinatown, Noe Valley, the Haight, and the Marina just south of the Golden Gate Bridge. Marina Gardens is centrally located within the Marina district, close to fine restaurants, shopping, the Palace of Fine Arts, the Marina Green, the Exploratorium, and the bay beaches. Fisherman's Wharf is a half hour walk or short bus ride away. The bed and breakfast itself is one of those Edwardian row houses so typical of San Francisco. Deb and Anton have turned the ground floor one-bedroom apartment into a self-contained hideaway with hardwood floors, fully-equipped kitchen, private phone line, loads of closet and storage space, garden view, and patio access through French double doors. It is perfect for the traveler who is looking for privacy with comfort and flexibility. The bedroom is especially cocoon-like with a queen bed surrounded by books and screened near the ceiling with a lace canopy. You'll enjoy getting to know the Marina, the city, and Deb and Anton.

Cats in residence; no pets; smoking outside only; children over six welcome; continental breakfast; TV/VCR CD player; private phone; robes provided; hot tub; weekly rate.

ROOM	BED	BATH	ENTRANCE	FLOOR	DAILY RATES S D EP+
A	1Q	Pvt	Sep	1G	$95 $100 $15

SAN FRANCISCO

Moffatt House   **(415) 661-6210**
Host: Ruth Moffatt   FAX: **(415) 564-2480**
431 Hugo Street, San Francisco, CA 94122
Between Fifth and Sixth Avenues near Golden Gate Park.

This pale blue Edwardian home is in close proximity to the popular neighborhood haunts of Ninth and Irving, Golden Gate Park, and U.C. Medical Center. Ruth Moffatt knows the area well and offers assistance with just about anything her guests might need. The four guest rooms are neat and cheerful, with artistic touches in the decor and, typically San Franciscan, shared split baths. The quiet, safe location of Moffatt House makes walking a pleasure and neighborhood shops, cafes, bakeries, and markets invite browsing. Ruth has an exercise discount that really pays off in a form most everyone can enjoy. Moffatt House pays a quarter a mile for any running or walking guests do in Golden Gate Park. Yes, Ruth puts the cash right in your hand! If you are just into watching runners and walkers, Ruth says the place to be is the finish line for the San Francisco Marathon or Bay to Breakers race. The city has dozens of shorter running and walking events to observe or enter. Moffatt House puts San Francisco at your feet —The possibilities are endless....

Cat in residence; kitchen privileges; crib available; one-night stays and late arrivals OK; Spanish, Italian, and French spoken; good public transportation and airport connections; inquire about parking; credit cards (V,MC,AMEX).

ROOM	BED	BATH	ENTRANCE	FLOOR	S	D	EP+
A	2T	Shd	Main	2	$39	$49	
B	1D	Shd	Main	2		$39	
C	1Q & 1T	Shd	Main	2	$49	$59	$10
D	1Q	Shd	Main	2	$49	$59	

DAILY RATES

SAN FRANCISCO - EAST BAY

Casabel   **(510) 236-5006**
Hosts: Sue and Julio Kaplan   FAX **(510) 215-5098**
8419 Bel View Ct., El Cerrito, CA 94530
In the El Cerrito Hills, overlooking Wildcat Canyon.

Sue and Julio greet you warmly, make sure you have everything you need, then go about their business. Your privacy is cherished at Casabel, an upscale yet homey bed and breakfast atop the East Bay hills. Sue and Julio's guest room, done in white with pastels of tan, green, and blue, is a spacious and relaxing place. Sit on the sofa— you can see across Wildcat Canyon to the rolling hills beyond; step onto the deck and the slope drops off to the oak and madrone of the canyon. Perhaps you'll see a rabbit, fox, coyote, or deer pass by, or horses grazing on the opposite slopes. To the left is San Pablo Bay, the northern portion of San Francisco Bay, and the hills of Napa and Sonoma; to the right are the upper reaches of Wildcat Canyon. Inside, you have a small kitchenette with stocked refrigerator, coffee maker, and microwave for quick snacks. An adjoining room is available with two additional twin futon beds to accommodate a family or two couples traveling together. Sue and Julio suggest hiking in Wildcat Canyon, touring the Napa wine country, and visiting the seashore at Point Reyes. Of course, all the urban amenities of San Francisco and the surrounding Bay Area are within easy reach of Casabel; Berkeley is a mere five minutes away.

No pets or smoking; children by arrangement; continental breakfast; TV/VCR; kitchenette; microwave; refrigerator; Spanish spoken. $125 for Room (A) with adjoining room.

ROOM	BED	BATH	ENTRANCE	FLOOR	DAILY RATES S D EP
A	1Q	Pvt	Main	LL	$75

SANTA BARBARA

Ocean View House   **(805) 966-6659**
Hosts: Carolyn and Bill Canfield
PO Box 3373, Santa Barbara, CA 93130-3373
Three blocks from the ocean.

    Bill and Carolyn Canfield offer guests an attractive private suite in their home. It has a bedroom, a shower bath, and an adjoining paneled den with a sofa bed. Interesting books and collections may be perused at your leisure. A generous Continental breakfast featuring fruit from backyard trees is served on the patio, a good vantage point for viewing the Channel Islands with a background of vivid blue. Close by are beaches and lovely Shoreline Drive, a popular place for joggers, skaters, cyclists, and sightseers. The harbor and downtown Santa Barbara are within three miles. The Canfields suggest visiting for two special local events: the summer Solstice and Parade Celebration, the weekend near June 21; and the "Old Spanish Days" Celebration, the first week in August. Kids visit so they can play in the backyard playhouse which is a big favorite for them. If you need a relaxing spot that the whole family can appreciate, Ocean View House has all the necessary ingredients.
    Dog and cat in residence; smoking on patio preferred; two TVs; refrigerator; ample street parking; *two-night minimum.*

ROOM	BED	BATH	ENTRANCE	FLOOR	DAILY RATES S	D	EP
A	1Q	Pvt	Sep	1G	$65	$70	$10

SANTA CLARA

Argonaut House   **(408) 244-4849**
Host: Marcia Doyle
2358 Fosgate Avenue, Santa Clara, CA 95050
In Santa Clara, near Pruneridge Golf Course.

Marcia's home in a quiet Santa Clara neighborhood is tucked away from busy streets, yet near the Silicon Valley in a neighborhood of 1950's Ranch-style homes. The pleasing guest room has a view of the quiet back yard and patio. The bath is just across the hall. You can relax in the bright living room with its stuffed furniture and pleasing skylight and fireplace, or in the family room, or on the patio and enjoy the roses in her well-maintained yard and garden. Nearby is the University of Santa Clara, and area attractions also include the Japanese Friendship Garden, Winchester Mystery House, San Jose Art Museum, San Jose Performing Arts Center, and hiking/biking along the San Francisco peninsula. Marcia particularly recommends the San Jose Rose Garden and the extra-special flower gardens at Filoli (near Woodside). Marcia knows the area well and will be glad to help you plan your visit.

No smoking, children, or pets; continental breakfast; AC; TV/VCR; fireplace; snacks and beverages always available.

ROOM	BED	BATH	ENTRANCE	FLOOR	S	D	EP
A	1D	Pvt	Main	1	$60	$75	

DAILY RATES

SONORA

Lavender Hill Bed & Breakfast (209) 532-9024
Hosts: Jean and Charlie Marinelli (800) 446-1333 x 290
683 South Barretta Street, Sonora, CA 95370
Central Sonora.

Set on a hill overlooking town and countryside, Lavender Hill Bed & Breakfast is a turn-of-the-century Victorian with period furnishings and plenty of old-fashioned comfort. Jean and Charlie provide an easy manner that make guests feel immediately at home, relaxed, and pampered. On the main floor there are spacious common areas where guests are welcome, as well as a formal dining room where three-course breakfasts are graciously served. Bedrooms on the second floor vary in size and combine the charm of sloped ceilings, papered walls, quilts, and floral themes. To visit Lavender Hill Bed & Breakfast is to enjoy the unhurried pace and abundant hospitality that make staying here an unqualified pleasure. When you are out and about in Sonora, Jean and Charlie suggest you take the carriage ride through the historic downtown.

No pets; smoking outside only; full breakfast; TV, books, and games available; porch swing; lawn furniture under shade trees; walk to shops and restaurants; off-street parking.

ROOM	BED	BATH	ENTRANCE	FLOOR	DAILY RATES S D EP+
Lavender	1K	Pvt	Main	2	$90
Primavera	1Q	Shd	Main	2	$70
Wildflower	1Q	Shd	Main	2	$70
Cabbage Rose	1Q	Pvt	Main	2	$80

SPRINGVILLE

Annie's Bed & Breakfast   (209) 539-3827
Hosts: Annie and John Bozanich
33024 Globe Drive, Springville, CA 93265
In the Sierra foothills off Highway 190.

    Annie and John offer B&B guests something delightfully unusual in lodging. Oh, all the comforts are here in abundance, but then...well...about the hosts...John is a horse trainer, saddlemaker, and also makes custom golf clubs. Annie, who takes dancing lessons, happens to love pigs. She has three. Two are potbelly pigs—Boo, a black potbelly who thinks she is the Queen; and Mr. Magoo, a near sighted white potbelly pig. The newest addition is Fannie, a Duroc mix speckled hog. They all love to do trick for treats. When John and Annie had their swimming pool built, they equipped it with spouting fountains all around, inside jets, and a place to install a volleyball net. Staying at Annie's is just plain fun—and each individually decorated room is just plain gorgeous. Full country breakfasts, cooked on an antique woodstove, are beautifully served. Here *everything* is a special treat. A special area event is the Apple Festival, the third weekend in October. A secret and special place to visit is the Balch Park redwood grove.

  No pets, not recommended for children under twelve, no smoking; full breakfast and afternoon refreshments; swimming pool; golf, fishing, boating, tennis, and hiking nearby; off-street parking; major credit cards; inquire about weddings, receptions, and small business meetings and dinner parties.

ROOM	BED	BATH	ENTRANCE	FLOOR	DAILY RATES S	D	EP
Ode's Room	1D	Pvt	Sep	1	$75	$85	$25
Boars Room	1D	Pvt	Sep	1	$75	$85	
Sows Room	2T	Pvt	Sep	1	$75	$85	

California

ST. HELENA

Judy's Bed & Breakfast (707) 963-3081
Hosts: Judy and Bob Sculatti
2036 Madrona Avenue, St. Helena, CA 94574
One-half mile west of Main Street, or Highway 29.

You'll get a warm, wine-country welcome at Judy's. Bob and Judy Sculatti have enjoyed their vineyard setting for many years. They've converted a spacious, private room at one end of their home to a B&B accommodation of great charm and air conditioned comfort. The large space is furnished with lovely antiques and a romantic brass bed. There is also a wood-burning stove with a glass door. Complimentary beverage and cheese are offered upon your arrival. Breakfast is served in your room or outside. Judy's is a gracious place to return to after a day of touring and tasting. To round out your perfect day, dine at one of the Napa Valley's superb restaurants.

No pets; no smoking preferred; TV; AC; off-street parking; Italian spoken; weekday rates $10 less; **KNIGHTTIME PUBLICATIONS SPECIAL RATE: 10% discount with this book.

ROOM	BED	BATH	ENTRANCE	FLOOR	DAILY RATES S	D	EP+
A	1Q	Pvt	Sep	1G		$95	$25

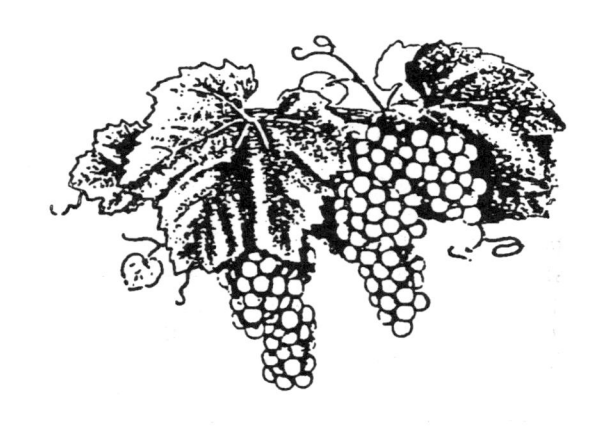

TAHOE CITY

Chaney House   (916) 525-7333
Hosts: Gary and Lori Chaney   FAX: (916) 525-4413
PO Box 7852, Tahoe City, CA 96145
4725 West Lake Blvd., overlooking the west shore of Lake Tahoe.

California

    Few homes around Lake Tahoe possess the unique sense of history that Chaney House has. Some of the Italian stonemasons who built Vikingsholm at nearby Emerald Bay in the twenties also worked on this impressive home. Eighteen-inch-thick stone walls, elaborately carved woodwork, Gothic arches, and a massive stone fireplace reaching to the top of the cathedral ceiling give the interior an old-world European flavor. Stone arches and walls outline the paths around the three patios; on one of these, superb breakfasts are served on mild days. Across the road, enjoy the private pier that juts out into the crystal clear water or take a bike ride on the path alongside the lake; in winter, choose from the many ski areas close at hand. Gary and Lori love the territory around them and they are well-versed on its wealth of outdoor and indoor activities for year-round pleasure including the Snowfest in March and music festival in July and August. Let the warmth of their hospitality enhance your next visit to spectacular Lake Tahoe.

    Dog in residence; no pets; children over twelve welcome; smoking outside only; full breakfast; TV/VCR; barbecue; off-street parking; sofa bed extra in *Master Suite*; additional lodging in quaint, European-style *Honeymoon Hideaway* with kitchen; two-night minimum on weekends.

ROOM	BED	BATH	ENTRANCE	FLOOR	DAILY RATES S	D	EP+
Jeanne's Room	1Q	Pvt	Main	1		$100	$20
Russell's Suite	1Q	Pvt	Main	2		$110	$20
Master Suite	1K	Pvt	Main	2		$120	$20
Honeymoon Hideaway	1Q	Pvt	Sep	2		$125	$20

TAHOE PARADISE

Chalet A-Capella (916) 577-6841
Hosts: Richard and Suzanne Capella
PO Box 11334, Tahoe Paradise, CA 95708
Near the intersection of Highways 89 and 50.

Richard and Suzanne's chalet-style home blends well with the Alpine scenery that surrounds it. You can go cross-country skiing from the doorstep, drive to a number of ski touring trails or downhill slopes in about thirty minutes, or fish right across the street in the Upper Truckee River. South Shore casinos are a short distance away. The interior woodwork and sloped ceilings of the upstairs guest quarters create a snug, rustic feeling. A bedroom and a private bath are just right for a couple. Summer or winter, Chalet A-Capella is a picture-perfect vacation spot.

No pets; no smoking preferred; TV; deck; off-street parking; Italian spoken; one-night stays, $5 extra; two-night minimum preferred.

ROOM	BED	BATH	ENTRANCE	FLOOR	DAILY RATES S / D / EP
A	1K	Pvt	Sep	2	$50

THREE RIVERS

Cort Cottage **(209) 561-4671**
Hosts: Gary and Catherine Cort **(209) 561-4036**
PO Box 245, Three Rivers, CA 93271
East of Visalia, near the entrance to Sequoia National Park.

The natural setting for this B&B is breathtaking. The inviting private cottage with a panoramic view of mountain and sky was built by architect/owner Gary Cort to fit snugly into a hillside next to the Corts' home. At sunrise and sunset, colors play off the rocks in a constantly changing show. In the spring, wildflowers bloom in profusion in the meadow below the cottage while the foothills become a brilliant green. A private outdoor hot tub is located, as Cathy Cort says, "directly under the Milky Way." The cottage is a splendid home base for exploring Sequoia/Kings Canyon National Park and it's Giant forest where you can witness trees that are the largest living things on earth. You'll feel dwarfed by their size and awed by their beauty—and love every minute of it. Sequoia has a myriad of hiking trails for all levels of foot travel. You can walk quietly under the redwoods, cross country ski or explore Crystal Cave. Those with an interest in art will want to visit the Cort Gallery in Three Rivers; it is "dedicated to the ideal that art is a part of every moment" and shows the work of local artists.

No pets; smoking outside on the deck only; sunken bathtub/shower; fully equipped kitchen; sofa bed in living room; hot tub; off-street parking; two-night minimum except for last-minute availability; credit cards (MC,V).

ROOM	BED	BATH	ENTRANCE	FLOOR	DAILY RATES S	D	EP
Cort Cottage	1Q	Pvt	Sep	1	$70	$75	$10

THREE RIVERS

The Garden Room (209)561-4853
Hosts: Mike and Celeste Riley
43745 Kaweah River Drive, Three Rivers, CA 93271
East of Visalia, near the entrance to Sequoia National Park.

Set among large oak trees at the end of a private road near the Kaweah River, The Garden Room is a self-contained guest accommodation that was architecturally designed to blend with the vintage home of Mike and Celeste Riley. Connected by a breezeway to their home, the unit was built partially around a large boulder that was integrated into the design and serves as a base for a free-standing fireplace. Cascading plants thrive among rocks that extend from the boulder. The total effect is ingeniously organic, with built-in furnishings and everything perfectly coordinated, from the forest green floral chintz fabric right down to the dishes. Mike's artistic touches highlight the decor: lovely oil paintings of rural scenes on the walls and stenciled designs on the wooden doors, dining table, and headboard. Above the bed, there's a large skylight, and beyond the sliding glass doors, a rock-enclosed garden patio. The Garden Room was custom-crafted for comfort; it's a place to bask in country seclusion surrounded by art and nature. Enjoy the area by walking the entrance road or strolling to the nearby llama ranch.

No pets; smoking outside only; full breakfast; TV; patio with chairs; coffee/tea-making area with small fridge; extra sleeping space on built-in seating; off-street parking; excellent hiking nearby; summer recreation at Lake Kaweah.

ROOM	BED	BATH	ENTRANCE	FLOOR	DAILY RATES S	D	EP
A	1Q	Pvt	Sep	1G		$75	$10

WATSONVILLE

Villa Carota   (408) 722-6075
Hosts: Elizabeth and Harold Carota
385 Protsman Way, Watsonville, CA 95076
Off Freedom Boulevard, near Highway 1.

    The Carotas' Mediterranean style home sits high on a hill overlooking Freedom Lake. It's convenient to the Santa Cruz beaches, and to the restaurants and shops of Carmel, Monterey, and Pacific Grove. The second floor room (A) is a one bedroom apartment with kitchenette. It's spacious, with modern decor and a private deck off the kitchen. The ground-floor room is wheelchair accessible and contains a large closet and bright brass bed. Breakfast is served family style, giving you a nice chance to chat with the gracious Carotas. Elizabeth is a watercolor artist, and her pictures hang throughout the house. Later, head outside to enjoy the garden and grape arbor while roaming the hilltop and enjoying the view. Elizabeth and Harold suggest beach walks, and hikes at Point Lobos near Carmel or at Fremont Peak in Hollister. California State College at Santa Cruz is nearby, and of course, the Monterey Bay Aquarium and Santa Cruz boardwalk are readily accessible.

    No pets; please, smoking outside only; children by arrangement; full breakfast; TV in each room; ground floor room (B) wheel chair accessible; patio; off street parking.

ROOM	BED	BATH	ENTRANCE	FLOOR	DAILY RATES S	D	EP+
A	1Q & 2T	Pvt	Sep	2		$90	$15
B	1Q	Pvt	Main	1		$75	

WATSONVILLE

Knighttime Bed & Breakfast (408) 684-0528
Hosts: Ray Miller and Diane Knight FAX: (408) 684-1859
890 Calabasas Road, Watsonville, CA 95076
Upper Monterey Bay Area.

    This well constructed custom home is set in a clearing on a hilltop surrounded by twenty-six acres of eucalyptus, redwood, and manzanita. It's just a few minutes from the beaches between Santa Cruz and Monterey. Built with conventional wood siding in the style of a New England log home, it has a pitched roof and wide porches. The bright interior is filled with art, pine and walnut cabinetry, and creature comforts. Eclectic furnishings include some antiques as well as reproductions, wicker, and new pieces tucked into inviting nooks and crannies. The main floor has a country French flavor, and the decor of the upper floor—the guests' private area—is strongly influenced by shells and the sea. Luscious shades of pink and peach prevail in the sitting room, large bath, commodious bedroom, and second bedroom that can sleep two additional persons in the same party. Ray and Diane enjoy guests from all walks of life. For activities, they suggest hiking, bird watching, and kayaking in Elkhorn Slough Natural Estaurine Research Reserve and always encourage guests to visit the nearby, excellent, Santa Cruz County wineries.

    No smoking; pets by arrangement; full breakfast on weekends, continental breakfast weekdays; off-street parking.

ROOM	BED	BATH	ENTRANCE	FLOOR	DAILY RATES S	D	EP
A	1T, 1D, 1Q	Pvt	Main	2	$65	$75	$25

WESTPORT

Howard Creek Ranch   **(707) 964-6725**
Hosts: Charles and Sally Grigg
PO Box 121, Westport, CA 95488
Three miles north of Westport on Highway 1.

Sally and Charles (Sunny) invite you to retreat to the romance of yesteryear at Howard Creek Ranch. Their ranch house was built in 1872 by Alfred Howard, newly arrived from the coast of Maine. At one time a stagecoach stop, it is now a quaint and cozy home filled with collectibles and antiques. The guest suites allow privacy, and the old fireplace inspires conversation and fun. The house is set in a wide, secluded valley at the mouth of Howard Creek. It faces the ocean and a wide, sandy beach where you can walk for miles at low tide. Several private, handcrafted redwood guest units on the forty-acre property offer additional accommodations. At this bed and breakfast resort, you can find your own pace and tune in to the natural beauty all around you. And not to be missed is the Westport rubber ducky race held in the creek on Mother's Day. An event to remember! Horseback riding is nearby on the beach or in the redwoods.

Various animals on property; full ranch breakfast; kitchen privileges by arrangement; barbecue; heated swimming pool; hot tub; sauna; massage by reservation; off-street parking; credit cards (V,MC,AMEX); skylights in most units; *Sun Room* has a balcony; *The Boat* is a boat; *Meadow Cabin* and *Beach House* are cabins with woodstoves; **KNIGHTTIME PUBLICATIONS SPECIAL: Stay 2 nights, get third night free, Sunday through Thursday, November 1 through May 15, excluding holiday periods. Mention offer immediately when reserving, present book upon arrival.

ROOM	BED	BATH	ENTRANCE	FLOOR	DAILY RATES S / D / EP+
Sun Room	1Q	Pvt	Sep	2	$95
Garden Room	1K & 1T	Pvt	Sep	1	$95
Loft Room	1Q	Shd	Main	2	$69
The Boat	1D	Pvt	Sep	1	$115
Meadow Cabin	1D	Pvt	Sep	1	$55
Beach House	1K & 1D	Pvt	Sep	1	$145

WHITTIER

Coleen's California Casa (310) 699-8427
Host: Coleen Davis
PO Box 9302, Whittier, CA 90608
Five minutes from I-605; thirty minutes east of downtown L.A.

Staying at Coleen Davis's contemporary hillside home is one pleasant surprise after another. Park in front, then make your way through the lush foliage to the back where you'll find a delightful patio/garden and the entrance to the private guest quarters. After settling in, join Coleen on the patio for wine and hors d'oeuvres. After dark you can view the lights of Whittier, and maybe the fireworks of Disneyland, from the large front deck (pictured) where ample breakfast specialties are served. If you're inclined to watch TV, write, or read in bed, the adjustable king-sized bed in Room A will please you. The Casa is a quiet retreat where families can share a private space and get all the help they need to plan a day's adventure in the booming L.A. area. You may even wind up with a little memento from Coleen to remind you of your wonderful visit; she's great with surprises. She did mention that close to Whittier, a historic Quaker landmark and home of Whittier College, there is a horseback riding, fishing; even skiing in the winter; close to California Casa you'll find Knotts Berry Farm and several museums

No pets; full breakfast; TV, robes in each room; use of fridge and microwave; off-street parking; wheelchair access; If rooms A & B are used as a suite, rate is $95; Room C is off the front deck, has a king bed and sitting room with sofa bed, if used as a suite, rate is $95; two-night minimum; one-night stays, $10 extra. Coleen operates a B&B reservation service: CoHost, America's Bed & Breakfast, she can help you with listings throughout California.

ROOM	BED	BATH	ENTRANCE	FLOOR	S	D	EP+
A	1K	Pvt	Sep	1G		$65	$15
B	2T	Pvt	Sep	1G		$65	
C	1K	Pvt	Sep	1G		$65	

(DAILY RATES)

YOSEMITE NATIONAL PARK

Waldschloss Bed & Breakfast   (209) 372-4958
Hosts: John and Betty Clark
7486 Henness Circle, Yosemite West, Y. N. P., CA 95389
Midway between Wawona and Yosemite Valley.

    Many who visit John and Betty Clark envy their unique location. Surrounded on three sides by the national park, their property is in a private development at 6400 feet, well away from the congestion of the valley yet ideally poised for exploring a variety of wonders. Waldschloss is a beautifully appointed mountain home with two distinctive accommodations. The spacious *Queen Room* done in ivory and lace features a collection of fine old quilts; it has a large bath with oak cabinetry. A detached two-floor *Suite* has a sitting room with a free-standing circular stairway leading to the sleeping quarters: a twin-bedded room with oak and brass furnishings, a ceiling fan, lace curtains, and fluffy bedspreads in ivory, pink, and blue. A full bath completes the *Suite*. Country silence, starry night skies, home cooking, freshly ironed cotton sheets, cozy comforters, a brick fireplace, and old toys tucked discreetly about enhance Waldschloss—a real Yosemite experience. Nearby is the Pioneer Yosemite History Center which commemorates the establishment of the national park.

    No pets; children by arrangement; smoking on deck only; full breakfast; TV/VCR; off-street parking; some German spoken; credit cards V,MC; *closed December-February*.

ROOM	BED	BATH	ENTRANCE	FLOOR	DAILY RATES S	D	EP+
Queen	1Q	Pvt	Main	1		$78	$15
Suite	2T	Pvt	Sep	1 & 2		$88	$15

DINING HIGHLIGHTS - CALIFORNIA

Please read "About Dining Highlights" on page ix.

ALBANY see East Bay

AMADOR CITY

Ballads; 14220 Highway 49; (209) 267-5403; California

Imperial Hotel; 14202 Highway 49; (209) 267-9172; Continental

Pelargonium; #1 Hanford Street (Highway 49 N) in Sutter Creek; (209) 267-5008; California

Teresa's; 1235 Jackson Gate Road in Jackson; (209) 223-1786; Italian/American

APTOS

Cafe Sparrow; 8042 Soquel Avenue; (408) 688-6238; French-style home cooking

Chez Renee; 9051 Soquel Avenue; (408) 688-5566; French/Continental

Palapas; 21 Seascape Village- Seascape Boulevard and Sumner Avenue; (408) 662-9000; Mexican seafood

Sanderlings; 1 Seascape Resort Drive; (408) 662-7120; ocean view fine dining

The Veranda; 8041 Soquel Avenue; (408) 685-1881; American/California

BERKELEY see East Bay

BIG SUR see Monterey

BISHOP

Brass Bell; 635 North Main Street; (619) 872-1200

Paradise Lodge; 15 miles north on Lower Rock Creek Road; (619) 387-2370; steak/seafood

Whiskey Creek; 524 North Main Street; (619) 873-7174

BOLINAS see Marin County

BOONVILLE

The Boonville Hotel; Highway 128; (707) 895-2210; California

CALISTOGA

All Seasons Cafe & Wine; 1400 Lincoln Ave.; (707) 942-9111; bistro/wine

Calistoga Inn; 1250 Lincoln Ave.; (707) 942-4101; Fresh seafood/American

Valeriano's Ristorante; 1457 Lincoln Ave. in the Mount View Hotel; Italian

CAMBRIA

The Brambles Dinner House; 4005 Burton Drive; (805) 927-4716; prime rib/seafood

Ian's Restaurant; 2150 Center Street; (805) 927-8649; American/extensive wine list

Main Street Grill; 603 Main Street; (805) 927-3194; excellent fast food and take-out orders

DINING HIGHLIGHTS - CALIFORNIA

CAMBRIA (continued)
Robin's; 4095 Burton Drive; (805) 927-5007; breakfast/lunch/dinner/varied ethnic and vegetarian dishes

The Sow's Ear; 2248 Main Street; (805) 927-4865; ribs/chicken/fish

CAPITOLA
Balzac Bistro; 112 Capitola Avenue; (408) 476-5035; informal Continental

Caffe Lido Bar & Ristorante; 110 Monterey Avenue, Capitola Village at the beach; (408) 475-6544; casual Italian

Gayle's Bakery & Rosticceria; 504 Bay Avenue; (408) 462-1200; baked goods/salads/hot entrees

Shadowbrook Restaurant; 1750 Wharf Road; (408) 475-1511; Continental

CARMEL see Monterey

CASTROVILLE
Central Texan Barbecue; 10749 Merritt Street; (408) 633-2285; -a vegetarian's nightmare-

CHICO
The Restaurant Albatross; 3312 The Esplanade; (916) 345-6037

Dancing Noodles; 131 Broadway; (916) 891-1383; pasta

R Fish & Company; 2539 The Esplanade; (916) 895-3474; seafood

The Sicilian Cafe; 1020 Main; (916) 345-2233

CONTRA COSTA COUNTY - CONCORD
Grissini; 1970A Diamond Boulevard; (510) 680-1700; northern Italian

CONTRA COSTA COUNTY - DANVILLE
Blackhawk Grille; 3540 Blackhawk Plaza Circle; (510) 736-4295; contemporary Mediterranean

Bridges Restaurant and Bar; 44 Church Street; (510) 820-7200; California with Asian influence

Cafe de Paris; 3407 Blackhawk Plaza Circle; (510) 736-5006; crepes

Faz; 400 South Hartz Avenue; (510) 838-1320; Mediterranean/Greek/Italian

Florentine Restaurant and Pasta Market; 3485 Blackhawk Plaza Circle; (510) 736-6060; Italian

Sen Dai; 101C Town & Country Drive; (510) 837-1027; Japanese

CONTRA COSTA COUNTY - LAFAYETTE
Duck Club; 3287 Mount Diablo Drive in the Lafayette Park Hotel; (510) 283-3700; regional American

Miraku; 3740 Mount Diablo Boulevard; (510) 284-5700; Japanese

Spruzzo! Ristorante; 210 Lafayette Circle; (510) 284-9709; Italian

Tourelle; 3565 Mount Diablo Boulevard; (510) 284-3565; Mediterranean bistro

Uncle Yu's Szechuan; 999 Oak Hill Road; (510) 283-1688

DINING HIGHLIGHTS - CALIFORNIA

CONTRA COSTA COUNTY - LIVERMORE
Wente Brothers Restaurant (Champagne Cellars); 5050 Arroyo Road; (510) 447-3696; California/summer concerts

CONTRA COSTA COUNTY - WALNUT CREEK
Il Pavone; 2291 Olympic Boulevard; (510) 939-9060; cucina Italiana

Mai Thai; 1414 North Main Street; (510) 937-7887

Max's Opera Cafe; 1676 North California Boulevard; (510) 932-3434; American/New York-style deli

Montecatini; 1528 Civic Drive; (510) 943-6608; Italian

Ristorante Toscano; 1520 Palos Verdes Mall; (510) 934-3737; Italian

Spiedini Northern Italian Ristorante; 101 Ygnacio Valley Road; (510) 939-2100; Italian

Vic Stewart's; 850 South Broadway; (510) 943-5666; steak

Wan Fu; 1375 N. Broadway; (510) 938-2288; elegant Szechwan/Mandarin

CORTE MADERA see Marin County

DANVILLE see Contra Costa County

DAVENPORT
New Davenport Cash Store Restaurant; Highway 1; (408) 426-4122; fresh home cooking, California style

EAST BAY - ALBANY
Enoteca Mastro; 933 San Pablo Avenue; (510) 524-4822; northern Italian/nouvelle northern California

EAST BAY - BERKELEY
Ajanta; 1888 Solano Avenue; (510) 526-4373; Indian

Cafe Fanny; 1603 San Pablo Avenue; (510) 524-5447; fresh, simple breakfasts/lunches

Chez Panisse; 1517 Shattuck Avenue; (510) 548-5525; California

Fatapple's; 1346 Martin Luther King Jr. Way; (510) 526-2260; American/burgers

Gertie's Chesapeake Bay Cafe; 1919 Addison Street; (510) 841-2722; Maryland and Louisiana seafood dishes

Ginger Island; 1820 Fourth Street; (510) 644-0444; Asian/California

Kirala Japanese Restaurant; 2100 Ward Street; (510) 549-3486

Lalime's; 1329 Gilman Street; (510) 527-9838; Mediterranean French

Plearn Thai Cuisine; 2050 University Avenue; (510) 841-2148

Rick & Ann's; 2922 Domingo Street; (510) 649-8538; American

Yujean's Modern Cuisine of China; 843 San Pablo Avenue; (510) 525-8557

EAST BAY - EMERYVILLE
Bucci's; 6121 Hollis Street; (510) 547-4725; Italian

Townhouse Bar & Grill; 5862 Doyle Street; (510) 652-6151; American

DINING HIGHLIGHTS - CALIFORNIA

EAST BAY - OAKLAND
Bay Wolf Restaurant; 3853 Piedmont Avenue; (510) 655-6004; California/Mediterranean
Cactus Taqueria; 5525 College Avenue; (510) 547-1305; Mexican
Chef Paul's; 4197 Piedmont Avenue; (510) 547-2175; French
Citron; 5484 College Avenue; (510) 653-5484; Mediterranean-influenced California
Creme de la Creme; 5362 College Avenue; (510) 420-8822; California/country French
Fornelli; 5891 Broadway Terrace; (510) 652-4442; Italian
Jade Villa; 800 Broadway; (510) 839-1688; Chinese/dim sum
La Brasserie; 542 Grand Avenue; (510) 893-6206; traditional French
Little Shin Shin; 4258 Piedmont Avenue; (510) 658-9799; Chinese
Nan Yang; 301 8th Street; (510) 465-6924; Indian/Chinese/Burmese home cooking
Nan Yang; 6048 College Avenue; (510) 655-3298; Indian/Chinese/Burmese home cooking
Olivetto; 5655 College Avenue; (510) 547-5356; Mediterranean
Sorabal; 372 Grand Avenue; (510) 839-2288; Korean
Ti Bacio Ristorante; 5912 College Avenue; (510) 428-1703; heart-healthy Italian
Zachary's; 5801 College Avenue; (510) 655-6385; Chicago pizza

EMERYVILLE see East Bay
EUREKA
Lazios Restaurant; 327 2nd Street; (707) 443-9717; California
Roys Italian club; 216 'D' Street; (707) 442-4574
The Sea Grill; 316 E Street in Old Town; (707) 443-7187; seafood/steaks
Tomo Japanese Restaurant; in the Hotel Arcata, Arcata; (707) 822-3223

GREENBRAE see Marin County
HALF MOON BAY
The Foglifter Restaurant; Corner of Eighth Street and Highway 1 in Montara; (415) 728-7905; eclectic menu
Pasta Moon; 315 Main Street; (415) 726-5125; homemade pasta and sauces
San Benito House; 356 Main Street; (415) 726-3425; French/northern Italian
Waves; 4230 Cabrillo Highway; (415) 726-9500; northern Italian/pasta/seafood/view dining

HEALDSBURG
Bistro Ralph; 109 Plaza Street; (707) 433-1380; American
Samba Java; 109A Plaza Street; (707) 433-5282; Caribbean
Tre Scalini; 241 Healdsburg Avenue; (707) 433-1772; fine Italian cuisine

DINING HIGHLIGHTS - CALIFORNIA

HEMET
Joe's The Sicilian; 41525 East Florida; (909) 766-5637; Italian

IDYLLWILD
Restaurant Gastrognome; 54381 Ridgeview Drive; (909) 659-5055; elegant dining/fresh fish/steaks/cocktails
Hidden Village; 25840 Cedar Street; (909) 659-2712; Mandarin Chinese
Pastries by Kathi; 54360 North Circle Drive; (909) 659-4359; specialty bakery/restaurant/breakfast/lunch/rural mountain ambiance
River Rock Cafe; 26290 Highway 243; (909) 659-5047; European bistro

INVERNESS
Barnabys by the Bay; 12938 Sir Francis Drake Boulevard; (415) 669-1114
Drake's Beach Cafe; Kenneth C. Patrick Visitor Center at Drake's Beach; (415) 669-1297; grilled fish/oysters/snacks/chowders
Grey Whale Pizza; 94937 Sir Francis Drake Boulevard; (415) 669-1244; pizza and antipasta salad
Manka's; 30 Callender Way at Argyle; (415) 669-1034; Continental/game

JACKSON see Amador City

KELSEYVILLE
Konocti Klines Oak Barrel; 6445 Soda Bay Road; (707) 279-0101; seafood
Lakewood Restaurant & Bar; 6330 Soda Bay Road; (707) 279-9450; French/American
Loon's Nest; 5685 Main Street; (707) 279-1812; American

KENTFIELD see Marin County

LAFAYETTE see Contra Costa County

LAKEPORT
Park Place Cafe; 50 Third Street; (707) 263-0444; homemade pasta/on the lake
Rainbow Restaurant & Bar; 2599 Lakeshore Boulevard; (707) 263-6237; American/lake view

LARKSPUR see Marin County

LIVERMORE see Contra Costa County

LOS ANGELES
Anarkali Indian Tandoori Restaurant; 7013 Melrose Avenue; (213) 934-6488
Authentic Cafe; 7605 Beverly Boulevard; (213) 939-4626; southwestern
Cafe des Artistes; 1534 North McFadden Place, Hollywood; (213) 461-6889; French (simple bistro-style)
Cafe Gale; 8400 Wilshire Boulevard; (213) 655-2494; eclectic menu
Cafe La Boheme; 8400 Santa Monica Boulevard; (213) 848-2360; California
Cafe Morpheus Bistro & Bakery; 180 North Robertson Boulevard, West Hollywood; (310) 657-0527; Franco-Italian
Campanile; 624 South La Brea Avenue; (213) 938-1447; Italian

DINING HIGHLIGHTS - CALIFORNIA

LOS ANGELES (continued)

Cha Cha Cafe; 656 North Virgil Avenue; (213) 664-7723; Caribbean

Chan Dara; 1511 North Cahuenga Boulevard; (213) 464-8585; Thai

Chopstix; 7229 Melrose Avenue; (213) 937-1111; Chinese

Cicada; 8478 Melrose Avenue; (213) 655-5559; country French

El Cholo; 1121 South Western Avenue; (213) 734-2773; Mexican

El Floridita; 1253 North Vine Street; (213) 871-8612; Cuban

El Mercadito; 3425 East First Street, East L.A.; (213) 268-3451; authentic Mexican

Emilio's Ristorante; 6602 Melrose Avenue; (213) 935-4922; Italian

Empress Pavilion; 988 North Hill St., Chinatown; (213) 617-9898; Chinese

Engine Company Number 28; 644 South Figueroa Street; (213) 624-6996; American

Flora Kitchen; 460 South La Brea Avenue; (213) 931-9900; California

Girogio; 114 West Channel Road, Santa Monica; (310) 459-8988; bustling cafe with lighter Italian cuisine

The Greek Connection; 133 North La Cienega Boulevard, Beverly Hills; (310) 659-2271

The Grill on the Alley; 9560 Dayton Way, Beverly Hills; (310) 276-0615; American

Hop Li Restaurant; 526 Alpine St. in Chinatown; (213) 680-3939; Chinese

Il Fornaio Cucina Italiana; 301 North Beverly Drive, Beverly Hills; (310) 550-8330

Il Piccolino; 641 North Highland Avenue; (213) 936-2996; Italian

Indigo; 8222-1/2 West Third Street; (213) 653-0140; California

Intermezzo; 6919 Melrose Avenue; (213) 937-2875; French

Jake & Annie's; 2702 Main Street, Santa Monica; (310) 452-1734; American

Kachina Grill; 330 South Hope Street; (213) 625-0956; southwestern

Katsu; 1972 North Hillhurst Avenue; (213) 665-1891; Japanese

Knoll's Black Forest Inn; 2454 Wilshire Boulevard, Santa Monica; (310) 395-2212; German

L.A. Trattoria; 8022 West Third Street; (213) 658-7607; Italian

La Luna; 113 North Larchmont Avenue; (213) 962-2130; Italian

Locanda Veneta; 8638 West Third Street, Beverly Hills; (310) 274-1893; Italian

Matsuhisa; 129 North La Cienega Boulevard, Beverly Hills; (310) 659-9639; Japanese

McCormick & Schmick's Seafood Restaurant; 600 Hope Place; (213) 629-1929

Mezzaluna; 9428 Brighton Way, Beverly Hills; (310) 275-6703; Italian

DINING HIGHLIGHTS - CALIFORNIA

LOS ANGELES (continued)
Mon Kees; 679 North Spring Street; (213) 628-6717; Chinese seafood

Monica's on Main; 2640 Main Street, Santa Monica; (310) 392-4956; American

Moustache Cafe; 8155 Melrose Avenue; (213) 651-2111; French

North Beach Bar & Grill; 111 Rose Avenue at Main Street, Venice; (310) 399-3900; old-fashioned steakhouse/contemporary California

Paru's Indian Vegetarian Restaurant; 5140 Sunset Boulevard; (213) 661-7600

Pazzia; 755 North La Cienega Boulevard; (310) 657-9271; Italian

Pho 79; 9200 Bolsa Avenue, Westminster; (714) 893-1883; Vietnamese

Plum Tree Inn; 937 North Hill Street; (213) 613-1819; Chinese

Rosalind's Ethopian; 1044 South Fairfax Avenue; (213) 936-2486; Ethiopian

Rose Cafe and Market; 220 Rose Avenue, Venice; (310) 399-0711; Continental

Rosso E N; 7371 Melrose Avenue; (213) 658-6340; Italian

17th Street Cafe on Montana; 1610 Montana Avenue, Santa Monica; (310) 453-2771; California

Sher-E Punjav Restaurant; 5370 Wilshire Boulevard; (213) 933-2031; Indian

Simply Thai; 1850 North Hillhurst Avenue; (213) 665-6958

Sonora Cafe; 445 South Figueroa Street; (213) 624-1800; Mexican

Tokyo Kaikan; 225 South San Pedro Street; (213) 489-1333; Japanese

Yamashiro; 1999 North Sycamore Avenue, Hollywood; (213) 466-5125; fine dining with spectacular view/Japanese

Ye Olde King's Head; 116 Santa Monica Boulevard, Santa Monica; (310) 451-1402; English pub fare

Zumayas; 5722 Melrose Avenue; (213) 464-0624; Mexican

LOS GATOS see also San Jose and Santa Clara
Andale Los Gatos; 21 North Santa Cruz Avenue; (408) 395-8997; light, healthy Mexican

Cafe Marcella; 368 Village Lane; (408) 354-8006; Italian trattoria

Pigalle; 27 North Santa Cruz Avenue; (408) 395-7924; French

Valeriano's Ristorante; 160 West Main Street; (408) 354-8108; Italian

MARIN COUNTY - BOLINAS
Bolinas Bay Bakery & Cafe; 20 Wharf Road; (415) 868-0211; eclectic menu

MARIN COUNTY - CORTE MADERA
Il Fornaio; 233 Corte Madera Town Center; (415) 927-4400; Italian

Savannah Grill; 55 Tamal Vista Boulevard; (415) 924-6774; American

MARIN COUNTY - GREENBRAE
Joe Lococo's; 300 Drake's Landing Road; (415) 925-0808; Italian

DINING HIGHLIGHTS - CALIFORNIA

MARIN COUNTY - KENTFIELD
Pacific Cafe; 850 College Avenue; (415) 456-3898; seafood
MARIN COUNTY - LARKSPUR
Lark Creek Inn; 234 Magnolia Avenue; (415) 924-7766; American
MARIN COUNTY - MILL VALLEY
The Avenue Grill; 44 East Blithedale Avenue; (415) 388-6003; American
Buckeye Roadhouse; 15 Shoreline Highway; (415) 331-2600; American
MARIN COUNTY - NICASIO
Rancho Nicasio; in Nicasio off Sir Francis Drake Boulevard; (415) 662-2219; meat specialties in western atmosphere
MARIN COUNTY - NOVATO
Dalecio; 340 Ignacio Boulevard; (415) 883-0960; Italian
MARIN COUNTY - OLEMA
Olema Inn Restaurant; 10000 Sir Francis Drake Boulevard at Highway 1; (415) 663-9559; Continental
MARIN COUNTY - SAN ANSELMO
Comforts; 337 San Anselmo Avenue; (415) 454-6790; eclectic menu
MARIN COUNTY - SAN RAFAEL
Pacific Tap and Grill; 812 Fourth Street; (415) 457-9711; American grill and beer garden
Rice Table; 1617 Fourth Street; (415) 456-1808; Indonesian
MARIN COUNTY - SAUSALITO
Arawan; 47 Caledonia Street; (415) 332-0882; Thai
North Sea Village; 300 Turney; (415) 331-3300; Chinese
MARIN COUNTY - STINSON BEACH
The Parkside; 43 Arenal Avenue; (415) 868-1272; casual neighborhood cafe/varied menu
Sand Dollar; 3458 Shoreline Highway; (415) 868-0434; simple seaside food
MARIN COUNTY - TIBURON
The Caprice; 2000 Paradise Drive, Waterfront Park; (415) 435-3400; Continental
Guaymas; 5 Main Street; (415) 435-6300; upscale Mexican
MARIPOSA
Chibchas; 2747 Highway 140, Catheys Valley; (209) 966-2940; Colombian
China Station; Highway 140 & Highway 49 South; (209) 966-3889; Chinese
Old Saw Mill; 5034 Coakley Circle; (209) 742-6101; varied and economical
Pizza Factory; Highway 140 and 5th Street; (209) 966-3112; pizza and Italian

DINING HIGHLIGHTS - CALIFORNIA

MENDOCINO
Bay View Cafe; Main Street; (707) 937-4197; breakfast/lunch/dinner/ocean view

Little River Restaurant; 7750 Highway 1, Little River; (707) 937-4945; 2 dinner seatings, chef's choice

MacCallum House Restaurant & Grey Whale Bar & Cafe; 45020 Albion Street; (707) 937-5763; Continental/fresh local ingredients, bistro menu

955 Ukiah Street; 955 Ukiah Street; (707) 937-1955; American

MILL VALLEY see Marin County
MONTARA see Half Moon Bay
MONTEREY - TOWN
Tarpy's Roadhouse; Highway 68 at Canyon Del Rey; (408) 647-1444; creative American country food

MONTEREY - BIG SUR
Deetjen's Big Sur Inn; Highway 1; (408) 667-2377; vegetarian/fish/meat

Glen Oaks Restaurant; Highway 1; (408) 667-2623; seafood/Continental

Nepenthe; Highway 1; (408) 667-2345; American

MONTEREY - CARMEL
Casanova Restaurant; Fifth Street between San Carlos and Mission; (408) 625-0501; country French/Italian

L'Escargot; Mission Street at Fourth; (408) 624-4914; French

La Boheme Restaurant; Dolores Street near 7th; (408) 624-7500; country European

Pacific's Edge; four miles south of Carmel on Highway 1 at Highlands Inn; (408) 624-3801; ocean view fine dining/regional California

Rio Grill; 101 Crossroads Boulevard; (408) 625-5436; creative American

MONTEREY - PACIFIC GROVE
Taste Cafe & Bistro; 1199 Forest; (408) 655-0324; Franco-Italian

MOSS LANDING
Maloney's Harbor Inn; Highway 1 at the bridge; (408) 724-9371; California/seafood

NICASIO see Marin County
NOVATO see Marin County
OAKHURST
Castillo's Mexican Restaurant; Highway 41 and Road 426; (209) 683-8000

Ducey's On the Lake; 39225 Marina Drive in Pines Village at Bass Lake; (209) 642-3131; steak/seafood

Erna's Elderberry House; Highway 41 and Victoria Lane; (209) 683-6800; Continental fine dining

Teresa's Place; 1235 Jackson Gate Road; (209) 223-1786; Italian/American

OAKLAND see East Bay

DINING HIGHLIGHTS - CALIFORNIA

OLEMA see Marin County
PACIFIC GROVE see Monterey
PALM SPRINGS
Alfredo's Italian Gardens; 385 South Palm Canyon Drive; (619) 325-4060; Italian
Cedar Creek Inn; 1555 South Palm Canyon Dr.; (619) 325-7300; American
Las Casuelas Terraza; 222 South Palm Canyon Drive; (619) 325-2794; Mexican
Otani, A Garden Restaurant; 1000 East Tahquitz Canyon Way; (619) 327-6700; Japanese
Thai Cuisine Siamese Gourmet; 4711 East Palm Canyon Drive at Gene Autry Trail; (619) 328-0057
PALO ALTO
Fresco; 3398 El Camino Real; (415) 493-3470; California
Gordon Biersch Brewing Company; 640 Emerson Street; (415) 323-7723; brewpub/California
PESCADERO
Duarte's Tavern; 202 Stage Road; (415) 879-0464; seafood/local specialties
PHILO
The Flood Gate Store & Grill; 1810 Highway 128; (707) 895-3000; regional dishes/grilled items
POINT REYES STATION
Point Reyes Road House; 10905 Highway 1; (415) 663-1277; oysters - everyway
Station House Cafe; 11180 Main Street (Highway 1); (415) 663-1515; American regional
RED BLUFF
The Green Barn; 5 Chestnut Avenue; (916) 527-9997; prime rib/fish/salads
REDDING
DeMercurio's Fine Dining; 1647 Hartnell Avenue; (916) 222-1307; French/Italian/American
Jack's Grill; 1743 California Street; (916) 241-9705; steakhouse
Nello's Place; 3055 Bechelli Lane; (916) 223-1636; Italian
SACRAMENTO
Biba Restaurant, Old Tavern Bldg.,; 2801 Capitol Avenue; (916) 455-2422; cucina Italiana
Capitol Grill; 2730 N Street; (916) 736-0744; California
Celestin's Caribbean; 2516 J Street; (916) 444-2423
Danielle's Village Creperie & Gallery; Fulton & Marconi, Town & Country Village; (916) 972-1911

DINING HIGHLIGHTS - CALIFORNIA

SACRAMENTO (continued)

Frank Fat's; 808 L Street; (916) 442-7092; Chinese - Sacramento's favorite

Harlow's Bar and Cafe; 2708 J Street; (916) 441-4693

Il Fornaio Gastronomia Italiano; 400 Capitol Mall; (916) 446-4100; Italian bistro

Mace's in the Pavillions Center; 501 Pavillions Lane; (916) 922-0222; California

SAN ANSELMO see Marin County

SAN DIEGO

Alexis Greek Cafe; 3863 Fifth Avenue; (619) 297-1777

Anthony's Seafood; 9530 Murray Drive, La Mesa; (619) 463-0368; fresh seafood in lake-side setting

The Belgian Lion; 2265 Bacon Street; (619) 223-2700; Belgian French

The Blue Crab Restaurant; 4922 North Harbor Drive; (619) 224-3000; seafood/lunch/dinner

Brigantine; 9350 Fuerte Drive, La Mesa; (619) 465-1935; varied menu

Busalacchi's Ristorante; 36813 Fifth Avenue; (619) 298-0119; Sicilian

Cafe Pacifica; 2414 San Diego Blvd.; (619) 291-6666; seafood/California

California Cafe Bar & Grill; 502 Horton Plaza; (619) 238-5440; California

California Cuisine; 1027 University Avenue; (619) 543-0790

Calliope's Greek Cafe; 3958 Fifth Avenue; (619) 291-5588

Canes California Bistro; 1270 Cleveland Avenue; (619) 299-3551

Cass Street Bar & Grill; 4612 Cass Street; (619) 270-1320; salad/soup/chili, great atmosphere

Celadon, a Thai Restaurant; 3628 Fifth Avenue; (619) 295-8800

Chez Odette; 3614 Fifth Avenue; (619) 299-1000; French

Chinese Garden Restaurant; 3057 Clairemont Drive, Clairemont Village; (619) 275-2888

Dansk Restaurant; 8425 La Mesa Boulevard, La Mesa; (619) 463-0640

El Bizcocho; 17550 Bernardo Oaks Drive, Rancho Bernardo; (619) 277-2146; Spanish

Fairouz Cafe & Gallery; 3166 Midway Drive #102; (619) 225-0308; Middle Eastern

Karinya Thai Restaurant; 4475 Mission Boulevard; (619) 270-5050; Thai

La Gran Tapa; 611 B Street; (619) 234-8272; Spanish

Little Tokyo; 3867 Fifth Avenue; (619) 291-8518; Japanese

Mandarin Plaza; 3760 Sports Arena Boulevard at Sports Arena Village; (619) 224-4222; Chinese

Montana's American Grill; 1421 University Avenue; (619) 297-0722

Osteria Panevino; 722 Fifth Avenue; (619) 595-7959; Tuscan

Petro's Place; 6618 Mission Gorge Road; (619) 280-4888; Greek

DINING HIGHLIGHTS - CALIFORNIA

SAN DIEGO (continued)

Quigg's Bar & Grill; 5091 Santa Monica Avenue, Ocean Beach; (619) 222-1101; seafood/pasta/steak/chicken

Rosaria Pizza; 8055 Clairemont Mesa Boulevard; (619) 565-8053; New York-style pizza

Saska's; 3768 Mission Boulevard, Mission Beach; (619) 488-7311; steak/seafood/late night dining

Thai Chada; 142 University Avenue; (619) 297-9548

Thee Bungalow; 4996 West Point Loma Boulevard; (619) 224-2884; Continental

Tokyo House; 980 Garnet Avenue; (619) 270-8828; Japanese

World Famous; 711 Pacific Beach Avenue, Pacific Beach; (619) 272-3100; seafood/steak/chicken

SAN FRANCISCO

Aqua; 252 California Street; (415) 956-9662; contemporary seafood

Baker Street Bistro; 2953 Baker Street; (415) 931-1475; neighborhood French

Boulevard; 1 Mission Street; (415) 543-6084; cutting-edge American

Brasserie Savoy; 580 Geary Street; (415) 474-8686; French/seafood

Buca Giovanni; 800 Greenwich Street; (415) 776-7766; Italian

Cafe For All Seasons; 350 West Portal Avenue; (415) 665-0900; American

Cafe Kati; 1963 Sutter Street; (415) 775-7313; international

Caffe Delle Stelle; 330 Gough Street; (415) 252-1110; informal Italian/live opera some evenings

Cha Cha Cha; 1805 Haight Street; (415) 386-5758; Caribbean

China House Bistro; 501 Balboa Street; (415) 752-2802; Chinese

City of Paris; 101 Shannon Alley in the Shannon Court Hotel; (415) 441-4442; Parisian-style brasserie

Cleopatra Restaurant; 1755 Noriega Street; (415) 753-5005; Middle Eastern

Compass Rose; Westin St. Francis Hotel at Union Square; (415) 774-0167; lunch/high tea/cocktails in splendid surroundings

Cypress Club; 500 Jackson Street; (415) 296-8555; contemporary regional American

Des Alpes; 732 Broadway; (415) 391-4249; Basque

The Flying Saucer; 1000 Guerrero Street; (415) 641-9955; neighborhood French

Fog City Diner; 1300 Battery St.; (415) 982-2000; contemporary American

Fringale; 570 Fourth Street; (415) 543-0573

Geva's; 482A Hayes Street; (415) 863-1220; contemporary Caribbean

Green's Restaurant; Fort Mason, on the water; (415) 771-6222; vegetarian

DINING HIGHLIGHTS - CALIFORNIA

SAN FRANCISCO (continued)

Hana Restaurant; 408 Irving Street; (415) 665-3952; neighborhood Japanese sushi bar

Harry Denton's; 161 Stewart Street; (415) 882-1333; American

The Helmand; 430 Broadway; (415) 362-0641; Afghanistani

Hong Kong Flower Lounge; 5322 Geary Blvd.; (415) 668-8998; Chinese

House of Nanking; 919 Kearney Street; (415) 421-1429; Chinese

Hyde Street Bistro; 1521 Hyde Street; (415) 441-7778; California

Jackson Cafe; 640 Jackson Street; (415) 982-2409; inexpensive prime rib/daily specials

Julie's Supper Club; 1123 Folsom Street; (415) 861-0707; American

Kabuto; 5116 Geary Boulevard; (415) 752-5652; sushi/Japanese

Kuleto's; 221 Powell Street (adjacent to Villa Florence Hotel); (415) 397-7720; Italian

L'Olivier; 465 Davis Street; (415) 981-7824; lighter classic French

La Bergerie; 4221 Geary Boulevard; (415) 387-3573; neighborhood French

La Folie; 2316 Polk Street; (415) 776-5577; upscale French

Le Central; 453 Bush Street; (415) 391-2233; French bistro/brasserie

Lulu; 816 Folsom Street; (415) 495-5775; Mediterranean

Manora's Thai Restaurant; 1600 Folsom Street; (415) 861-6224

McCormick & Kuleto's; 900 Northpoint in Ghirardelli Square; (415) 929-1730; upscale seafood/California

Michelangelo Cafe; 579 Columbus Avenue; (415) 986-4058; hearty Italian

Moose's; 1652 Stockton Street; (415) 989-7800; American

One Market; 1 Market Street; (415) 777-5577; American

Oriental Pearl; 760 Clay Street; (415) 433-1817; Chinese

Palio D'Asti; 640 Sacramento Street; (415) 395-9800; regional Italian

Panos'; 4000 24th Street; (415) 824-8000; Greek

PJ's Oyster Bed; 737 Irving Street; (415) 566-7775; seafood/cajun

Roosevelt Tamale Parlor; 2817 24th Street; (415) 550-9213; Mexican

Rosemarino; 3665 Sacramento Street; (415) 931-7710; neighborhood Mediterranean

Square One; 190 Pacific Street; (415) 788-1110; multi-ethnic cuisine

Stars Cafe; 555 Golden Gate Ave.; (415) 861-7827; light food/fish & chips

The Stinking Rose; 325 Columbus Ave.; (415) 781-7673; garlic specialties

Stoyanof's Cafe & Restaurant; 1240 Ninth Avenue; (415) 664-3664; Greek/Mediterranean/seafood

Tart to Tart; 641 Irving Street; (415) 753-0643; neighborhood cafe/coffees/baked goods

Thep Phanom Restaurant; 400 Waller Street; (415) 431-2526; Thai

DINING HIGHLIGHTS - CALIFORNIA

SAN FRANCISCO (continued)
Tuba Garden; 3634 Sacramento Street; (415) 921-8822; California

Vertigo; 600 Montgomery, at the base of Transamerica Bldg.; (415) 433-7250; seafood

Wu Kong Restaurant; 101 Spear Street, 1 Rincon Center; (415) 957-9300; shanghai Chinese

Yaya; 1220 9th Avenue; (415) 566-6966; Mesopotanian

Zuni Cafe; 1658 Market Street; (415) 552-2522; Mediterranean

SAN JOSE see also Santa Clara & Los Gatos
Eulipia Restaurant & Bar; 374 South First Street; (408) 280-6161; California

Gordon Biersch Brewing Company; 33 East San Fernando Street; (408) 294-6785; brewpub/California

Il Fornaio; 302 South Market Street in the Hotel Sainte Claire; (408) 271-3366; Italian

SAN LUIS OBISPO
Cafe Roma; 1819 Osos Street; (805) 541-6800; cucina rustica Italiana

SAN MATEO
Bella Mangiata Caffe; 233 Baldwin Avenue; (415) 343-2404; Italian

Buffalo Grill; 66 Hillsdale Mall on 31st Avenue; (415) 358-8777; American home cooking

Cafe for all Seasons; 50 East Third Avenue; (415) 348-4996; American

Capellini Ristorante; 310 Baldwin Avenue; (415) 348-2296; Italian

Eposto's Four Day Cafe; 1119 South B Street; (415) 345-6443; Italian

Jo Ann's B Street Cafe; 30 South B Street; (415) 347-7000; American

Max's Bakery and Kitchen; 111 East Fourth Avenue; (415) 344-1997; American

SAN RAFAEL see Marin County

SANTA BARBARA
Andria's Harborside Restaurant; 336 West Cabrillo Boulevard; (805) 966-3000; seafood

Bay Cafe Seafood Restaurant and Fish Market; 131 Anacapa; (805) 963-2215; seafood

Cold Spring Tavern; 5995 Stagecoach Road; (805) 967-0066; American/game

Enterprise Fish Company; 225 State Street; (805) 962-3313; seafood

La Super-Rica Taqueria; 622 North Milpas; (805) 963-4940; tacos/Mexican

Mousse Odile; 18 East Cota; (805) 962-5393; French

Paradise Cafe; 702 Anacapa; (805) 962-4416; seafood/California

SANTA CLARA see also Los Gatos and San Jose
Birk's; 3955 Freedom Circle; (408) 980-6400; classic American grill

DINING HIGHLIGHTS - CALIFORNIA
SANTA CRUZ
Cafe Bittersweet; 2332 Mission Street; (408) 423-9999; Italian/French/American home cooking/desserts/espresso/wine bar

Casablanca Restaurant; 101 Main Street, overlooking beach; (408) 426-9063; Continental cuisine/elegant atmosphere

Crow's Nest; 2218 East Cliff, by beach at Santa Cruz Yacht Harbor; (408) 476-4560; seafood/steaks/oyster bar

Hollins House; 20 Clubhouse Road; (408) 459-9177; Continental

India Joze; 1001 Center Street; (408) 427-3554; Asian/Middle Eastern

Linda's Seabreeze Cafe; 542 Seabreeze; (408) 427-9713; varied menu/breakfast/lunch

O'mei Restaurant; 2361 Mission Street; (408) 425-8458; Chinese

SAUSALITO see Marin County
SEBASTOPOL
Mom's Apple Pie; 4550 Gravenstein Highway North; (707) 823-8330; American home cooking

SONORA
Bella Union Dining Saloon; 18242 Main Street in Jamestown; (209) 984-2421; game dishes and a variety of specials

Carmela's; 221 South Stewart; (209) 532-8858; homestyle Italian

SONORA
City Hotel Restaurant; Main Street in Columbia; (209) 532-1479; nouvelle California

Coyote Creek Cafe; 177 South Washington; (209) 532-9115; international/healthy preparations

Diamondback Grill; 110 South Washington; (209) 532-6661; great burgers and innovative daily specials

Hemingway's Cafe; 362 South Stewart; (209) 532-4900; American/French

La Tortuga; 11914 Highway 49; (209) 532-2386; creative Italian trattoria

Michelangelo; 18228 Main Street in Jamestown; (209) 984-4830; Italian trattoria

SOQUEL
Ranjeet's; 3051 Porter Street; (408) 475-6407; California

Theo's; 3101 North Main Street; (408) 462-3657; French

Tortilla Flats; 4616 Soquel Drive; (408) 476-1754; Mexican

SPRINGVILLE
Golden Rice Bowls; 34961 Highway 190; (209) 539-3828; Chinese

Our Place; 35498 Highway 190; (209) 539-3225; sandwiches/pizza/barbecue

Springville Inn Restaurant; 35634 Highway 190; (209) 539 1708; steak/seafood/pasta/lamb

DINING HIGHLIGHTS - CALIFORNIA

ST. HELENA
Pairs; 1420 Main Street; (707) 963-7566; California/southwest
Terra; 1345 Railroad Avenue; (707) 963-8931; California
Tra Vigne; 1050 Charter Oak; (707) 963-4444; rustic Italian
Trilogy; 1234 Main Street; (707) 963-5507; American

STINSON BEACH see Marin County
SUTTER CREEK see Amador City
TAHOE CITY
Chambers Landing; 6300 Chambers Lodge Road, Homewood; (916) 525-7262; Mediterranean (summer only)

La Playa; 7046 North Lake Boulevard, Kings Beach; (916) 546-5903; creative fresh seafood

Pheifer House; 760 River Road; (916) 583-3102; German

River Ranch; Highway 89 at Alpine Meadows Road; (916) 583-4264; Continental/seafood

Swiss Lakewood; 5055 West Lake Boulevard; (916) 525-5211; Continental

West Shore Cafe; 5180 West Lake Boulevard, Homewood; (916) 525-5200; Continental (open summer only)

THREE RIVERS
The Gateway; 45978 Sierra Drive/Highway 198; (209) 561-4133; steaks/seafood/riverside setting

Staff of Life; 41651 Sierra Drive; (209) 561-4937; lunches/homemade soups/salads/sandwiches with vegetarian accent

White Horse Inn; 42975 Sierra Drive; (209) 561-4185; American

TIBURON see Marin County
VISALIA
The Vintage Press Restaurante; 216 North Willis Street; (209) 733-3033; California

WALNUT CREEK see Contra Costa County
WATSONVILLE
Amanda's Cafe; 1047 Freedom Boulevard; (408) 763-1448; American

Cilantros; 1934 Main Street, Watsonville Square; (408) 761-2161; Mexican

WESTPORT
DeHaven Valley Farm; One mile south of Howard Creek Ranch; (707) 961-1660; prix fixe, four course dinners

How shall I know unless I go
To China and Cathay
Whether or not this blessed spot
Is blest in every way.

--Edna St. Vincent Millay

Traveling makes a man wiser,
but less happy.

--Thomas Jefferson

Oregon

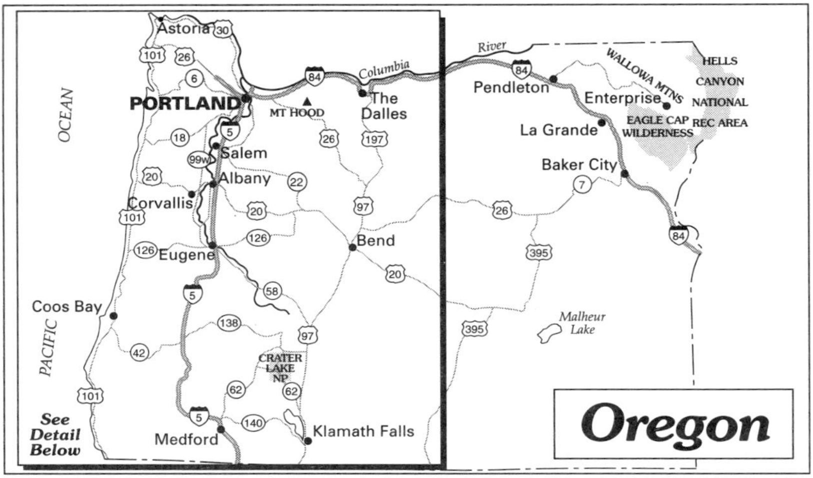
Oregon
Astoria
PORTLAND
MT HOOD
The Dalles
Columbia
River
OCEAN
PACIFIC
Salem
Albany
Corvallis
Eugene
Bend
Coos Bay
CRATER LAKE NP
Medford
Klamath Falls
See Detail Below
Pendleton
Enterprise
La Grande
Baker City
WALLOWA MTNS
EAGLE CAP WILDERNESS
HELLS CANYON NATIONAL REC AREA
Malheur Lake

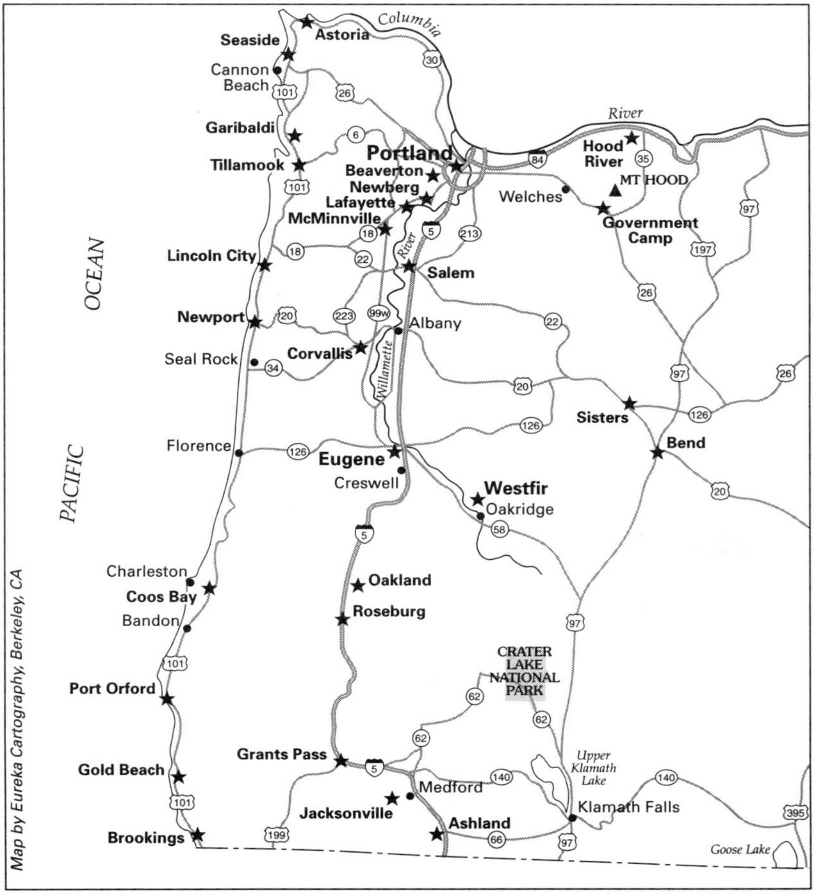
Columbia
River
Seaside
Astoria
Cannon Beach
Garibaldi
Tillamook
Portland
Beaverton
Newberg
Lafayette
McMinnville
Hood River
MT HOOD
Welches
Government Camp
OCEAN
PACIFIC
Lincoln City
Salem
Newport
Albany
Seal Rock
Corvallis
Willamette River
Sisters
Bend
Florence
Eugene
Creswell
Westfir
Oakridge
Charleston
Coos Bay
Bandon
Oakland
Roseburg
CRATER LAKE NATIONAL PARK
Port Orford
Grants Pass
Gold Beach
Jacksonville
Medford
Upper Klamath Lake
Klamath Falls
Ashland
Brookings
Goose Lake
Map by Eureka Cartography, Berkeley, CA

ASHLAND

The Woods House Bed & Breakfast Inn   **(800) 435-8260**
Hosts: Françoise and Lester Roddy   FAX: **(541) 482-7912**
333 North Main Street, Ashland, OR 97520   **(541) 488-1598**
In the historic district, four blocks from theaters.

This beautifully renovated 1908 Craftsman home has a welcoming heart that you feel as soon as you enter the front door. Françoise and Lester Roddy have restored the home's natural charm and added many comforts, services, and aesthetic pleasures that show up in each facet of the inn—from the inviting common living and dining rooms to the special, individually fashioned bedrooms to the exquisite terraced gardens. Romantic touches include fresh flowers, lovely antiques, lace canopies, and luxurious fabrics. Two accommodations are on the main floor, two on the upper floor, and two in the carriage house. At The Woods House, you'll have plenty of privacy, extravagant breakfasts, and some of the warmest hospitality around. The Roddy's suggest visiting the Pacific Northwest Natural History Museum or joining their murder mystery weekends held three times a year including New Year's Eve and Valentines Day.

Dog and cats on premises; no pets, but kennels nearby; smoking outside only; full or Continental breakfast; living room, front porch and garden areas for guests' relaxation; credit cards (V, MC); airport pickup in Ashland. *Note: Rates vary from $65 to $112 depending on season and day. RESERVE WELL IN ADVANCE DURING SHAKESPEARE FESTIVAL MONTHS, ESPECIALLY MAY - SEPTEMBER.

ROOM	BED	BATH	ENTRANCE	FLOOR	DAILY RATES S D EP+
Courtyard	1Q	Pvt	Sep	1	
Victoria	1Q & 1T	Pvt	Main	1	
Bouquet	1Q & 1T	Pvt	Main	2	*See
Monet	1Q & 1T	Pvt	Main	2	note
Cottage	1Q	Pvt	Sep	1G	
Cupid's Chamber	1K & 1T	Pvt	Sep	1G	

ASTORIA

The Inn-Chanted Bed & Breakfast (503) 325-5223
Hosts: Richard and Dixie Swart (800) 455-7018
707 Eighth Street, Astoria, OR 97103
In the historic area near Flavel House.

Dramatically situated where the mighty Columbia meets the Pacific, Astoria has the distinction of being the oldest town west of the Mississippi. Its early importance in the lumber trade prompted the construction of many fine Victorian homes overlooking the river. The Inn-Chanted bed and breakfast is one of the loveliest of these "painted ladies", with lots of nooks and crannies, interesting angles, and gingerbread trim. Wood moldings, medallions, and columns, silk brocade wallcoverings, crystal chandeliers, and other Victorian fancies abound, capturing the formality of a bygone era without sacrificing the comfort of guests. View passing ships from any of the three individually tailored accommodations, including the huge, romantic *Cherubs Chamber* suite that spans the front of the house. Richard and Dixie strive to pamper and, yes, enchant you with their special service, food, and accommodations. They would like to invite you to join them for the April Crab Festival, June Scandinavian Festival, or August regatta.

No pets; smoking outside only; full breakfast with a variety of options; TV in each room; deck/garden area; ample street parking; major credit cards; off-season discounts; airport pickup (Astoria/Warrenton); family accommodations in *The Sanctuary* or *Cherubs Chamber*.

ROOM	BED	BATH	ENTRANCE	FLOOR	DAILY RATES S	D	EP+
Victorian View	1Q	Pvt	Main	2	$75	$80	
The Sanctuary	1Q & 2T	Pvt	Main	2	$85	$90	
Cherubs Chamber	1Q & 2T	Pvt	Main	2	$105	$110	

BEAVERTON

The Yankee Tinker Bed & Breakfast   (503) 649-0932
Hosts: Jan and Ralph Wadleigh   (800) 846-5372
5480 SW 183rd Avenue, Beaverton, OR 97007
Ten miles west of Portland.

In the common surroundings of their quiet suburban neighborhood, Jan and Ralph Wadleigh offer a most uncommon bed and breakfast experience. They meet their guests' needs in a variety of ways, providing comforts, services, and luxuries far exceeding what one might expect. Local wines and cheeses may be enjoyed in the congenial ease of the guest sitting room. Bouquets of fresh flowers are displayed throughout the house, and each of the three guest bedrooms has its own special flair created with New England antiques and collectibles. Lovely quilts, bed linens, and family heirlooms add to the warm ambiance. A great night's sleep is followed by morning fare made up of specialties that the Wadleighs have developed just for their guests. The pleasant surprises and personalized care found at The Yankee Tinker gives Yankee hospitality a whole new meaning. Jan and Ralph suggest visiting in the spring to best see the area's many rhododendron gardens.

No pets or smoking; full breakfast; TV, fireplace, and writing desk in sitting room; AC; telephone in each room; rollaway bed available; large deck and lovely gardens; wineries, good restaurants, golf courses, public swimming pool, tennis courts, parks, and hiking trails in vicinity; good public transportation; off-street parking; major credit cards; 10% discount to business travelers.

ROOM	BED	BATH	ENTRANCE	FLOOR	S	D	EP+
Massachusetts	1Q	Pvt	Main	1G		$70	$10
Maine	1Q	Shd	Main	1G		$60	$10
New Hampshire	1T	Shd	Main	1G	$50		$10

BEND

The Sather House   (541) 388-1065
Host: Robbie Giamboi
7 NW Tumalo Avenue, Bend, OR 97701
Three blocks from downtown Bend and the Deschutes River.

The historic Sather house is conveniently close to downtown Bend, the Mt. Bachelor ski bus, and the Deschutes River. Robbie has carefully restored this stately green-and-white Colonial Revival home, built in 1911, and occupied by the Sather family for 75 years. Located in a quiet neighborhood of older homes, it provides a welcome alternative to other Bend accommodations. The rooms are uniquely furnished in elegant turn-of-the-century style. The plants and many large, sunny windows of the Garden Room bring the outside in. In the comfy den, you can play a friendly board game or two, or step into the living room, and settle in by the fireside with a good book—just the thing after a brisk day exploring the local lakes and mountains. Sather House is the perfect place to absorb the history of Bend and the high desert. Robbie has many suggestions on Bend's dining, activities, and area attractions. She specially suggests the weekly free summer-evening concerts in nearby Drake Park along the Deschutes River, and visiting the High Desert Museum.

No pets; children 12 and older; smoking outside only; full breakfast; TV/VCR; fireplace; library, off street parking; credit cards (MC,V,DS).

ROOM	BED	BATH	ENTRANCE	FLOOR	S	D	EP+
Garden Room	1K	Shd	Main	2		$85	$12
English Room	2T or 1K	Shd	Main	2		$75	
Victorian Room	1Q	Pvt	Main	2		$85	
Country Room	1D	Pvt	Main	2		$75	

BROOKINGS

Oceancrest House (800) 769-9200
Hosts: Georgine Paulin and Ronya Robinson (541) 469-9200
15510 Pedrioli Drive, Harbor, OR 97415
email: innkeep@harborside.com
3 1/2 miles north of the California border near Highway 101.

Oceancrest House provides two spacious rooms especially set up for privacy. Short stairs lead to the *Blue Room* with its panoramic view of the coast and Pelican Bay south to Point St. George off Crescent City. The ground floor *Rose Room* has glass doors opening onto a deck overlooking the beach and a very large bath. The house is not just ocean view, its oceanfront with 77 stairs (with two benches for resting) descending to a secluded beach protected by a rocky point. Low tide reveals an extensive network of tide pools to examine. Should dramatic winter storms threaten, your room is complete with TV/VCR, book and video library, games, tapes and tape deck, microwave, coffee maker, and stocked fridge—and always, the every-changing ocean view. Awaken to a breakfast tray of fresh fruit and baked goodies at your door; Ronya or Georgine are close by to suggest local activities or places to visit such as the Stout Redwood Grove, which was background for the Ewoks battle in <u>Star Wars</u>. Whether hiking a trail, hot tubbing under the stars, or just curling up with solitude and a good book, you'll find contentment at Oceancrest.

Cats in residence in the host's private quarters; no pets; smoking outside only; extended continental breakfast; TV/VCR/Tape Deck; board games; microwave; coffee maker; stocked guest refrigerator; hot tub; golf course; credit cards (MC,V,DS); member PAII.

ROOM	BED	BATH	ENTRANCE	FLOOR	S	DAILY RATES D	EP+
Rose	1Q	Pvt	Sep	1G		$89	$20
Blue	2Q	Pvt	Sep	2		$89	$20

COOS BAY

Upper Room Chalet   (541) 269-5385
Hosts: Carl and Barbara Solomon
306 North Eighth Street, Coos Bay, OR 97420
Central Coos Bay near Mingus Park (good jogging around the lake).

On a quiet little street near downtown, surrounded by evergreen and rhododendron, is the warm family home of Carl and Barbara Solomon. A piano in the foyer, a living room with cushy places to sit, a fireplace, and country Victorian decor combine to create the essence of hospitality. Family antiques, dolls, mementos, and photos fill the house. Each upstairs bedroom has a focal point: *Carleen's Room*, a colorful patchwork quilt; *Annette's Room*, two iron day beds done up in ivory eyelet and mauve; and the *Master Suite*, a king-sized antique brass bed, and private bath with clawfoot tub. The Solomons' big country kitchen is the heart of the house, a magnet for people who appreciate its old-time ambiance and camaraderie—not to mention the comfort foods, such as biscuits, gravy, berries, dumplings, or homemade pies, that are served. The Upper Room is minutes from the ocean and lakes. Carl and Barbara advise the Christmas season is great to stay and visit Shore Acres Gardens with thousands of lights and a Christmas Carols concert every night.

No pets; no alcohol; children seventeen and older; smoking outside only; full country breakfast; candlelight dinners catered by Heavenly Cuisine; tennis courts across street; off-street and street parking; North Bend Municipal airport and bus pickup; credit cards (V, MC); corporate rates; lodging tax included in rates.

ROOM	BED	BATH	ENTRANCE	FLOOR	DAILY RATES S	D	EP
Carleen's Room	1D	Shd	Main	2	$60	$65	
Annette's Room	2T	Shd	Main	2	$60	$65	
Master Suite	1K	Pvt	Main	2	$70	$75	
Raggedy Ann Room	1T	Shd	Main	1	$40		

CORVALLIS

Abed and Breakfast   **(541) 757-7321**
Hosts: Neoma and Herb Sparks   FAX: **(541) 753-4332**
2515 SW 45th Street, Corvallis, OR 97333
Three miles southwest of downtown Corvallis on the Corvallis Country Club golf course.

    Swinging gently on deck chairs, watching the golfers play the fourth green, or sinking into red velvet Empire love seats in front of the fire—it doesn't get much better than this. Actually, it does when you add Neoma's breakfast, served on bright china and crystal place settings at a long table with a view of the coastal range in the distance. Breakfast may end with fresh fruit pie or cinnamon rolls. The rooms in this well-kept, comfortable, contemporary home are decorated with dried wreaths and flowers, cozy quilts, and family antiques. The mixture of old and new reflects the mixed land use in this rural neighborhood. On 45th street you'll find small farms and orchards to the west, casual homes fronting the private golf course to the east. Herb and Neoma suggest biking and strolling the neighborhood. Farther afield, you can visit local wineries, tour the last steam-powered lumber mill in Oregon, and explore the campus of nearby Oregon State University. Upon your return, enjoy the private spa adjoining the house—just another of the many amenities of Abed and Breakfast.

    No pets; smoking outside only; children over 8 welcome; full breakfast; TV/VCR; CD player; fireplace; robes provided; spa; complementary juices and beverages; major credit cards.

ROOM	BED	BATH	ENTRANCE	FLOOR	DAILY RATES S	D	EP
Neoma's Room	1K	Pvt	Main	2	$68	$78	
Nancy's Room	1K	Pvt	Main	2	$62	$72	
Blake's Room	2T	Shd	Main	2	$55	$65	
Susan's Room	1Q	Shd	Main	2	$55	$65	

EUGENE

The Country House   **(541) 895-3924**
Hosts: Michael and Susie Hanner
30930 Camas Swale Road, Creswell, OR 97426
From I-5 exit 182, go west straight through Creswell, six miles on Camas Swale Road.

    Tranquility is the specialty of the Country House. The large, rambling home of Michael and Susie provides a special retreat from the cares and concerns of life. Set on a forested ridge and surrounded by acres of trees, you can loose yourself on the trails which wind through the woods. Or visit the hot tub, set at the edge of the forest, and enjoy the panoramic views across meadows and farms of the Camas Valley. For croquet fans, an English croquet lawn has been carved out of a small glen in the woods. Indoor recreation, in the game room, includes a pool table, bumper pool table, board games, and TV/VCR. The over-stuffed furniture in the bright and airy living room is just right for curling up with a book from the extensive library. Special snack trays including decadent chocolate truffles are in each room. The Sunrise room is a bright cherry yellow with a dormer "high ceiling", graciously decorated, with an ensuite bath. The Hanners suggest bicycling along the Willamette River bike trails during your stay.
    No pets; smoking outside; children 12 or older welcome; full breakfast; Guest refrigerator with beverages; robes provided; TV/VCR; Game room; Fireplace; Croquet court; hiking trails; hot tub; resident dogs and cats; air-conditioned.

ROOM	BED	BATH	ENTRANCE	FLOOR	S	D	EP+
Sunrise	1K	Pvt	Main	2	$75	$85	$10
A	1K	Pvt	Main	2	$75	$85	$10

Daily Rates

EUGENE

The House in the Woods   (541) 343-3234
Hosts: George and Eunice Kjaer
814 Lorane Highway, Eugene, OR 97405
Southwest Eugene, South Hills area.

The Lorane Highway is a thoroughfare for joggers and cyclists and a convenient route to downtown Eugene, three miles away. The House in the Woods is set back from the road, with a periphery of fir and oak trees, an abundance of azaleas and rhododendrons, and some formally landscaped open areas. Friendly wildlife still abounds on the two acres. Long-time residents Eunice and George Kjaer have restored their 1910 home to its original quiet elegance. There are hardwood floors with Oriental carpets, high ceilings, lots of windows, and three covered porches (one with a swing). A large, comfortable parlor is most pleasant for visiting, listening to music, or reading. Guest rooms are tastefully decorated. The house and grounds are so peaceful and relaxing that you may be compelled to stay put, but parks, cultural events, outdoor recreation, and good restaurants can be pointed out by your versatile hosts. The Kjaers suggest Mt. Pisgah Arboretum and hiking trails of the Howard Buford Recreation Area as good places to start your explorations

No pets; children by prior arrangement; smoking on outside covered areas; full breakfast (Continental-style for late risers); TV; piano; music library; public transportation; off-street parking; winter rates.

ROOM	BED	BATH	ENTRANCE	FLOOR	DAILY RATES S	D	EP+
Maria's Room	1Q	Pvt	Main	1	$40	$65	
Ivy Room	1Q	Pvt	Main	2	$65	$75	

GARIBALDI

Pelican's Perch Bed & Breakfast (503) 322-3633
Hosts: Dianna and Bill Moore
PO Box 543, Garibaldi, OR 97118
114 East Cypress Avenue, south of Garibaldi on Highway 101, opposite the Old Mill Marina.

Rustic Pelican's Perch, nesting at the edge of Tillamook Bay, invites you to sample its interior comforts, such as the rich Southern antiques and Primitives that lend the rooms their special warmth. The *Sunshine Suite's* windowed sitting bay captures the afternoon sun and boasts an old-fashioned claw foot tub/shower and soft, romantic lighting. The *Tidepool Room* takes its name from a luxurious two-person jacuzzi overlooking the bay. *Storm Catcher* and *Moon Watcher*, both second floor suites, also have bay views, separate bedrooms with antique double beds, private baths, and well-stocked kitchenettes. Dianna serves a full breakfast on the sun porch amidst winding greenery and local art pieces. Dianna and Bill suggest you experience the ocean with hands-on crabbing, clamming, fishing, and exploring the beaches and barrier spit along the sea. Then return to the Perch to soak away your cares and tired muscles in the hot tub, while behind you, the fishing boats enter and leave the harbor. It's a life you could really get used to.

Dog in residence; no pets; smoking outside only; children over 12 welcome; full breakfast; TV/VCR in each room; 2 kitchenette equipped suites; hot tub; off-street parking; picnic lunches available; area for cooking your "catch"; credit cards (MC,V).

ROOM	BED	BATH	ENTRANCE	FLOOR	S	D	EP+
Tide Pool	1Q	Pvt	Main	1		$83	
Sunshine	1Q	Pvt	Main	1		$78	
Stormwatcher	1D & 1Q	Pvt	Main	2		$78	$15
Mooncatcher	1D & 1Q	Pvt	Main	2		$78	$15

DAILY RATES

GOLD BEACH

Endicott Gardens (541) 247-6513
Hosts: Mary and Beverly Endicott
95768 Jerrys Flat Road, Gold Beach, OR 97444
Four miles east of U.S. 101.

Endicott Gardens is the setting for a small nursery and the home of Mary and Beverly Endicott. Bed and breakfast accommodations have been constructed in a separate wing of the house. Each of the four comfortable bedrooms has its own pleasing personality and a private bath. Two rooms, (3) and (5) open onto a deck that is blessed with a forest and mountain view. As one might expect, the grounds are spectacular with flowers and shrubs. Breakfast on the deck is a delight, but in cool weather Mary presents the morning fare in the dining room near the crackle and warmth of the fireplace. Guests are provided with some thoughtful amenities, and the cordial climate is spiced with humor. Endicott Gardens offers the traveler all this plus a chance to unwind in a quiet, natural environment.

No pets; TV available; Rogue River, ocean, and forest recreation nearby; off-street parking; airport pickup (Gold Beach).

ROOM	BED	BATH	ENTRANCE	FLOOR	DAILY RATES S	D	EP
(3)	1Q	Pvt	Sep	1G	$45	$55	$10
(4)	1Q & 1T	Pvt	Sep	1G		$65	$10
(5)	1Q	Pvt	Sep	1G	$45	$55	$10
(6)	1Q	Pvt	Sep	1G	$45	$55	$10

GRANTS PASS

Flery Manor Bed & Breakfast (541) 476-3591
Hosts: Marla and John Vidrinskas FAX: (541) 471-2303
2000 Jumpoff Joe Creek Road, Grants Pass, OR 97526
One and a half miles off Interstate 5, ten minutes from Grants Pass.

Get away from the hurried world...retreat to the comfort and hospitality of Flery Manor. Nestled on a peaceful and secluded mountainside near the Rogue River, Flery Manor is filled with family antiques and original artwork. Floor to ceiling arched windows bring the outside in with views of the surrounding forest-covered mountains of this rural valley. Extensive decks invite you outdoors to enjoy the seven acres of grounds. For an extra touch of elegance and romance, Marla has unique canopies over every bed. *Sweet Dreams* abounds with satin and lace inviting romance. Spacious *Moonlight Suite* features a canopied king bed, fireplace, glass shower, jacuzzi tub, sitting room, and private deck for enjoying sunsets and silvery moonlit vistas. The *Windsor Room's* queen bed has a dramatic beveled and etched glass, lighted headboard with delicate lace canopy. Healthy, three-course breakfasts are served in style on china, crystal, and silver, set on heirloom linens. Flery Manor is elegant, yet comfortable, secluded, yet accessible. Ideal for that special event, wedding, or business retreat.

No pets or smoking; children over eight welcome with special accommodations; full breakfast; AC; robes provided; fireplace; piano; library; games; decks; hiking; wildlife and bird watching; Russian, German, Lithuanian spoken; credit cards (MC,V).

ROOM	BED	BATH	ENTRANCE	FLOOR	DAILY RATES S D EP+
Sweet Dreams	1Q	Pvt	Main	2	$85
Windsor Room	1Q	Pvt	Main	2	$85
Moonlight Suite	1K	Pvt	Main	2	$110

HOOD RIVER

Cascade Avenue Bed & Breakfast (541) 387-2377
Hosts: Lisa and Mike Ward
823 Cascade Avenue, Hood River, OR 97031
West of downtown, within walking distance of town.

Mike and Lisa's quaint, historic English cottage near downtown Hood River is quite cozy, and you can see the famous Columbia River gorge, now a wind surfing mecca, right from the living room. Above a vee in the gorge rises Mt. Adams, namesake of the *Mt. Adams* room. As the sun sets in *Mt. Adams*, a soft yellow glow falls over the antique goldleafed queen headboard and gilded chair. Spacious *East Wind* catches the morning sun; it's favored with a river view and colorful quilts with matching area rugs accenting the hardwood floors. A skylight brightens the shared tile shower/bath. Cascade B&B has a snug little herb and flower garden. A few blocks south is the rich agricultural Hood River Valley rising to the dramatic north side of Mount Hood. After Lisa's hearty breakfast, head for the many local activities. Mike and Lisa suggest wind surfing (of course!), white-water rafting, hot springs, golfing, year-round skiing, and sampling the fresh local fruit and produce.

No pets; smoking outside only; children over 6 welcome; full breakfast; AC; robes; fireplace; patio; garden; barbecue; off-street parking; accessible by rail.

ROOM	BED	BATH	ENTRANCE	FLOOR	S	D	EP+
East Wind	2T & 1Q	Shd	Main	2	$65	$75	$15
Mt. Adams	1Q	Shd	Main	2	$65	$75	

DAILY RATES

Oregon

JACKSONVILLE

Reames House 1868 (800) 207-0269
Hosts: George Winsley and Charlotte Harrington-Winsley
PO Box 128, Jacksonville, OR 97530 (541) 899-1868
Three short blocks east of town at 540 East California Street.

Reames House 1868 is just four blocks from the center of Jacksonville, a well preserved gold rush town on the National Register of Historic Places. Encircled by a white picket fence, spacious lawns, and perennial flower gardens, the Queen Anne beauty is also on the Historic Register. It has a fine array of exterior woodwork and an interior enhanced with handsome antiques. Accommodations on the second floor share a lovely sitting room with telephone for guests. Exquisite wall stenciling sets the tone for the decor, and period details combined with flair give each bedroom a charm all its own. Reames House 1868 offers superb hospitality to attendees of the celebrated Britt Music Festivals as well as year-round visitors who just want to steep themselves in the history of colorful Jacksonville. George and Charlotte suggest visiting during the holiday season to enjoy Jacksonville's beautiful Christmas decorations and events.

No pets; children by arrangement; smoking outside only; full breakfast; AC; Ashland, fifteen miles away; day trips to Crater Lake National Park, Oregon Caves National Monument, and Rogue River rafting; off-street parking; *Colonial and Peachtree Rooms* available as a suite at $160. Shared bath rate $80. Reduced off-season rates November through April.

ROOM	BED	BATH	ENTRANCE	FLOOR	DAILY RATES S	D	EP+
Colonial Room	1Q	Shd/Pvt	Main	2		$90	
Peachtree Room	2T	Pvt	Main	2		$90	
Goldstrike Room	1Q	Shd/Pvt	Main	2		$90	
Victoria Room	1Q	Pvt	Main	2		$90	

LAFAYETTE

Kelty Estate (503) 864-3740
Hosts: Ronald and JoAnn Ross (800) 867-3740
PO Box 817, Lafayette, OR 97127
At 675 3rd Street, in the center of the Yamhill County wine region.

Lafayette was an early farming settlement where the James Keltys first built their rural Gothic farmhouse in 1872. In 1934, son Paul Kelty—then prominent editor of *The Oregonian* in Portland—bought back his boyhood home, refurbished it in the colonial style, and used it as a summer home. Most recently, Ronald and JoAnn Ross's painstaking restorations have left the interior with a new feeling, while graceful architectural details and selected antiques recall another era. The proud white house with green trim is surrounded by lush lawns, gardens, and trees. Choose one of two lovely corner bedrooms where soft pastels create a soothing ambiance. Guests enjoy gathering around the living room fireplace, on the front porch, or in the beautiful back yard. Kelty Estate is a gracious way station for travelers who appreciate a warm welcome and immaculate accommodations.

No children, pets, or smoking; full breakfast; popular Lafayette Antique Mall diagonally across from B&B; off-street parking.

ROOM	BED	BATH	ENTRANCE	FLOOR	DAILY RATES S	D	EP
A	1Q	Pvt	Main	2		$65	
B	1Q	Pvt	Main	2		$65	

LINCOLN CITY

The Brey House Ocean View Bed & Breakfast (541) 994-7123
Hosts: Milt and Shirley Brey
3725 NW Keel, Lincoln City, OR 97367
North of town center, across the street from the ocean.

Seeking a casual, relaxing place by the ocean to unwind? A homey respite right across the street from a walk-forever beach is The Brey House, where Milt and Shirley Brey's guests appreciate the do-as-you-please atmosphere, the walking-distance proximity to shops and restaurants, and the unobstructed ocean view from most every room. A nautical theme prevails throughout the house. The dining room with ocean views on three sides is the perfect place to enjoy the extravagant breakfasts Milt whips up. The ground-floor accommodation may be used by a family or group; it has two bedrooms, a family room with a pool table, comfy places to sit, a fireplace, and a TV/VCR, as well as a full kitchen, and guests are welcome to use the hot tub. The *Captains Room* and *Admirals Room* on the second and third floors have unforgettable ocean views. Milt and Shirley recommend attending the kite flying championships in July.

No pets; smoking restricted; full breakfast; hot tub; fishing, golf, hiking, antique shopping and more nearby; off-street parking; credit cards (V,MC,D); midweek rates.

ROOM	BED	BATH	ENTRANCE	FLOOR	S	D	EP+
Sunroom	1Q	Pvt	Sep	1	$75	$85	
Cascade Room	1Q	Pvt	Sep	1	$55	$65	
Captains Room	1Q	Pvt	Sep	2	$75	$85	
Admirals Room	1Q	Pvt	Sep	3	$75	$85	
Deluxe Suite, 1Q, 2 baths, Living room with fireplace						$125	

McMINNVILLE

Alderstreet Bed & Breakfast (503) 472-8418
Hosts: Nancy and Armand de Rosset
707 Alder Street, McMinnville, OR 97128
Near downtown McMinnville just off Highway 99.

Granddaughter Nicole likes lavender. So it's fitting that *Nicole's Room* is subdued shades of same—a soft, pleasant touch that makes for a soothing room particularly comfortable with it's fireplace and settee that makes into a single bed if there is an extra person. The dressing area, walk-in closet, and bath are ample and comfy, a feeling extending throughout the home. Nancy's personal touches are everywhere from the hand-quilted bedspreads to sponge-painted walls. *Fred's Old Room*, a two-room suite, with queen bed in one room, a twin in the second room, is ideal for families. The backyard and deck are private and spacious allowing easy relaxation away from the pressures of travel during the summer. Relax in front of the living room fireplace during the winter. McMinnville is the center of the Willamette wine country and home to Linfield College. Nancy and Armand suggest wine tasting in the area, and visiting nearby Lawrence Art Gallery, and Lafayette Antique Mall while staying in their pleasant retreat.

Dogs and cats in residence; no pets; smoking outside only; children by prior arrangement; full breakfast; AC; TV; Fireplace in *Nicole's* room; airport pickup available.

ROOM	BED	BATH	ENTRANCE	FLOOR	DAILY RATES S	D	EP
Nicole's Room	1Q & 1T	Pvt	Main	2		$75	$15
Fred's Old Room	1Q & 1T	Pvt	Main	2		$65	$25

MOUNT HOOD AREA

Falcon's Crest Inn   (503) 272-3403
Hosts: BJ and Melody Johnson   (800) 624-7384
P.O. Box 185, Government Camp, OR 97028
87287 Government Camp Loop Highway.

See Mount Hood "up close and personal" from BJ and Melody Johnson's Falcon's Crest Inn, a rustic yet luxurious all-wood structure featuring deluxe accommodations and fine dining. The central area of the house is a vast, open space with a vaulted ceiling and several sitting areas geared to comfort and conversation. Savor the magical mountain setting from almost every room. There are guest rooms on each of the inn's three levels, the upper ones opening to the surrounding balcony. Antiques and family heirlooms enhance each room's individual theme. The whole house is chock full of personality—a reflection of the gregarious hosts, who have as good a time as the guests. Meal preparation is, however, taken seriously, and wonderful candlelight dinners are offered in addition to lavish mountain breakfasts. BJ and Melody suggest visiting Ski Bowl's summer action park or hike to Ramona Falls. In the winter, snowshoe around Trillium Lake.

No pets; smoking on decks only; older, well-behaved children welcome; full breakfast; candlelight dinners by advance reservation; corporate, private, and mystery parties a specialty; year-round skiing, golf, hiking, and lake activities nearby; Timberline Lodge and Oregon Trail nearby; off-street parking; major credit cards; airport shuttle from Portland International.

ROOM	BED	BATH	ENTRANCE	FLOOR	DAILY RATES S	D	EP+
Mexicali Suite	1Q	Pvt	Main	1G		$179	
Master Suite	1Q	Pvt	Main	2		$169	
Safari Room	1Q	Pvt	Main	2		$95	
Cat Ballou Room	1K	Pvt	Main	3		$99.50	
Sophia Room	2T	Pvt	Main	3		$99.50	

NEWBERG

Secluded Bed & Breakfast (503) 538-2635
Hosts: Del and Durell Belanger
19719 NE Williamson Road, Newberg, OR 97132
Yamhill County wine region.

Oregon's growing stature as a wine-producing state is enhanced by a visit to its premier grape-growing region in Yamhill County. Whether you're making a quick stop between Portland and the coast or staying long enough to savor the fruits of the vine, Secluded Bed & Breakfast is an ideal stop. It's a woodsy retreat with quiet, natural surroundings and abundant seasonal wildlife. Del and Durell Belanger are long-time residents of the county. Among other things, Durell is a skilled violin maker and Del a fabulous cook. They know some excellent places to send you for dinner, and later you'll have a great sleep in wonderful country silence. They also want you to know that there are excellent wineries in the area and also great antique shops.

No pets; smoking outside only; full breakfast; living room with fireplace and TV/VCR; AC; off-street parking; airport pickup (Newberg, McMinnville); master suite with queen bed, private bath, and balcony available on request at $60; master suite with shared bath, $45 on request.

ROOM	BED	BATH	ENTRANCE	FLOOR	DAILY RATES S	D	EP
A	1D	Shd	Main	2		$50	
B	1Q	Pvt	Main	2		$60	

NEWBERG

Spring Creek Llama Ranch and Bed & Breakfast
Hosts: Melinda and Dave Bossuyt   (503) 538-5717
14700 NE Spring Creek Lane, Newberg, OR 97132
Yamhill County wine region.

Not far off the beaten path but seeming to be worlds away, Spring Creek Llama Ranch is set at the dead end of a private road on twenty-four acres of garden, field, and forest. Bed and breakfast takes place in a spacious contemporary home with cathedral ceilings and huge windows offering a feast of greenery. In this fresh atmosphere, enjoy a morning meal of home-baked treats and seasonal produce from the garden. A restful night is assured in one of two rooms: *Spring Meadow*, done in cheerful pastels and animal prints, or *Red Cloud*, a autumn-hued room with a large window overlooking a bank of fern, rhododendron, Douglas fir, and willow. Outside in the barn complex and yard, make friends with some of the Van Bossuyt family's llamas. It's easy to become totally enchanted while taking a Llama Walk along winding pathways through evergreen forest. You may even get to meet Red Cloud. Nearby is the boyhood home of Herbert Hoover, Champoeg State Park which commemorates the home of Oregon's statehood, and George Fox College. Wineries, restaurants, and antique shops are nearby.

No pets except other llamas; children welcome; no smoking; full breakfast; TV available; AC; patio. Inquire about family rates.

ROOM	BED	BATH	ENTRANCE	FLOOR	DAILY RATES S	D	EP
Spring Meadow	1D	Pvt	Main	1		$60	
Red Cloud Room	1Q	Pvt	Main	2		$75	$20
Red Cloud Suite, Red Cloud Room plus Toon Room with 2T						$130	

NEWPORT

Oar House Bed & Breakfast (541) 265-9571
Host: Jan LeBrun (800) 252-2358
520 SW 2nd Street, Newport, OR 97365
At the intersection of Hurbert and SW 2nd Street in the Nye Beach area of Newport.

This historic home has lived many lives since the turn of the century: family home, boarding house, bordello, and now bed and breakfast. Built by the Bradshaw family of timbers from a Newport shipwreck, the 5,600 square foot home is a treasure trove of hidden staircases, angled halls, and many doors. The staircase to the cupola cut into the roof is a vivid reminder of the steep "ladder" stairs found on ships, stairs best descended by backing down. The cupola's view sweeps across Newport's Nye Beach to Yaquina Head, north of the city. The rooms are nicely spaced, affording privacy along with ocean views and private baths. *Captain's Quarters* has a comfortable sitting room with stuffed furniture; a bath with large shower and bidet. *Starboard Cabin* offers an excellent northerly view along the Newport Coast to Yaquina Head, from both the room itself and from the ensuite bath. Jan suggests enjoying the sunset from the cupola before dining at one of the many fine Newport restaurants. She also suggests visiting the Oregon Coast Aquarium, currently home of Keiko, the killer whale star of the movie Free Willy.

No pets, smoking or children; full breakfast; fireplace; TV with 2 movie channels; library; deck; off-street parking; credit cards (MC,V); *Rates vary from $90 to $120, double, depending on season, day, and availability.

ROOM	BED	BATH	ENTRANCE	FLOOR	DAILY RATES S D EP+
Chart Room	1Q	Pvt	Main	2	
Starboard Cabin	1Q	Pvt	Main	2	*See
Captain's Quarters	1Q	Pvt	Main	2	Note
Master Stateroom	1Q	Pvt	Main	3	

NEWPORT

Tyee Lodge (541) 265-8953
Hosts: Mark and Cindy McConnell
4925 NW Woody Way, Newport, OR 97365
In the Agate Beach area of northern Newport.

Shielded from the winds by Yaquina Head, Tyee Lodge looks down on the sandy beach which lies south of the headland and extends to Newport Harbor jetty. From the front yard, past gardens and barbecue, down a short winding trail to the beach, turn right to arrive at the headland and tide pools, left for the 2-mile walk to Newport town itself. That's one of the charms of Tyee Lodge: far enough away to be quiet and secluded, yet easily near Newport's restaurants, attractions, and activities. Each of Tyee's five rooms is named for one of the coastal Indian tribes, and each boasts an ocean view, an ensuite bath with window or skylight, and a roomy queen bed. *Chinook* benefits from a fireplace, as well, and both *Chinook* and *Yaquina* feature sunny southward views. Mark and Cindy want you to know it's easy to walk (or bike) to Yaquina Head right from the lodge. At the lookout you can whale watch, bird watch, and explore the tide pools being created in an abandoned, old quarry. Also, in Newport you can enjoy charter fishing and, with luck, bring home a salmon for the barbecue.

No pets; smoking outside only; full breakfast; fireplace; fireplace in *Chinook* room; microwave and refrigerator available; French, German, Spanish spoken; credit cards (MC,V).

ROOM	BED	BATH	ENTRANCE	FLOOR	DAILY RATES S	D	EP+
Chinook	1Q	Pvt	Main	2	$115	$120	
Yaquina	1Q	Pvt	Main	2	$94	$99	
Siletz	1Q	Pvt	Main	2	$94	$99	
Tillamook	1Q	Pvt	Main	2	$94	$99	
Alsea	1Q	Pvt	Main	2	$94	$99	

OAKLAND

Beckley House Bed & Breakfast (541) 459-9320
Hosts: Karene and Rich Neuharth
PO Box 198, Oakland, OR 97462
3 blocks east of downtown Oakland, at 338 SE 2nd Street.

Oregon abounds with small historic towns, and one of the nicest and most accessible is Oakland, just a mile off I-5 between Roseburg and Eugene. It's a town where you'll want to stay and explore, and Beckley house, a classic late-1800's Revival Victorian, is just the place to do it. When you arrive, Karene and Rich greet you at the door with flowers—a lovely welcome to their lovely home furnished with comfortable period antiques. The sunny *Garden Suite* features a sitting room day bed, and flanking the queen bed are unique gas-and-electric lamps. Browsing through the collection of vintage 1930's magazines recalls the old weeklies that put pictures to the radio news. Gently rock in the secluded, covered patio swing or step out the front door into this venerable neighborhood, and you'll swear you've stepped back in time as well. The Neuharths suggest visiting local wineries and covered bridges, and taking a horse-drawn carriage tour of Oakland.

Resident cats; no pets; smoking outside; children welcome; full breakfast; TV; air conditioned.

ROOM	BED	BATH	ENTRANCE	FLOOR	DAILY RATES S	D	EP
Garden Suite	1Q & 1T	Pvt	Main	2		$80	$10
Spring Suite	1Q	Pvt	Main	2		$70	

PORT ORFORD

HOME by the SEA   **(541) 332-2855**
Hosts: Alan and Brenda Mitchell
PO Box 606-K, Port Orford, OR 97465
444 Jackson Street.

Alan and Brenda Mitchell built their contemporary wood home on a spit of land overlooking a stretch of Oregon coast that could take your breath away. The arresting view, seen below, may be enjoyed from both lovely bedrooms and from the Sunspace where the Mitchells get to know their guests. Queen-sized Oregon Myrtlewood beds and cable TV are featured in both accommodations which make ideal quarters for two couples traveling together. It's a short walk to restaurants, public beaches, historic Battle Rock Park, and the town's harbor— the home port of Oregon's only crane-launched commercial fishing fleet. Port Orford is a favorite of windsurfers as well of whale, bird, and storm watchers. It's an enchanting discovery, and so is HOME by the SEA.

No pets, children, or smoking; full breakfast; cable TV; laundry privileges; phone jacks in rooms; off-street parking; Macintosh spoken, Telnet available, CompuServe ID#72672,1072; credit cards (V,MC).

ROOM	BED	BATH	ENTRANCE	FLOOR	S	DAILY RATES D	EP+
Blue Suite	1Q	Pvt	Main	2		$85	$10
Coral Room	1Q	Pvt	Main	2		$75	

PORTLAND

The Clinkerbrick House   (503) 281-2533
Hosts: Peggie and Bob Irvine
2311 NE Schuyler, Portland, OR 97212
Near Lloyd Center, Convention Center, and Coliseum.

In a quiet residential neighborhood just minutes from downtown Portland, discover the warm country comfort of The Clinkerbrick House. The 1908 Dutch Colonial offers all the pleasures of a welcoming, family environment, along with an extra measure of privacy for guests: a separate outside entrance, allowing one to come and go freely. The second-floor accommodations include a full kitchen/TV room and three spacious bedrooms. On the door of each room is a decoration hinting at the perfectly executed theme within. The *Garden Room* has a private bath, a small deck, and a botanical flavor. The *Strawberry Room*, with antiques and stenciled walls, shares a bath off the hallway with The *Rose Room*, a romantic haven done in pink roses and white wicker. Delicious full breakfasts are served in the bright, cheerful dining room. For the traveler who likes feeling independent and pampered at the same time, Bob and Peggie Irvine have created the unique hospitality of The Clinkerbrick House.

No pets or smoking; full breakfast (special dietary needs accommodated); rollaway bed, $15; good area for walking or jogging; good public transportation; off-street and street parking; credit cards (V,MC).

ROOM	BED	BATH	ENTRANCE	FLOOR	DAILY RATES S	D	EP+
Garden Room	1Q	Pvt	Sep	2	$55	$65	$15
Strawberry Room	1Q	Shd	Sep	2	$40	$50	
Rose Room	1Q & 1T	Shd	Sep	2	$40	$50	$15

PORTLAND

Georgian House Bed & Breakfast   **(503) 281-2250**
Host: Willie Ackley   FAX: (503) 281-3301
1828 NE Siskiyou, Portland, OR 97212
Near Lloyd Center, Convention Center, Blazer Arena/Coliseum

Portland has only three true Georgian Colonial homes; one of them is Georgian House Bed & Breakfast. This authentic beauty, built in 1922, is red brick with white columns and dark blue shutters. It stands on a double corner lot in a fine, old, quiet, northeast Portland neighborhood. Willie Ackley has expertly restored the home with every exquisite detail. Her tasteful use of interior colors serves to enhance classic features such as leaded glass windows, built-in china cabinets, heavy moldings, oak floors, a sun porch, and a fireplace. A graceful stairway leads to the second-floor guest quarters. Each of the antique-furnished bedrooms is a singularly charming creation. The romantic *Lovejoy Suite* is a light, spacious bed/sitting room with a canopy bed, French windows, a color TV, a ceiling fan, and a view of the lovely grounds. There is a wide deck and gazebo overlooking the gardens featured in *Better Homes and Gardens Magazine*. If staying on a weekend, Willie says you will enjoy shopping at the Saturday Market in Old Town and Pioneer Place, then have dinner at one of many fine restaurants in Portland.

No pets; children welcome; smoking outside only; full breakfast; TV/VCR in common area; robes provided; crib available; extra-long beds in *Pettygrove Room*; good public transportation, train and airport connections; off-street and street parking; credit cards (V,MC). One bed in *Captain Irving Room* is a futon, rate for four, $100.

ROOM	BED	BATH	ENTRANCE	FLOOR	S	D	EP+
Lovejoy Suite	1Q	Pvt	Main	2		$85	
Pettygrove Room	1K or 2T	Shd	Main	2	$60	$65	
Eastlake Room	1Q	Shd	Main	2	$60	$65	
Captain Irving Room	2Q	Shd	Main	LL	$60	$65	

PORTLAND

Portland Guest House   (503) 282-1402
Host: Susan Gisvold
1720 NE Fifteenth Avenue, Portland, OR 97212
Closest B&B to Lloyd Center, Convention Center, and Blazer Arena/Coliseum.

An 1890 Victorian renovated with conspicuous care, Portland Guest House accommodates travelers who appreciate the historical sense it conveys, the many conveniences and comforts it offers, and the aesthetic pleasures of its decor. Susan welcomes guests to enjoy the parlor, the dining room, and the garden. The interior is fresh, light, and airy, with plenty of white and discreet accents of mauve, gray, rose, and blue. Floral designs and tapestries share space with wonderful, carefully chosen art and antiques. Outfitted with heirloom linens, the guest rooms are especially appealing. There is a spacious family accommodation on the home's lower level, and the two rooms with a shared bath have private balconies. The most recent additions are two air conditioned suites with private baths on the third floor, one with a view of Mt. Hood, the other with a view of downtown Portland.

No pets; children in family room and third floor suites only; smoking outside only; full breakfast; private phone in each room; FAX service, shopping, dining, and light rail service nearby; bus stop at the corner; off-street parking; major credit cards.

ROOM	BED	BATH	ENTRANCE	FLOOR	DAILY RATES S	D	EP+
A	1Q & 2T	Pvt	Main	LL	$75	$85	$10
B	1D	Pvt	Main	2	$65	$75	
C	1Q	Pvt	Main	2	$65	$75	
D	1Q	Shd	Main	2	$45	$55	
E	1D	Shd	Main	2	$45	$55	
F	1Q & 1T	Pvt	Main	3	$75	$85	$10
G	1Q & 1T	Pvt	Main	3	$75	$85	$10

Oregon

ROSEBURG

House of Hunter   (541) 672-2335
Hosts: Jean and Walt Hunter   (800) 541-7704
813 SE Kane Street, Roseburg, OR 97470
Bordering downtown Roseburg.

On a quiet residential street in the company of other historic homes, House of Hunter is a classic Italianate built at the turn of the century. In 1990 Walt and Jean Hunter made extensive renovations, preserving the home's essential character while adding modern attributes to enhance its ease and comfort, resulting in a light, airy, expansive atmosphere. The lovely guest rooms, each named for one of the hosts' daughters, feature English wardrobe closets and antique accents. Inspired by their own B&B travels, the Hunters offer their guests such treats as early morning coffee and goodies delivered to the second floor alcove, followed by a full breakfast served in the dining room. The grand room on the main floor is for the use of guests, as is a putting green, and the patio, surrounded by the flower garden. With a stay of two days, the Hunters offer free use of their raft on the Umpqua River. A special event recommended by the Jean and Walt is the Christmas Festival of Lights in Roseburg. Anytime of the year you will find a warm welcome.

No pets; children over ten welcome; smoking outside only; full breakfast; AC; TV/VCR; laundry facilities; walk to downtown shops, restaurants, and churches; off-street parking; credit cards (V,MC); airport shuttle (Roseburg).

ROOM	BED	BATH	ENTRANCE	FLOOR	S	D	EP+
Charlene's Room	1Q	Pvt	Main	2	$65	$70	$15
Debra's Room	1Q	Pvt	Main	2	$65	$70	$15
Ronette's Room	1K	Shd	Main	2	$50	$55	$15
Pamela's Room	2T	Shd	Main	2	$45	$50	$15
Ronette's & Pamela's as Suite		Pvt	Main	2	$70	$75	$15
Grandma's Suite	1Q & 1D	Shd	Main	2	$70	$75	$15

SALEM

Cottonwood Cottage Bed & Breakfast (503) 362-3979
Hosts: Bill and Donna Wickman (800) 349-3979
960 E Street NE, Salem, OR 97301
Central Salem near the Capitol and downtown.

From E Street it's a quick walk to downtown, the state capitol, Willamette University, and Amtrak. You might expect a busy neighborhood, but the quiet street has fine homes, many large trees, and lush lawns. The eye is drawn to Cottonwood Cottage, a delightful old Georgian house with a comfortable, quaint look and quiet appeal. Guest rooms feature comforters for cold winter nights and air conditioning for warm summer evenings. Tired of touring? Pass a rosy summer evening on the backyard deck in the cool shade of Cottonwood's namesake, a venerable grandfather cottonwood tree; or just relax in the living room. Bill takes pride in his hearty breakfasts with lovely place settings and soft music to suit your mood. Salem is a varied place; besides the capitol and university, Bill and Donna suggest visits to Mission Mill Museum, Gilbert House Children's Museum (the Erector Set folks), and nearby Silver Falls State Park with ten marvelous waterfalls, six of them well over 100 feet high. A more convenient location in Salem would be very hard to find.

No pets; smoking outside only; no children; full breakfast; AC; TV in each room; off street parking; credit cards (MC,V,DS); member Oregon B&B Guild.

ROOM	BED	BATH	ENTRANCE	FLOOR	DAILY RATES S / D / EP+
A	1Q	Shd	Main	2	$60
B	1T	Shd	Main	3	$55

SEASIDE

Summer House (503) 738-5740
Hosts: Jack and Lesle Palmeri (800) 745-2378
1221 North Franklin, Seaside, OR 97138
On the north end of Seaside, one block from the beach.

In bustling Seaside, quiet is a luxury. A tranquil environment is one of the many assets of Summer House, a completely renovated vacation home with a history of beach side hospitality. It has a wood shingled exterior, ample decking, and latticed and trellised garden areas burgeoning with flowers and vegetables. The interior is clean and modern with plenty of natural light and a subtle Southwest flavor. The *Garden Room*, a romantic haven on the main level, features a fireplace, sitting area, and small kitchenette. Other lovely rooms express different themes: *Sunrise* (with mountain view, fireplace, and refrigerator), *The Taj*, *Whispering Seas*, and *Victorian Lace*. No matter which room you have, each has a television and private bath. Jack's breakfast cuisine is the essence of fresh-from-the-garden goodness. He and Lesle provide superb, year-round hospitality at Summer House. During your stay practice your kite flying for the Seaside kite flying contest in June or enjoy wonderful beach combing.

Please, no pets, smoking, or children under twelve; full breakfast; shopping, dining, ocean and river activities, whale and bird watching, golfing, horseback riding, and more nearby; off-street parking; credit cards (V,MC,DS).

ROOM	BED	BATH	ENTRANCE	FLOOR	DAILY RATES S	D	EP+
The Garden Room	1Q	Pvt	Main	1		$100	
Victorian Lace	1D	Pvt	Main	1		$70	
Whispering Seas	1Q	Pvt	Main	2		$80	
The Taj	1Q	Pvt	Main	2		$80	
The Sunrise Room	1Q	Pvt	Main	2		$90	

SISTERS

Cascade Country Inn   (541) 549-INNN (4666)
Hosts: Judy and Victoria Tolonen   (800) 316-0089
PO Box 834, Sisters, OR 97759
15870 Barclay Drive, 1/4 mile NE of Sisters, adjoining Sisters Eagle Airport, a general airport for small planes only.

Whether you fly into Sisters Eagle Airport or whether you drive, expect a special B&B experience at Cascade Country Inn. Designed exclusively as a bed and breakfast, the home shows attention to every detail, from ample closets to spacious suites boasting spectacular views of the volcanic Cascades. Judy and Victoria have put time and talent into their handcrafted ceramic tiles, delicate stenciling, sweeping murals, and exquisite stained glass transoms. Relax in *Mi Amor*, with its romantic fireplace and bubbling jacuzzi. Enjoy *Lifestyles of the Fish and Famous*, ideal for family or dorm-style use. Or fly into the *Wild Blue Yonder*, inside the airplane hangar near the main house. It features a glass-topped coffee table made from a radial aircraft engine and spiral staircase leading to a roomy loft with queen bed. Perhaps *Granny's Garden* or *Country Fair* best suit your style—whatever you choose, it's definitely one-of-a-kind. Judy and Victoria suggest attending Sisters special events; the June Rodeo, July Quilt Show, or September Jazz Festival. The McKenzie/Santiam Pass auto tour is a drive that shouldn't be missed.

No pets or smoking; children welcome; evening refreshments, full breakfast; Refrigerator; robes provided; bicycles available; TV/VCR; Porch swing; *My Heart's Delight* room handicapped accessible; 2-night minimum summer weekends; winter discounts.

ROOM	BED	BATH	ENTRANCE	FLOOR	DAILY RATES S	D	EP+
Mi Amor	1Q	Pvt	Main	2	$120	$125	
Granny's Garden	1Q	Pvt	Main	2	$95	$100	
Country Fair	1Q	Pvt	Main	2	$95	$100	
Life-styles	1Q & 5T	Pvt	Main	2	$35/person min 3		
My Heart's Delight	1Q	Pvt	Main	1G	$95	$100	
Wild Blue Yonder	1Q	Pvt	Sep	1G	$95	$100	$10

Oregon

TILLAMOOK

Blue Haven Inn (541 842-2265)
Hosts: Joy and Ray Still
3025 Gienger Road, Tillamook, OR 97141
South of Tillamook on Highway 101, turn west on Gienger Road opposite the Air Museum access road.

Tillamook is a must-stop on the Oregon Coast. It has some of the best oysters on the West Coast, world-famous local cheeses, access to the remarkable Three Capes Loop drive along the coast, and bucolic farmland scenery as well. Where to stay? Blue Haven Inn is an excellent choice. This attractive country home on two acres, off the main highway, has healthy green lawns and white picket fences. The large common rooms are somewhat formal yet with a light, open feeling. Room themes derive from limited-edition collectors plates adorning the walls, augmented with antiques and collectibles. Enjoy breakfast in the dining room, leisure on the porch swing, and the all-around gracious hospitality of Joy and Ray Still. The Stills say visiting the world's largest cheese factory is a must-see. The coast's tallest waterfall, spectacular Munson Falls, is nearby, as is the Air Museum. August brings the exciting, the one-and-only, Pig and Ford Race—just another unique reason to visit Tillamook!

No pets; smoking outside only; children by arrangement; full or continental breakfast for guest's preference; fireplace; TV/VCR video tape library; telephone; robes for share bath rooms; off street parking.

ROOM	BED	BATH	ENTRANCE	FLOOR	DAILY RATES S	D	EP
Tara	1D	Shd	Main	2	$55	$60	
La Femme	1Q	Shd	Main	2		$60	$10
Of the Sea	1Q	Pvt	Main	2		$75	$10

WESTFIR

Westfir Lodge, A Bed & Breakfast Inn　　　(541) 782-3103
Hosts: Gerry Chamberlain and Ken Symons
47365 First Street, Westfir, OR 97492
Three miles from Highway 58 on Westfir Road.

Westfir? Where's Westfir? Westfir is a former logging town west of Oakridge between Eugene and Crater Lake on Highway 58. Westfir Lodge is reason enough to go there. Built in 1923 as offices for the Westfir Lumber Company, the building was remodeled in 1990 into a wonderful English-style bed and breakfast. You'll walk into a grand re-creation of the Victorian era with elaborately carved antique couches, ornate chandeliers and lamps, gilded picture frames, and guest rooms with Victorian furnishings and high headboards. Ken and Gerry will make you immediately comfortable. Fluffy robes are provided for the private baths located, in true English fashion nearby, down the hall. British scones and sausages, made using marvelous recipes from Ken's mother, start the day. When you tear yourself from the breakfast and antiques, you'll find many recreation activities close by. Fishing, boating, winter skiing, kayaking, and mountain biking are here or simply stroll the longest covered bridge in all Oregon. Perhaps later, discover one of the many cool and picturesque waterfalls in the area. Ken and Gerry suggest taking the Auderheide Scenic Drive to Highway 126 and will provide a descriptive audio tape of the drive. However you get to Westfir, be sure to stay at Westfir Lodge.

No pets, kennel nearby; smoking outside only; well-behaved children welcome; full English breakfast; AC; TV/VCR; robes provided; Oakridge airport pickup; two ground floor rooms handicapped accessible.

ROOM	BED	BATH	ENTRANCE	FLOOR	DAILY RATES S	D	EP
A	1Q	Pvt	Main	1G	$45	$65	
B	1Q	Pvt	Main	1G	$45	$65	
C	1Q	Pvt	Main	1G	$45	$65	
D	1Q	Pvt	Main	1G	$45	$65	
E	1T & 1Q	Pvt	Main	2		$65	$15
F	2T	Shd	Main	2	$45	$65	
G	1T & 1Q	Pvt	Main	2		$65	$15

DINING HIGHLIGHTS - OREGON

Please read "About Dining Highlights" on page ix.

ALOHA
Nonna Emilia; 17210 SW Shaw; (503) 649-2232; Italian

ASHLAND
Chateaulin; 50 East Main Street; (541) 482-2264; French

House of Thai; 1667 Siskiyou Boulevard; (541) 488-2583; authentic Thai

Monet; 36 South Second Street; (541) 482-1339; French

New Sammy's Bistro; 2210 South Pacific Highway, Talent; (541) 535-2779; country French

Plaza Cafe; 47 North Main Street; (541) 488-2233; seafood/pasta/vegetarian specialties

ASTORIA
Cafe Uniontown; 218 West Marine Drive; (503) 325-8708; varied menu

Pier 11 Feed Store Restaurant & Lounge; 77 11th Street, waterfront at foot of Tenth and Eleventh; (503) 325-0279; seafood specialties

Victoria Dahl's; 2921 Marine Drive; (503) 325-7109; salad/sandwich lunches/Italian pasta dinners/espresso drinks

BANDON
Bandon Boatworks; South Jetty; (541) 347-2111; seafood

Lord Bennett's; 1695 Beach Loop Road; (541) 347-3663; Continental/seafood

Sea Star Bistro; Second Street, Old Town; (541) 347-9632; creative house-made dishes

BEAVERTON
The Grapery; 4190 SW Cedar Hills Boulevard; (503) 646-1437; Northwest Continental

McCormick's Fish House & Bar; 9945 SW Beaverton-Hillsdale Highway; (503) 643-1322; extensive seafood menu

BEND
Deschutes Brewery; 1044 NW Bond; (541) 382-9242; brew pub

Honkers Restaurant; 805 Industrial Way; (541) 389-4665; steak & seafood

Pine Tavern; the foot of NW Oregon Street downtown Bend; (541) 382-5581; steak/seafood/pasta

BROOKINGS
Bistro Gardens; 1103 Chetco Avenue; (541) 469-9750; contemporary Continental

Caffe Fredde; 1025 Chetco Avenue (U.S. 101); (541) 469-3733

Chives Restaurant; 1025 Chetco Avenue; (541) 569-4121; contemporary Continental

Great American Smokehouse & Seafood; 15657 Highway 101 South; (541) 469-6903; seafood

Hog Wild Cafe; 16158 Highway 101 South in Harbor; (541) 469-8869; homestyle

DINING HIGHLIGHTS - OREGON

CANNON BEACH
Bistro Restaurant & Bar; 263 North Hemlock Street; (503) 436-2661; northwest eclectic

Cafe de la Mer; 1287 South Hemlock Street; (503) 436-1179; northwest/French

CHARLESTON
Ceryn's Seafood; ; (541) 888-3251; fresh seafood

Portside; 8001 Kingfisher Road at Charleston Boat Basin; (541) 888-5544; fresh seafood/some Chinese dishes

CLACKAMAS
Nonna Emilia Cafe Italiano; 16691 SE McLoughlin Boulevard; (503) 786-1004

COOS BAY
Benettis; 260 South Broadway; ; Italian

Blue Heron Bistro; 100 Commercial; (541) 267-3933; Continental

Heavenly Cuisine; 361 East 2nd Street, Coquille; (541) 396-5396; prime rib/seafood

Kum-Yon's; 835 S. Broadway; (541) 269-2662; Japanese/Chinese/Korean

Pacific Grill and Steakhouse; 1313 North Bayshore Drive; (541) 267-2799; seafood/steaks

Teske's Germania; 647 SE Jackson Street; (541) 672-5401; German

CORVALLIS
The Gables; 1121 NW 9th; (541) 752-3364; seafood

Michael's Landing; 603 NW 2nd; (541) 754-6141; seafood/Continental

Oasis; 2315 NW Kings Boulevard; (541) 754-1850; Mediterranean/Lebanese

DUNDEE
Alfies Wayside Inn; 1111 N Highway 99W; (503) 538-9407

The Red Hills; 276 Highway 99W; (503) 538-8224; provincial

Tina's; 760 Highway 99W; (503) 538-8880; Continental

EUGENE
Chanterelle; 207 East Fifth Street; (541) 484-4065; fresh fish/pasta

Chez Ray's; 1473 E.Nineteenth Avenue at Agate; (541) 342-8596; European

Excelsior Cafe; 754 East Thirteenth Avenue; (541) 342-6963; Continental

The French Horn Cafe & Bakery; 1591 Willamette in L&L Market; (541) 343-7473; soups/breads/takeout items

The Gazebo Restaurant; 1646 East Nineteenth Street; (541) 683-6661; middle eastern

Jamie's Great Hamburgers; 2445 Hilyard; (541) 342-2206

North Bank; 22 Club Road; (541) 343-5622; steak/seafood/pasta

DINING HIGHLIGHTS - OREGON

EUGENE (continued)
Oregon Electric Station; 27 East Fifth Avenue; (541) 485-4444; steak/seafood/pasta
West Brothers Bar B Que; 844 Olive Street; (541) 345-8489; regional American
Zenon Cafe; 898 Pearl Street; (541) 343-3005; international/great desserts

FLORENCE
Traveler's Cove; 1362 Bay Street; (541) 997-6845; light meals and snacks

GARIBALDI VICINITY
ArtSpace; 5th Street & Highway 101 in Bay City; (503) 377-2782; innovative daily specials with an emphasis on the local fresh catch
Blue Sky; 154 Laneda Street in Manzanita; (503) 368-5712; seafood with a spicy Asian accent

GEARHART see Seaside

GOLD BEACH
Rod 'n' Reel; on Rogue River at Jot's Resort, Wedderburn; (541) 247-6823; varied menu for breakfast/lunch/dinner
Rogue Landing; 94749 Jerrys Flat Road; (541) 247-6031; seafood and steaks

GRANTS PASS
Bistro; 1214 NW Sixth Street; (541) 479-3412; Italian/deep dish pizza
Blue Heron Restaurant; 330 Merlin Avenue; (541) 479-6604
Hamilton House; 344 NE Terry Lane; (541) 479-3938; seafood/pasta/fowl/beef
Maria's Mexican Kitchen; 105 NE Mill Street; (541) 474-2429
Matsukaze; 1675 NE Seventh Street; (541) 479-2961; Japanese
Paradise Guest Ranch Inn; 7000 Monument Drive; (541) 479-4333; Continental
Pongsri's Thai-Chinese Cuisine; 1571 NE Sixth Street; (541) 479-1345
R-Haus Restaurant & Bistro; 2140 Rogue River Highway; (541) 474-3335; steak/seafood/vegetarian

HILLSBORO
Reedville Cafe; 21935 SW Tualatin Valley Highway; (503) 649-4643; casual

HOOD RIVER
6th Street Bistro; 509 Cascade Avenue; (541) 386-5737
Big City Chicks; 1302 13th Street; (541) 387-3811; world cuisine
Pasquale's Ristorante; 102 Oak Street; (541) 386-1900; Italian
Rio Grande Mexican Restaurant; 2nd & Cascade; (541) 386-5737; Mexican

JACKSONVILLE
Bella Union; 175 West California Street; (541) 899-1770; California/pizza
Jacksonville Inn Dinner House; 175 East California Street; (541) 899-1900; Continental/northwest

DINING HIGHLIGHTS - OREGON

JACKSONVILLE (continued)
McCully House Inn Restaurant; 240 East California Street; (541) 899-1942; creative American/historic home atmosphere

LAKE OSWEGO
Amadeus; 148 B Avenue at Second; (503) 636-7500; Continental

LINCOLN CITY
Audrey's Restaurant; 1725 SW Highway 101; (541) 994-6210; Continental

Bay House; 5911 SW Highway 101; (541) 996-3222; Continental/seafood

Dory Cove Restaurant; 5819 NW Logan Road; (541) 994-5180; clam chowder/seafood

Kernville Steak & Seafood House; 186 Siletz Highway; (541) 994-6200

Kyllo's Seafood & Grill; 1110 NW First Court; (541) 994-3179

Otis Cafe; Highway 18 at Otis Junction; (541) 994-2813; old-fashioned country cooking

McMINNVILLE
Augustine's; Highway 18; (503) 843-3225; Continental

Golden Valley Brewery & Pub; 980 East 4th Street; (503) 472-2739; brew pub

Nick's Italian Cafe; 521 East Third Street; (503) 434-4471

Rogers Seafood Restaurant; 2121 East 27th Street; (503) 472-0917

Sir Hinkleman, A Restaurant; 729 East Third Street; (503) 472-1309; picnics/lunch/catering

Umberto's; 828 North Adams Street; (503) 472-1717; traditional Italian

NEWBERG
Ixtapa Restaurant; 307 East First Street; (503) 538-5956; Mexican

The Noodle; 2320 Portland Road; (503) 538-0507; exceptional pasta dinners

Pasquale's Italian Restaurant; 111 West First Street; (503) 538-0910

NEWPORT
Canyon Way Bookstore and Restaurant; 1216 SW Canyon Way; (541) 265-8319; innovative dishes include fresh fish/salads/desserts/more

Chowder Bowl; 728 NW Beach Drive; (541) 265-7477; chowder/light lunches

Cosmos; 740 West Olive; (541) 265-7511; chowder & light lunches

Newport Bay Coffee Co.; 706 SW Hurbert Street; (541) 265-4090; seafood

Sylvia Beach Hotel; 267 NW Cliff; (541) 265-5428; fixed price & menu/Continental

Whales Tale; 452 SW Bay at Bay & Hurbert; (541) 265-8660; seafood

OAKLAND
Old Town Cafe; 116 NE Locust Street; (541) 459-4989; Italian

Tequita's; 875 West Central in Sutherlin; (541) 459-3314; Mexican

Tolly's; 115 NE Locust Street; (541) 459-3796; Continental

DINING HIGHLIGHTS - OREGON

OCEANSIDE
Roseanna's Oceanside Cafe; 1490 Pacific NW; (503) 842-7351; seafood/pasta

PORT ORFORD
The Port and Starboard Restaurant; US 101 at Madrona; (541) 332-4215; local seafood/steaks/pizza

The Sixes River Hotel; 93316 Sixes River Road, Six miles north of Port Orford; (541) 332-3900; French Continental/seafood

The Truculent Oyster; U.S. 101 at Sixth and Jefferson; (541) 332-9461; local seafood/steaks

PORTLAND
Alexis; 215 West Burnside Street; (503) 224-8577; Greek

Bread & Ink Cafe; 3610 SE Hawthorne Boulevard; (503) 239-4756; Continental

Elizabeth's Cafe; 3135 NE Broadway; (503) 281-8337; Continental

Genoa; 2832 SE Belmont Street; (503) 238-1464; fine Italian cuisine

Heathman Bakery & Pub; 901 SW Salmon; (503) 227-5700; designer pizza/brew pub

Jake's Famous Crawfish; 401 SW Twelfth; (503) 226-1419; northwest seafood

McCormick & Schmick's Oak Street Restaurant; 235 SW First Avenue; (503) 224-7522; extensive seafood menu

Papa Haydn; 5829 SE Milwaukie; (503) 232-9440; killer desserts

Winterborne; 3520 NE 42nd; (503) 249-8486; intimate dining/fine seafood

ROSEBURG
Los Dos Amigos; 537 SE Jackson Street; (541) 673-1354; Mexican

Saigon Restaurant; 719 SE Jackson Street; (541) 440-6658; Vietnamese

SALEM
Inn at Orchard Heights; 695 Orchard Heights NW in West Salem; (503) 378-1780; Continental

Mortons; 1128 Edgewater in West Salem; (503) 585-1113; American

SANDY
The Ivy Bear; 54735 East Highway 26; (503) 622-3440; Czechoslovakian

SEAL ROCK
Yuzen Japanese; Highway 101; (541) 563-4766

SEASIDE
Great Wall Restaurant; 4340 Highway 101 North in Gearhart; (503) 738-4108; Chinese

The Oceanside Restaurant; 1200 North Marion Drive in Gearhart; (503) 738-7789

DINING HIGHLIGHTS - OREGON

SISTERS

Coyote Creek Cafe; 497 Highway 20; (541) 595-9514

The Kokanee Cafe; in Camp Sherman; (541) 595-6420

Sisters Hotel; 105 West Cascade Street; (541) 549-7427; steak/seafood/pasta

WELCHES

Chalet Swiss; Highway 26 on Welches Road; (503) 622-3600; Swiss/northwest/fresh seafood

The Resort at the Mountain; 68010 East Fairway (at base of Mount Hood); (503) 622-3101; informal dining in the Tartans or elegant dining in the Highlands

It is good to have an end to journey toward;
But it is the journey that matters in the end.

--Ursula K. LeGun

To me, travel is a triple delight: anticipation, performance, and recollection.

--Ilka Chase

WASHINGTON

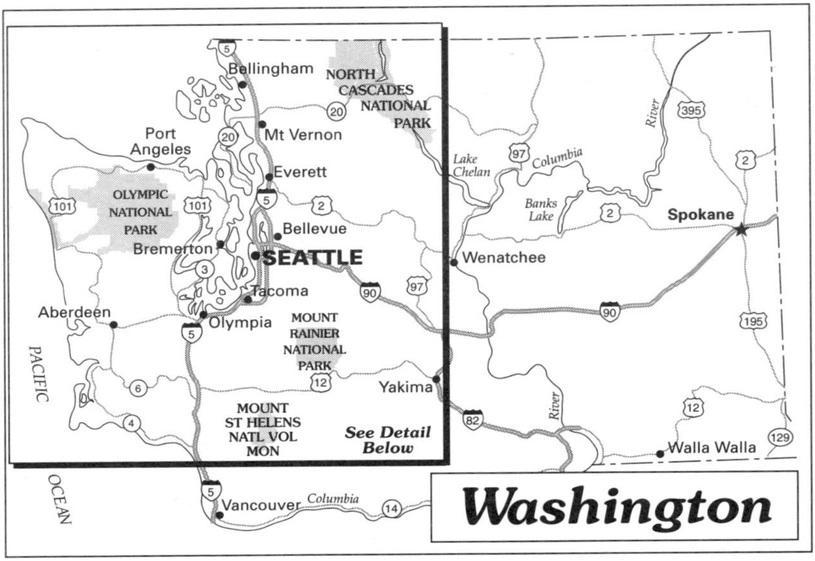
Washington
Bellingham
NORTH CASCADES NATIONAL PARK
Port Angeles
Mt Vernon
Everett
OLYMPIC NATIONAL PARK
Bellevue
Bremerton
SEATTLE
Tacoma
Aberdeen
Olympia
MOUNT RAINIER NATIONAL PARK
PACIFIC
OCEAN
Yakima
MOUNT ST HELENS NATL VOL MON
See Detail Below
Vancouver
Columbia
Lake Chelan
Columbia
River
Banks Lake
Spokane
Wenatchee
River
Walla Walla
5
20
101
2
3
90
97
12
6
4
82
14
395
195
129

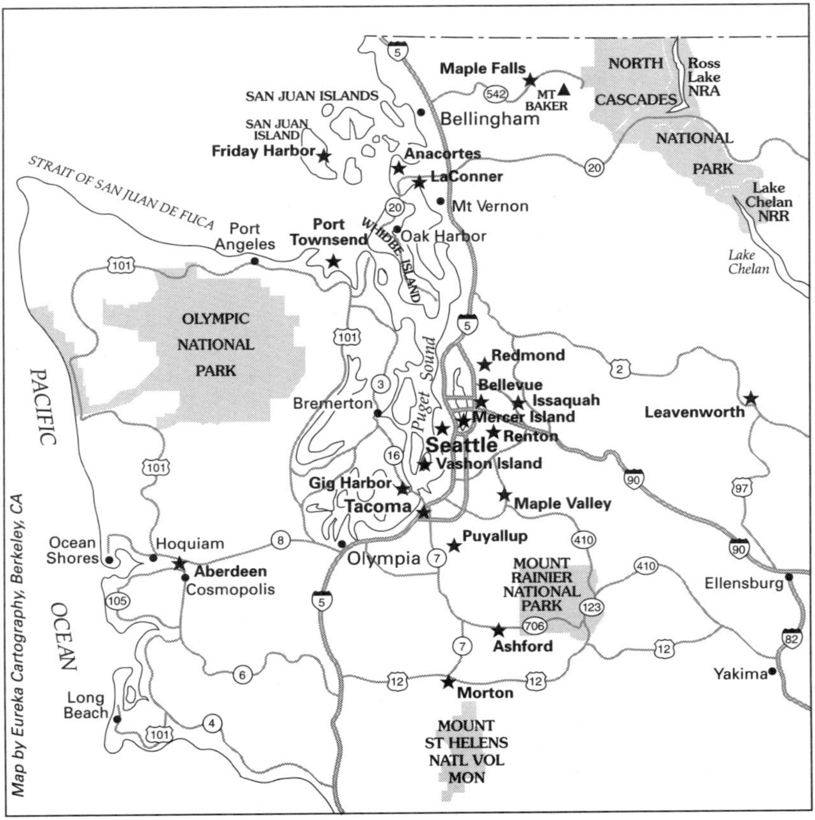
Maple Falls
MT BAKER
NORTH CASCADES
Ross Lake NRA
NATIONAL PARK
SAN JUAN ISLANDS
SAN JUAN ISLAND
Friday Harbor
Bellingham
Anacortes
LaConner
STRAIT OF SAN JUAN DE FUCA
Mt Vernon
Port Angeles
Port Townsend
WHIDBEY ISLAND
Oak Harbor
Lake Chelan NRR
Lake Chelan
OLYMPIC NATIONAL PARK
PACIFIC
Puget Sound
Redmond
Bellevue
Issaquah
Bremerton
Mercer Island
Renton
Leavenworth
Seattle
Vashon Island
Gig Harbor
Tacoma
Maple Valley
Ocean Shores
Hoquiam
Puyallup
Aberdeen
Cosmopolis
Olympia
MOUNT RAINIER NATIONAL PARK
Ellensburg
OCEAN
Ashford
Yakima
Long Beach
Morton
MOUNT ST HELENS NATL VOL MON
Map by Eureka Cartography, Berkeley, CA

ABERDEEN

Cooney Mansion Bed & Breakfast   (360) 533-0602
Hosts: Judi and Jim Lohr
1705 Fifth Street, Cosmopolis, WA 98537
In Cosmopolis, just south of Aberdeen.

   The Cooney Mansion is truly a mansion. Nothing small about this 1908 home built to showcase the wood from lumber baron Neil Cooney's mill. Some of the original furnishings, still in daily use, were made in the Cooney mill with wood we marvel at today. The private baths have their original fixtures as well, all in good working order. Now that's craftsmanship! The 600 square foot *Cooney Suite* is complete with fireplace, enclosed porch, sitting area, and a bathroom larger than most bedrooms. The tub-showers's original 10 inch showerhead yields a gentle, luxurious rain shower. The *Hemlock, Spruce,* and *Cedar* rooms have views of the 18-hole public golf course. Surrounding gardens make for captivating weddings, and receptions of all kinds are held in the ballroom. Relax in the sauna, jacuzzi, and exercise rooms, or get out for some golf, tennis, and hiking to the mill pond waterfall. An easy drive has you enjoying Grays Harbor Historic Seaport, and fishing, kayaking, and horseback riding along the ocean beaches.

   No pets; smoking outside only; children over 10 with prior arrangement; full lumber baron breakfast; TV/VCR; games; player piano; fireplace; fireplace in Cooney Suite; personal checks not accepted; major credit cards; special Dickens Christmas Dinner; special vacation packages.

ROOM	BED	BATH	ENTRANCE	FLOOR	S	D	EP+
Cooney Suite	1K	Pvt	Main	2		$125	$20
Cedar Room	1Q	Pvt	Main	2		$85	$20
Spruce Room	1Q	Pvt	Main	2		$80	
Alder Room	1Q	Pvt	Main	2		$75	
Hemlock Room	1T & 1D	Pvt	Main	2		$65	$20

Washington

ANACORTES

Albatross Bed & Breakfast (360) 293-0677
Hosts: Barbie and Ken (800) 622-8864
5708 Kingsway West, Anacortes, WA 98221
Across from Skyline Marina on Fidalgo Island.

When this home was built in the twenties, almost at water's edge, it was well constructed of solid cedar and survives today as a gracious haven of hospitality. The Albatross Bed & Breakfast provides excellent views of the boat launch area, the sea, and the San Juan Islands. Each comfortable, commodious guest room has a bath, an original painting, a lap blanket, thick carpeting, and a quiet, restful atmosphere. Antiques, fine art, and collectibles are displayed throughout the home. There is a vast selection of books and games, and a spacious living room offers a fireplace, a TV/VCR, and an inspiring panorama. Ken and Barbie do everything possible to ensure a pleasant stay for their guests, who appreciate especially the made-from-scratch breakfasts featuring local flavors. A sincere welcome and an array of thoughtful extras make staying here a rich experience. The Albatross offers a romantic package which includes two nights lodging, a sunset sail aboard the "Charisma", flight over the San Juan Islands, and special 2 for 1 dinner.

Smoking outside only; full breakfast; recreational opportunities close by, including sailboat cruises aboard hosts' 46-foot "Charisma"; travel information available; transportation to ferries (one mile away); off-street parking; credit cards (V,MC); winter rates.

ROOM	BED	BATH	ENTRANCE	FLOOR	S	D	EP+
Scarlett O'Hara	1Q	Pvt	Main	1		$85	$20
Victoria's Secret	1K	Pvt	Main	1		$85	
Captain's Hideaway	1K	Pvt	Main	1		$85	
Monet's Garden Retreat	1Q	Pvt	Main	1		$85	$20

ANACORTES

Channel House   (360) 293-9382
Hosts: Dennis and Pat McIntyre   (800) 238-4353
2902 Oakes Avenue, Anacortes, WA 98221
Overlooking Guemes Channel, five minutes from ferry docks.

Channel House is a joyous discovery for anyone traveling to this corner of the country. It's a home of unusual character; every guest room is uniquely situated for gazing out at the channel and the San Juan Islands. Shiny wood floors with Oriental rugs, fine antique furnishings, a library, and three fireplaces create an atmosphere of classic European elegance. Owners since 1986, Pat and Dennis McIntyre have preserved the flavor of the house while adding their own touches to make it their family home. They are former restaurateurs who take pride in the quality and variety of the breakfasts they serve, usually before a crackling fire. *Victorian Rose* and *Country Rose* are in the Rose Cottage, adjacent to main house; the individually decorated quarters feature fireplaces and private baths with whirlpool tubs. A memorable treat for guests is outdoor hot-tubbing with a view of island sunsets. All in all, staying at Channel House is an experience to be savored.

No pets; children over twelve OK; no smoking; full breakfast; evening refreshments; off-street parking; major credit cards.

ROOM	BED	BATH	ENTRANCE	FLOOR	DAILY RATES S	D	EP+
Island View Room	1K & 1T	Pvt	Main	2	$79	$89	$20
Garden View Room	1Q	Pvt	Main	2	$69	$79	
Canopy Room	1Q	Pvt	Main	1	$69	$79	
Grandma's Room	1Q	Pvt	Main	1	$59	$69	
Victorian Rose Room	1Q	Pvt	Sep	1		$95	
Country Rose Room	1Q	Pvt	Sep	1		$95	

Washington

ASHFORD

Mountain Meadows Inn   **(206) 569-2788**
Host: Chad Darrah
P.O. Box 291, Ashford, WA 98304
Six miles from entrance to Mount Rainier National Park.

The enchantment of Mountain Meadows Inn starts the minute you turn off the main highway to the clearing where this 1910 Craftsman-style home stands in a meadow encircled by forest and country quiet. It overlooks a stream-fed pond edged with cattails. The sturdy, character-filled house features a kaleidoscope of heart warming images and artistic touches. Chad Darrah, an engineer for "Rail-Link Railroad," displays a life-long collection of railroad paraphernalia. In 1991 he added two guest units (A and B) in a new building next door, and one has a full kitchen. Back at the main house, hearty breakfast fare is prepared on an old, wood-fired cook stove. Other old-fashioned pleasures include gathering 'round the campfire in the evening, visiting on the wide front porch, or reading hearth side in the living room. The property is a magical place to explore, and, of course, the mountain beckons and is only 6 miles away. Chad suggests the Mt. Rainier Scenic Railroad and Northwest Trek as nearby local activities for his guests.

Dog, cats, pigs, chickens, and ducks on property; no pets; children over ten welcome; no smoking in building; full breakfast; VCR in living room; player piano; pond has small dock, trout, and catfish; hiking trail to old National town site; off-street parking; credit cards (V,MC).

ROOM	BED	BATH	ENTRANCE	FLOOR	DAILY RATES S	D	EP+
Sunnybrook	1Q	Pvt	Main	1		$95	
Millpond	1K & 2T	Pvt	Main	1		$85	$15
Mt. Berry	1Q	Pvt	Main	1		$75	$15
A	1Q	Pvt	Sep	2		$75	$15
B	1D & 1T	Pvt	Sep	2		$75	$15

BELLEVUE (Near Seattle)

A Cascade View Bed & Breakfast (206) 883-7078
Hosts: Marianne and Bill Bundren
13425 NE 27th Street, Bellevue, WA 98005
Northern Bellevue near Bridal Trails State Park.

The Bundren's contemporary home, just a short 15 minute drive east of Seattle, is worlds apart from the Seattle urban environment. From its forested rolling hills, you can see the green lawns and rose garden, apple trees, and beyond to the Cascade peaks on the far horizon. The ground-floor *Garden Room* has direct garden and patio access; the fireplace, queen bed, and contour chair lend cozy comfort within. The *Rose Room* features a white iron queen bed and wonderful garden view. The Bundrens on their many travels have acquired a wealth of interests. Bill, a former ship's captain, has seen much of the world and is now a pilot in Puget Sound. Marianne, a former teacher who loves entertaining, radiates warmth and gracious hospitality; her healthy and delicious breakfasts may include apples from their own trees, and certainly, some Starbucks coffee. Nearness to Microsoft headquarters makes Cascade View first choice if you are visiting the software company. Suggested activities include antique shopping, guided horseback riding, and jogging nearby trails, and don't forget to sample the excellent Bellevue dining and lush wineries nestled in the Cascade foothills.

Dog in residence; no pets or smoking; children welcome; full breakfast; AC; TV with cable in Garden Room; fireplace in Garden Room; use of deck and garden.

ROOM	BED	BATH	ENTRANCE	FLOOR	S	D	EP+
Garden Room	1Q	Pvt	Main	1		$90	$15
Rose Room	1Q	Pvt	Main	1		$75	$15

DAILY RATES

BELLEVUE (Near Seattle)

Petersen Bed & Breakfast   **(206) 454-9334**
Hosts: Eunice and Carl Petersen
10228 SE Eighth, Bellevue, WA 98004
Fifteen minutes east of Seattle.

Though some think of Bellevue simply as part of suburban Seattle, it has come into its own in recent years as a major business and shopping area with its fair share of fine dining establishments and horticultural displays. In a quiet, established neighborhood, Eunice and Carl Petersen open their warm and inviting home to bed and breakfast guests. On the lower (daylight) level of the house you'll find two pretty, relaxing rooms with down comforters and tasteful decorator touches. Spend leisure moments on the large deck—perhaps in the steamy spa—that overlooks beautifully landscaped grounds. After a wonderful night's rest, enjoy a generous home-style breakfast in the atrium kitchen. Then you should be able to face the day with a smile.

Smoking outside only; full breakfast; TV/VCR; hot tub; one mile from Bellevue Square shopping; good public transportation; off-street parking; one-night stays, $10 extra.

ROOM	BED	BATH	ENTRANCE	FLOOR	DAILY RATES S D EP+
Queen Room	1Q	Shd	Main	LL	$55
King Room	1K or 2T	Shd	Main	LL	$55

GIG HARBOR

Peacock Hill Guest House   (800) 863-2318
Hosts: Suzanne and Steve Savlov   (206) 858-3322
9520 Peacock Hill Avenue, Gig Harbor, WA 98332
Above the marina in Gig Harbor.

Suzanne and Steve Savlov moved to the Puget Sound area from their Sedona bed-and-breakfast to resume a B&B career in Gig Harbor. Quite a change from warm Arizona to the cooler Northwest, yes, but they've created a pleasant, comfortable home overlooking the marina. At Peacock Hill, Steve and Suzanne maintain an attractive home with a Southwestern decor. The whole lower level, and part of the upper, is for guests. The downstairs suite has a four-poster queen bed and private bath with large shower; adjacent is a large living room with TV, VCR, CD player, small fridge, heated floors, fireplace, and wonderful view of the harbor. Upstairs, the contemporary bedroom is light and airy, with both queen and day bed. Breakfast is in the dining room or on the scenic patio. Afternoons, Suzanne serves coffee and homemade goodies. The Savlovs suggest boating and kayaking, and the summer community theater is just two blocks away. Peacock Hill is convenient to many fine attractions: Poulsbo, a Scandinavian village; Mts. Ranier and St. Helens; the ferry to Seattle's Pike Place Market; and a 5-mile bike ride through Tacoma's Point Defiance Park.

No pets or smoking; children by arrangement; full breakfast; TV in each room; VCR; fireplace; off-street parking.

ROOM	BED	BATH	ENTRANCE	FLOOR	DAILY RATES S	D	EP+
Upstairs	1T & 1Q	Pvt	Main	1G		$75	$10
Downstairs Suite	1Q	Pvt	Sep	LL		$95	

Washington

ISSAQUAH

Mountains and Planes Bed and Breakfast   (800) 231-8068
Host: Elizabeth FitzGerald   (206) 392-8068
100 Big Bear Place NW, Issaquah, WA 98027
On Squak Mountain, 1 mile west of the historic center of Issaquah.

Issaquah's modern history began in the late 1800's as a coal mining center. You won't see any coal being mined today, but you'll find this living/shopping hub exciting, and Elizabeth's home on Squak Mountain is convenient headquarters while exploring the area. Elizabeth has lived in various countries, and it shows: one room has a Chinese influence, another, the *Pink Room* a British flavor. *Chinese Room* and *Pink Room* share a bath and the aviation room, which serves as a TV/sitting room with cozy wood stove, aircraft pictures, books and videos, and a seat from a plane built for the king of Saudi Arabia. The *Icon Room* has a private bath, hand-painted stenciling, and a more American decor; it's near the dining room, the East Indian parlor, and the mountain-view deck. Elizabeth is enthusiastic about area activities—the Village Theatre, historic Gilman Village shopping, Boehm's Chocolate Factory, wineries, hang gliding—and it seems there's always some event, such as Issaquah Days in mid-May, the Fourth of July celebration, and Salmon Days in October. Plan to attend and when you do, stay at Mountains and Planes!

Smoking outside only; pets by arrangement; children by arrangement; full breakfast tailored to suit your taste.; TV and phone in *Icon room*; phone in *Chinese Room*; TV; FAX available; extended stay discount, one night stay surcharge; credit cards (MC,V,AMEX).

ROOM	BED	BATH	ENTRANCE	FLOOR	DAILY RATES S	D	EP+
Icon Room	1Q	Pvt	Main	1		$55	
Pink Room	2T	Shd	Main	LL	$38	$49	
Chinese Room	1Q	Shd	Main	LL		$49	

LA CONNER

The White Swan Guest House (360) 445-6805
Host: Peter Goldfarb
1388 Moore Road, Mount Vernon, WA 98273
Six miles from La Conner, on Skagit River.

Peter Goldfarb made a major shift in life style when he moved from New York City to the quiet countryside of the Pacific Northwest, but adapted to hosting quite easily. He bought a handsome Victorian home, badly in need of attention, and gave it his all. Keeping its charm and character intact, Peter's inspired renovations turned it into the jewel it is today. My favorite aspect of the decor is the bold use of color throughout the house. Vivid hues of a country garden create a cheerful environment, a lift to the spirit on dull days. Comfortable rooms are uniquely decorated, featuring Peter's large collection of antique samplers. Outside, English-style country gardens with seating areas and lots of flowers enhance the grounds. To the rear of the property is the wonderful, private, *Garden Cottage* with its own kitchen, deck, and gorgeous views of the farmlands. Mother Nature has richly endowed the surrounding landscape—it's great for walking along the river, cycling, and observing wildlife. Peter suggests kayaking excursions in summer, eagle viewing in winter, and the Tulip Festival in April as special activities for his guests. Any way you look at it, The White Swan is a find.

Dogs in residence; smoking outside only (porch); homemade chocolate chip cookies all day; three rooms share two baths on second floor; double futon sofa bed extra in cottage; off-street parking; credit cards (V,MC).

ROOM	BED	BATH	ENTRANCE	FLOOR	DAILY RATES S	D	EP+
Yellow	1K	Shd	Main	2	$65	$80	
Pink	1Q	Shd	Main	2	$65	$80	
Peach	1Q	Shd	Main	2	$65	$80	
Garden Cottage	1Q	Pvt	Sep	1 & 2	$125	$150	$20

LEAVENWORTH

Bosch Garten Bed & Breakfast   (509) 548-6900
Hosts: Myke and Cal Bosch   FAX: (509) 548-6076
9846 Dye Road, Leavenworth, WA 98826
Four tenths of a miles east of downtown Leavenworth.

   Bosch Garten Bed and Breakfast is a true garden spot, smack in the middle of a pear and apple orchard. Myke has a perennial garden, a wildflower garden, and a rose garden complete with three arbors to display the roses she so carefully tends. Inside, a ti plant grows in a sunny window beside a fifteen foot Norfolk Pine. The pine, topped once, now has three shoots stretching toward the ceiling. High windows offer a marvelous view up the Wenatchee River Valley to Wedge Mountain and the Cascade peaks. The peaks provide a dramatic setting for the Bavarian town of Leavenworth, where you'll find European atmosphere, German food, shopping, skiing (two nearby downhill and cross country ski areas), river rafting, hiking, rock climbing, and golf. Activity is the byword in Leavenworth. There's always something happening, and later you can ease your sore muscles in the steamy hot tub. Rooms all have mountain views, ensuite baths, and decor to match their names. The seasonal Maifest, Autumn Leaf, and Christmas lighting ceremonies, suggests Cal, are especially nice to see and are good times to visit.

   No pets or smoking; children by prior arrangement; full breakfast; fireplace; cable TV in each room; telephone; AC; hot tub; library; tennis rackets; bikes; credit cards (V,MC,DS).

ROOM	BED	BATH	ENTRANCE	FLOOR	DAILY RATES		
					S	D	EP+
Northwest	1K & 2T	Pvt	Main	2	$80	$95	$25
Southwest	1K	Pvt	Main	2	$75	$90	$25
Midwest	1K	Pvt	Main	2	$70	$85	$25

MAPLE FALLS

Yodeler Inn (206) 599-2156
Hosts: Jeff and Bethnie Morrison (800) 642-9033
P.O. Box 222, Maple Falls, WA 98266
Twenty-six miles east of Bellingham in Mount Baker foothills.

    Yodeler Inn seems a natural part of the ambiance in the little alpine village of Maple Falls. With the omnipresence of Mount Baker, the surrounding area is a vacation wonderland with year-round adventures to pursue. Here Jeff and Bethnie Morrison aim to provide "a relaxing environment to sleep, eat, and play in." Their homey inn has one guest room with its own entrance, country decor, and a hot tub just outside the door; a spacious living room with a fireplace may also be used. An intimate private cottage (B) on the property provides additional accommodation. It's a pleasant surprise to find several good restaurants, and one great one, nearby. Some local activities include Alpine and cross-country skiing, river rafting, mountain climbing, fishing, photography, and many hiking trails. Nearby points of interest to visit include Silver Lake, the Nooksack River, and Nooksack Falls. Your hosts can suggest many more.

    Two cats in residence; smoking outside only; full breakfast; kitchenette in cottage; TV/VCR available; off-street parking; credit cards (V,MC).

ROOM	BED	BATH	ENTRANCE	FLOOR	DAILY RATES S	D	EP+
A	1Q	Pvt	Sep	1	$35	$65	
B	1D & 1T	Pvt	Sep	1	$35	$65	

MAPLE VALLEY

Maple Valley Bed & Breakfast (206) 432-1409
Hosts: Clarke and Jayne Hurlbut
20020 SE 228, Maple Valley, WA 98038
Nineteen miles due east of Sea-Tac International Airport.

After a demanding week at work or a day of hard traveling, how satisfying to find that perfect haven in the country for a few days of pampered relaxation—Maple Valley Bed & Breakfast. Jayne and Clarke Hurlbut have fashioned a rustic family home of outstanding warmth and charm. Built by Clarke, it stands in a clearing in the woods, surrounded by a carpet of neat green lawn. The later addition of an "eagles' aerie" lends a fairy tale quality. Walls of warm cedar, a huge stone fireplace, open-beamed ceilings, and many interesting angles give the house its singular appeal, and two gabled guest rooms on the second floor couldn't be more endearing. The decor is country Americana, very well done. Each room has lacy curtains, antiques, and nostalgia pieces, as well as French doors that open to a large deck. Featured in the *Cedar Log Room* are a hand hewn four-poster log bed and a pedestal sink; in *Cedar Branch Room*, beautiful heirloom quilts cover the beds. An upstairs sitting room and adjoining TV area are great for reading, playing games, working puzzles, and viewing the wildlife pond through binoculars. Attention to detail is the essence of what's so special at Maple Valley Bed & Breakfast. Far be it from me to spoil all the surprises. During your visit, be sure to visit Black Diamond, an old coal-mining town with its famous bakery and nearby Green River Gorge.

Outdoor peacocks, chickens, cats, and dog; no pets; smoking outside only; full breakfast; crib available; barbecue area; basketball; hiking; nature walks; available for outdoor weddings; off-street parking.

ROOM	BED	BATH	ENTRANCE	FLOOR	DAILY RATES S	D	EP+
Cedar Log Room	1Q	Shd	Main	2	$65	$15	
Cedar Branch Room	1D & 1T	Shd	Main	2	$60	$15	

MERCER ISLAND (Near Seattle)

Duck-In Bed & Breakfast   **(206) 232-2554**
Hosts: Ruth and Ron Mullen
4118 - 100th Avenue, SE, Mercer Island, WA 98040
Waterfront, on the east side of the island.

Removed from urban frenzy, on the bank of Lake Washington, this inviting, cozy cottage makes a great little getaway spot. Take it easy in lounge chairs on the sloping green lawn, grill some fish for dinner, or even send out for pizza—you'll probably want to stay put for a while. Guests have the cottage, full of homey touches, to themselves. There are two bedrooms separated by a bathroom and an office. Facing the water is the living/dining room. You'll find nice table linens, a well-stocked kitchen, and all kinds of thoughtful amenities (picnic basket, sewing basket, binoculars, books and games, etc.). Ron and Ruth Mullen encourage snooping in every nook and cranny, really making yourself at home. At the Duck-In, you'll have plenty of privacy in a waterfront setting with all the necessary comforts and many unexpected ones.

No pets; smoking outside only; TV/VCR; desk and private phone; full kitchen with stove, dishwasher, and microwave; off-street parking.

ROOM	BED	BATH	ENTRANCE	FLOOR	DAILY RATES S	D	EP+
A	1Q & 2T	Pvt	Main	1		$95	$10

MERCER ISLAND (Near Seattle)

Mole House Bed & Breakfast   (206) 232-1611
Hosts: Don and Petra Walker
3308 West Mercer Way, Mercer Island, WA 98040
On the west shore of the island.

It would take an album full of pictures to capture the many facets of Mole House. The rambling contemporary Northwest home overlooks Lake Washington, Seattle, and the Olympic Mountains. It is made up of several distinct sections that are harmoniously linked together by the hosts' collection of art, antiques, and family heirlooms. Don, a native of Seattle, and Petra, who emigrated from West Germany in 1986, extend caring hospitality in a refined atmosphere. Here you can have all the privacy you need, invite friends in for a visit, or enjoy the interesting company of Don and Petra. The three guest accommodations are on different levels of the house. *Eagle* is on the main level, The *Garden Suite* has a sitting room and opens onto a brick patio, and *The Apartment* is a totally self-contained space with a deck and a panoramic view of the lake. Park-like surroundings, soft music, and elegant breakfasts contribute to the sensual delight of staying at Mole House. It is in every respect a rare find. The Walkers encourage you to come and enjoy the great jogging on Mercer Island.

No pets; well-behaved children welcome; no smoking; full breakfast; *The Apartment* has a sofa bed, telephone, and kitchen with stocked fridge; cable TV in each room; patios, decks, and gardens; ten minutes from Seattle, twenty from airport; good public transportation and airport connections; off-street parking; German spoken.

ROOM	BED	BATH	ENTRANCE	FLOOR	DAILY RATES S	D	EP+
Eagle	1D	Pvt	Main	1		$55	
Garden Suite	1D	Pvt	Main	LL		$65	
The Apartment	1D	Pvt	Main & Sep	2		$70	$5

MORTON

St. Helens Manorhouse   (360) 498-5243
Host: Susyn Dragness   (800) 551-3290
7476 Highway 12, Morton, WA 98356
5.8 miles east of Morton on Highway 12, just past mile marker 103 - on the right (south).

St. Helens Manorhouse is a grand old 1910 farmhouse. Turning off Highway 12, you'll see it atop the hill surrounded by a white running fence. An European emigrant named Uden built the house as headquarters for his thousand-acre truck farm and as home to Anna Senn, his mail-order Swiss bride. The four rooms on the second floor all maintain their farmhouse charm with high ceilings and period decor. The original wavy, etched leaded glass still graces the windows overlooking a profuse landscape of flowers, herbs, and berries. Susyn includes the herbs and berries in her generous breakfasts. Bear, cougar, deer, elk, and an array of birds, including a pair of bald eagles, live at nearby Cowlitz Wildlife Preserve. Relax in the parlor, or step out to the columned front porch to enjoy the outdoors—then stroll to the gazebo, and among the many trees: dogwood, walnut, chestnut, apple, plum. For adventure, there's hang gliding, boating, and wind surfing. Susyn also suggests the calmer pleasures of the wildlife preserve, or fishing for silvers at Riffe or Mayfield Lake, and in the fall, picking chantrels and morels in the surrounding forests.

Dog and cat in residence; no pets; children 10 and over; smoking outside only; full breakfast; TV/VCR; fireplace; airport pickup at the Morton airport.

ROOM	BED	BATH	ENTRANCE	FLOOR	DAILY RATES S	D	EP+
Sophie's Choice	1Q	Shd	Main	2		$59	
The Twins	2D	Shd	Main	2		$59	$15
Winterthur	1Q	Pvt	Main	2		$69	
Limoges	1Q	Pvt	Main	2		$69	

Washington

PORT TOWNSEND

Holly Hill House   **(206) 385-5619**
Host: Lynne Sterling
611 Polk Street, Port Townsend, WA 98368
Historic Uptown District.

This Christmas-card-perfect 1872 Victorian stands on a corner lot with tall holly trees and other plantings from long ago. The lawn is encircled by a white picket fence flanked by roses, and a flower-lined path leads to the front door of Holly Hill House. The second-floor guest rooms are havens of comfort and pleasure, with florals and laces and wonderful views. Overlook the gardens from *Lizette's Room*, or Admiralty Inlet and the Cascades from the *Colonel's Room* or *Billie's Room*. Equally attractive newer rooms in the Carriage House include the *Morning Glory* and the *Skyview*. Sumptuous breakfasts are prepared in the large country kitchen, then served with a gracious air in the formal dining room. Both here and in the living room, notice the original stippled woodwork that was the rage in the house's heyday. Some furnishings are antiques, some reproductions, but the accent is on livability. Lynne wants guests to fully relax and enjoy the whole house and the gardens. She mentions the music festivals and the Wooden Boat Show as special activities to enjoy in the area.

No pets; children over twelve welcome; smoking outside only; full breakfast; queen sofa bed extra in Room A; off-street parking; credit cards (V,MC). Inquire about special off-season packages such as wine-tasting (Ms. Sterling makes an award-winning Merlot) and mystery weekends; intimate weddings and honeymoon packages available.

ROOM	BED	BATH	ENTRANCE	FLOOR	S	D	EP+
Colonel's Room	1K	Pvt	Main	2		$125	$20
Billie's Room	1Q	Pvt	Main	2		$86	
Lizette's Room	1Q & 1T	Pvt	Main	2		$78	$12
Skyview Room	1Q	Pvt	Sep	1		$78	
Morning Glory Room	1Q	Pvt	Sep	1		$72	

(DAILY RATES)

PUYALLUP

Hart's Tayberry House   **(206) 848-4594**
Hosts: Ray and Donna Hart, Sandy Hart Hammer
7406 - 80th Street East, Puyallup, WA 98371
Puyallup/Tacoma area.

   The authenticity of this Victorian charmer is almost palpable, so it's surprising to learn that the home is in fact a reproduction. The original no longer stands, but it was built by a leading pioneer in the area. Unusual care was taken in its re-creation here on a hillside overlooking rich farmlands. Intricately carved exterior woodwork and a wrap-around porch with a gazebo are a perfect prelude to the turn-of-the-century details inside. Upstairs, the front Balcony Room offers fresh air and a view. The smaller but oh-so-sweet Heart Room is just down the hall. A bathroom off the hallway has an old-fashioned chain-pull toilet and a clawfoot tub. A spacious suite spans the back of the house. Lovingly combined wallpapers, rugs, linens, and furnishings give each room a romantic warmth. A friendly, hospitable stay in quiet rural surroundings awaits you at Hart's Tayberry House.

   No pets; children over twelve welcome; smoking outside only; small refrigerator in suite; AC; elevator; walk to city park and tennis courts; off-street parking; senior discount.

ROOM	BED	BATH	ENTRANCE	FLOOR	DAILY RATES S	D	EP+
A	1Q	Shd	Main	2		$55	
B	1D	Shd	Main	2		$45	
C	1Q	Pvt	Main	2		$65	$10

REDMOND

A Cottage Creek Inn Bed & Breakfast   (206) 881-5606
Hosts: Jeanette and Steve Wynecoop
12525 Avondale Road, Redmond, WA 98052
30 minutes from Seattle in the suburban area near Redmond and Bellevue.

Would you enjoy an English Tudor manor with expansive lawns? A pond with fountain and gazebo in a quiet country setting yet near an urban center? If so, Cottage Creek Inn is the place to stay. You'll cross the namesake Cottage Creek shortly after turning off Avondale Road going down the long driveway that leads to this secluded home. Lawns reach to the edge of the creek, where you can see salmon spawn in the fall. The manor is set in a tall conifer grove, and hiking trails lead into the woods. It's tailor-made for small, intimate weddings. Many lovely brides have donned their veils and lace in front of the fully-mirrored closet doors in the *Bride's Room*. The large *Stephanotis Room* has gables jutting out from the roof, which creates a lot of little nooks inside, and the skylights lend a cheery atmosphere. Steve's wildlife and marine artwork is displayed throughout the house which has traditional decorating with some antiques and lace. The courtyard fountain lulls you to sleep, and in the morning, you wake up refreshed and renewed for another day of exploration.

No pets; smoking outside only; children by arrangement (10 or older suggested); extended continental breakfast; credit cards (V,MC,AMEX); FAX available.

ROOM	BED	BATH	ENTRANCE	FLOOR	S	D	EP+
Bride's Room	1Q	Pvt	Main	2		$75	$15
Rose Room	1Q	Shd	Main	2		$65	$15
Stephanotis Room	1Q	Shd	Main	2		$85	$15

RENTON

Holly Hedge House—A Private Retreat
Hosts: Lynn and Marian Thrasher **Voice/Fax: (206) 226-2555**
908 Grant Avenue South, Renton, WA 98055
On Renton Hill overlooking Renton and the Green River Valley.

Step into Holly Hedge House and feel the meticulous quality and care that created this English country style, five room cottage. Remarkably, Holly Hedge House was built by Marian's grandfather in 1901, and has been in the family ever since. Marian and Lynn live next door and enjoy telling about the neatly sculptured front Holly hedge, growing strong since the turn of the century, taking over the original wood fence. The cottage is reserved for one couple at a time, and that couple gets everything: book library, CD library, video library, TV/VCR, fully-stocked kitchen (including cookbooks, coffee maker, and espresso machine), whirlpool tub-shower, hot tub, large decks, fireplace, swimming pool, recliner chairs, and a solid four-poster queen bed. Floors are light oak with matching cabinets. The rose-print curtains, linens, and wainscoting selected by Marian as part of the interior decor won a Waverly fabric decorating award (October '95 issue of Country Inns). Holly Hedge House's hilltop location is less than 10 minutes from Sea-Tac Airport and 20 minutes from downtown Seattle; jogging paths and biking trails are in walking distance. Visit Holly Hedge House and experience a quality bed and breakfast stay.

No pets; smoking outside only; full breakfast; TV/VCR/CD with library; fireplace; spa; robes provided; pool; deck; full kitchen; bikes; tennis rackets; credit cards (V,MC). Two night minimum.

ROOM	BED	BATH	ENTRANCE	FLOOR	DAILY RATES S / D / EP
Holly Hedge House	1Q	Pvt	Sep	1	$98

Washington

SAN JUAN ISLAND - FRIDAY HARBOR

Tower House Bed & Breakfast (360) 378-5464
Hosts: Chris and Joe Luma
1230 Little Road, Friday Harbor, WA 98250
Three and one-half miles from ferry landing.

On a quiet country road overlooking the San Juan Valley, Tower House rests on ten acres of rural beauty. Chris and Joe Luma offer a gracious bed and breakfast experience for one or two couples at a time. Luxuries and little surprises grace the vintage home, which manages to be both cozy and elegant. Choose the spacious *Sun Room*, a light and airy creation in peach and cream; it has its own solarium/library with an antique desk and a marvelous sunrise view. Or choose the mauve and ecru *Tower Room*, with antique furnishings that complement the spectacular stained glass of the tower windows. A tufted window seat encircles the tower; a sunset view can be savored from here or from the wide veranda. Chris and Joe pride themselves on their breakfast cuisine and assure that even people on special diets like vegan or gluten-free can enjoy a full breakfast served on china with crystal, silver, and antique linens. They suggest visiting in May when the weather is usually great, the island green, the wildflowers are in bloom, the Orca whales are most active, yet tourist traffic is still low. Caring hospitality and superb accommodations ensure a memorable stay at Tower House.

Cat in residence; no pets, children, or smoking; full breakfast; snacks and beverages always available; great hikes and wildlife viewing from Tower House; off-street parking; major credit cards.

ROOM	BED	BATH	ENTRANCE	FLOOR	S	DAILY RATES D	EP+
Tower Room	1Q	Pvt	Main	1		$115	
Sun Room	1Q	Pvt	Main	1		$95	

SEATTLE

The Bacon Mansion (206) 329-1864
Hosts: Daryl King and Tim Stiles (800) 240-1864
959 Broadway East, Seattle, WA 98102 FAX: (206) 860-9025
Capitol Hill.

Built in 1909 by Cecil Bacon, this classical house, combining Edwardian and Tudor styling, has been returned to much of its original grandeur and offers refined comfort to all who enter. The Bacon family crest in red and white stained glass enhances the front entrance. The extensive, carefully preserved woodwork, a 3,000-crystal chandelier, marble fireplaces, handsome library, and magnificent living and dining rooms will delight the connoisseur and casual observer alike. On the floors above are six most pleasant guest rooms offering great variety in decor, size, bed type, and price. The premier accommodation is the *Capitol Suite*, a huge area that features a view of the Space Needle, a sun room with a hide-a-bed, a private bath, a beautiful fireplace, and pine and wicker furnishings. Believe me, the Bacon Mansion is a lot to live up to, but Daryl and Tim pull it off seamlessly.

Smoking outside only; some rooms with fireplaces; TV and telephone in each room; exercise equipment; near bus route; off-street and street parking; Shuttle Express from airport; major credit cards; off-season rates; *Carriage House* (across patio) is a two-story retreat with a living room with hide-a-bed, bedroom, and bath.

ROOM	BED	BATH	ENTRANCE	FLOOR	S	D	EP+
Carriage House	1Q & 1D	Pvt	Sep	1 & 2		$125	$25
Capitol Suite	1Q & 1D	Pvt	Main	2		$119	$20
Venetian Room	1D	Pvt	Main	2	$92	$99	
Rose Room	1Q	Pvt	Main	2	$84	$92	
Garden Suite	1Q & 1T	Pvt	Main	LL	$84	$92	$15
Fountain Room	1Q & 1T	Pvt	Main	LL	$84	$92	$15
Clipper Room	1D	Pvt	Main	2	$84	$92	
Iris Room	1Q	Shd	Main	3	$70	$79	
Cabin Room	1D	Shd	Main	3	$65	$74	

Washington

SEATTLE

Capitol Hill House Bed & Breakfast (206) 322-1752
Host: Mary Wolf
2215 East Prospect, Seattle, WA 98112
In the Capitol Hill district of Seattle.

Mary Wolf's stately brick home on a quiet, tree-lined street is in one of Seattle's most prestigious neighborhoods. This handsome red brick structure houses luxury accommodations filled with family heirlooms, tapestries, and oriental rugs. You'll enjoy wandering the house, admiring the enchanting French Romance art. Two pretty guest rooms plus a spacious master suite with nursery and dressing room occupy the second floor. Mary serves breakfast in style, and later you can relax on the private patio, or perhaps take a stroll to the tennis courts. Refined comfort, convenient location (near the University of Washington, Volunteer Park, the Convention Center, and downtown Seattle): both are yours at Capitol Hill. Mary suggests visiting the Seattle Art Museum, the Seattle Asian Art Museum, Seattle Center, and the Pike Place Market while you stay at Capitol Hill.

Ages welcome by arrangement; full breakfast; TV and phone in each room; fireplace; refrigerator and washer/dryer use permitted.

ROOM	BED	BATH	ENTRANCE	FLOOR	S	D	EP+
Queen	1Q	Shd	Main	2		$55	
King	1K or 2T	Shd	Main	2		$65	$15
Master Suite	1K or 2T	Pvt	Main	2		$75	$15

SEATTLE

Dibble House   (206) 783-0320
Host: Sue Gregor
7301 Dibble Avenue NW, Seattle, WA 98117
Off Interstate 5, north of Seattle.

When visiting a large city such as Seattle, it is great to be conveniently located so that you can find the sights easily. Dibble House, in historic Ballard, is a 1920-style red brick home close to Puget Sound, Green Lake, the Seattle Center, and the Seattle Zoo. The combination of accessibility, a welcoming home, an accomplished and charming hostess is what a bed and breakfast is all about. Sue has run Dibble House for nine years and her special touches are everywhere. She has an eye for treasurers other people miss at garage sales and antique auctions. The living room is large with comfortable chairs, a telephone, TV/VCR, and fireplace. The adjoining dining room has picture windows overlooking apple trees and flower gardens. Sue has been in the catering business for twelve years and welcomes small weddings and meetings at Dibble House. The bedrooms are decorated with an old-fashioned flair and each has unusual antiques. A cot and porta crib can fit in any room. Sue suggests going to the nearby Government Locks to watch boats being lowered from Lake Union to Puget Sound—interesting, fun, and FREE!

Cat in residence; pets with prior arrangement; smoking outside only; children welcome; full breakfast; TV/VCR; two telephones; crib; cot; airport shuttle to door; bus to downtown; discount for extended stays; open year round.

ROOM	BED	BATH	ENTRANCE	FLOOR	DAILY RATES S D EP+
Jenna	1Q	Pvt	Main	1	$65
Suzanne	1Q	Shd	Main	2	$55
Alyssa	2T	Shd	Main	2	$55
Violet	1Q	Shd	Main	2	$55
Rose	2T	Shd	Main	2	$55

Washington

SEATTLE

Mildred's Bed & Breakfast (206) 325-6072
Hosts: Mildred and Melodee Sarver
1202 Fifteenth Avenue East, Seattle, WA 98112
Capitol Hill, facing east side of Volunteer Park.

If ever a place could tug at your heartstrings, Mildred's would do it. It's the ultimate trip-to-Grandmother's fantasy come true. A large, double-turreted, white Victorian possessed of a friendly charm, it's the perfect setting for Mildred Sarver's caring hospitality. Three guest rooms on the upper floor couldn't be prettier. Lace curtains, stained glass, and antiques add to the ambiance of warmth and security. An alcove adjacent to the guest rooms offers the convenience of a drop-down ironing board with full-length mirrored door, a refrigerator, makings for tea and coffee, a sink, and a telephone. Mildred's special touches and lavish breakfasts make her guests feel truly pampered.

No pets; smoking in restricted areas; full breakfast; TV available; fireplace and grand piano in living room; 40-acre park across street, good for walking or jogging; ample street parking; good public transportation; Shuttle Express from airport; major credit cards.

ROOM	BED	BATH	ENTRANCE	FLOOR	S	D	EP+
A	1Q	Pvt	Main	2	$75	$85	$15
B	1Q	Pvt	Main	2	$75	$85	$15
C	1Q	Pvt	Main	2	$75	$85	$15

SEATTLE

Prince of Wales (206) 325-9692
Host: Carol Norton   FAX: (206) 322-6402
133 Thirteenth Avenue East, Seattle, WA 98102 (800) 327-9692
Capitol Hill.

From this handsome turn-of-the-century home you can easily reach the city's conference sites and all the downtown attractions you'll want to visit. Equally well-suited for business or vacation travelers, Prince of Wales has home-like comfort with hints of royalty throughout. Enjoy a relaxing stay in the *Princess Suite*, the *King's Room*, the *Queen's Room*, or the top-floor *Prince's Retreat*, which features a clawfoot tub, a city and mountain view, and a private deck. The cheerful, friendly atmosphere of the home is enhanced by interesting collections, handcrafted collages, and touches of whimsy. A delicious full breakfast rounds out the generous hospitality offered by Carol. But most impressive of all is the view—a stunning panorama of the city skyline, Olympic Mountains, and Puget Sound, with the Space Needle in the foreground. Three of the four guest rooms feature this ever-present reminder that you couldn't be anywhere but Seattle. Carol notes you are in walking distance of the Capitol Hill attractions including ethnic restaurants, shops, and coffee houses and suggests visiting the neighborhood while staying at Prince of Wales.

Cat and dog in residence; no pets or smoking; full breakfast; fireplace in living room; private garden; good public transportation; local limousine from airport; off-street and street parking; guest phone; major credit cards; two-night minimum *May 15-October 15.*

ROOM	BED	BATH	ENTRANCE	FLOOR	DAILY RATES S	D	EP+
Queen's Room	1Q	Pvt	Main	2		$80	
King's Room	1Q	Pvt	Main	2		$90	
Princess Suite	1Q & 1T	Pvt	Main	2		$100	$15
Prince's Retreat	2Q	Pvt	Main	3		$110	$15

Washington

SPOKANE

Marianna Stoltz House (509) 483-4316
Hosts: Phyllis and Jim Maguire (800) 978-6587
East 427 Indiana, Spokane, WA 99207
Central Spokane, historic Gonzaga University area.

Phyllis and Jim Maguire have the good fortune to live in the 1908 American foursquare classic home in which Phyllis grew up. She named it Marianna Stoltz in honor of her mother. Now one of Spokane's historic landmarks, it has the feel of a big, old-fashioned family home that's comfortable through and through. Period furnishings, handsome woodwork, leaded glass cabinets, and a lovely tile fireplace enhance the gracious interior. Accommodations are all on the second floor, and guests are welcome to come and go as they please; the front entrance is theirs alone. Beds are covered with the wonderful collection of old quilts that Phyllis so generously shares. Fond memories of Marianna Stoltz House might include visiting or reading on the wide, wraparound verandah or breakfasting on Stoltz House strada, peach Melba parfaits, or Dutch babies. These and other pleasures await you at this popular in town B&B. The Maguires suggest you ride the hand-carved carousel in Riverfront Park or enjoy the 39 mile river-front jogging and bicycling trail.

No pets; no children under twelve; smoking outside only; full breakfast; cable TV in each room; AC; choice of shower or clawfoot tub; good public transportation and airport connections; off-street parking; all major credit cards.

ROOM	BED	BATH	ENTRANCE	FLOOR	S	D	EP+
A	1K & 1T	Shd	Main	2	$55	$65	$15
B	1Q	Shd	Main	2	$50	$60	
C	1Q	Pvt	Main	2	$60	$70	
D	1Q	Pvt	Main	2	$65	$75	

TACOMA

Commencement Bay Bed & Breakfast   (206) 752-8175
Hosts: Sharon and Bill Kaufmann   email: greatviews@aol.com
3312 North Union Avenue, Tacoma, WA 98407
Just 30 miles south of Seattle in historic North Tacoma, near Point Defiance Park, scenic waterfront areas, and the Washington State Historical Museum.

From its elevated position, this stately Colonial home affords a breathtaking view of Commencement Bay and Mount Rainier beyond. Bill and Sharon keep the gardens tended, their home immaculate, and the welcome mat always out for guests. Upon arrival, you'll make one pleasant discovery after another: elegantly appointed guest rooms; a variety of common areas for relaxing, and even conducting business; a deck with a hot tub; a game room; and hospitality that makes you feel your every need has been anticipated. The Kaufmanns' generosity extends to helping visitors discover the wealth of historical, cultural, and natural assets that make the area an increasingly attractive and interesting destination. The daffodil floral parades held each April are particularly colorful and visual treats. A stay at Commencement Bay Bed & Breakfast couldn't be a better introduction.

Small dog in residence; no pets; children over twelve OK; outdoor smoking area; full breakfast; robes provided; cable TV/VCR; phones; office for business use; public transportation; historic districts, nature trails, parks, zoo, aquarium, universities, boating marinas, antique shops, restaurants, theaters and more nearby; ample parking; major credit cards; Shuttle Express from Sea-Tac airport; ferry, and Amtrak pickup. *Special winter rates Oct. 1 - May 31 except holidays and local special events.

ROOM	BED	BATH	ENTRANCE	FLOOR	DAILY RATES S D EP+
Myrtle's Room	1Q	Pvt	Main	2	$105*
Jessie's Room	1Q	Pvt	Main	2	$95*
Laurie's Room	1Q	Pvt	Main	2	$85*

TACOMA

The Villa   **(206) 572 1157**
Hosts: Becky and Greg Anglemyer
705 N 5th Street, Tacoma, WA 98403
In the Stadium Historic District, close to downtown.

The grandeur and majesty of the Villa's arched windows, columned entryway, and imposing appearance might lead you to expect stiff formality, but once inside, the light and casual elegance put you immediately at ease. Greg and Becky are so friendly and welcoming, you're soon like family. The Villa is in the National Historic Register and an official city of Tacoma "Grand House". The mansion's four magnificent guest rooms are grand in scale but furnished to retain warmth and intimacy. The *Bay View Suite* boasts sweeping views of Commencement Bay and the Olympic Mountains, and has a four-poster king bed, fireplace, private bath, and veranda. The *Garden Suite* has a wrought-iron queen bed, airy sitting room, garden-view veranda, and private bath with original shower fixtures. The wonderful grounds feature many lovely Pacific Northwestern flowering plants. This special B&B experience is simply not to be missed. Greg and Becky suggest you visit Tacoma's recently revitalized antique row and downtown, or dine along the Ruston Way waterfront before sampling the theater or Tacoma Symphony.

Dog and cat in residence; no pets; no smoking in house or on grounds; children over 12 welcome; full breakfast; TV; CD player in each room; fireplace in Bay View Suite; credit cards (MC,V).

ROOM	BED	BATH	ENTRANCE	FLOOR	S	D	EP+
Bay View Suite	1K	Pvt	Main	2		$125	
Rice Bed Room	1Q	Pvt	Main	2		$85	
Garden Suite	1T & 1Q	Pvt	Main	2		$100	$10
The Maid's Quarters	1Q	Pvt	Main	3		$75	

VASHON ISLAND

Angels of the Sea Bed & Breakfast　　　(206) 463-6980
Host: Marnie Jones　　　(800) 798-9249
26431 99th Avenue SW, Vashon, WA 98070
Near Dockton Harbor on Vashon Island.

Would you like to start your day deliciously breakfasting to a heavenly harp? If so, Angels of the Sea is *the* B&B for you! Accomplished harpist Marnie Jones rings in the morning with a melodious private concert in the sanctuary of this country church turned bed-and-breakfast. Afterwards, Vashon Island, southwest of Seattle, awaits exploration. Vashon is accessible by ferry from Seattle, Tacoma, and Kitsap— cares just slip away as you glide across the cool waters to the peaceful isle. The church itself, with its belfry and Gothic windows, is pure serenity set in tranquil woods and meadows. Rooms are bright and filled with angels and mementos of the sea and shore, and share a bath and the living room with TV/VCR (video tapes galore), fridge, coffee maker, and laundry. Marnie suggests hiking island trails to discover lovely beaches and forests. On Saturdays, Vashon's yard sales and country market offer a myriad of beguiling treasures. And Vashon also has kayaking and boating, perhaps even in Marnie's classic 18-ft. sailboat. Angels of the Sea—a serenely different retreat.

Dog in residence; no smoking; children welcome; full breakfast; TV/VCR with tapes; pickup at Dockton Harbor; sailboat; off-season rates; special rates for both rooms; credit cards (MC,V,DS).

ROOM	BED	BATH	ENTRANCE	FLOOR	S	D	EP+
Whale Room	1Q	Shd	Sep	1		$85	$10
Dolphin Room	2T	Shd	Sep	1		$75	$10

DAILY RATES

Washington

DINING HIGHLIGHTS - WASHINGTON

Please read "About Dining Highlights" on page ix.

ABERDEEN
Billy's; 322 East Heron Street; (360) 533-7144; American

Bridges Restaurant; 112 North G Street; (360) 532-6563; seafood/prime rib/pasta

Golden Dragon Cafe; 212 East Wishkah; (360) 533-6966; Chinese

Mazatlan; 202 East Wishkah; (360) 532-0940; Mexican

ANACORTES
Boomer's Landing; 209 T Avenue; (360) 293-5109; seafood

Charlie's; 5407 Ferry Terminal Road; (360) 293-7377; prime rib/steaks/seafood

The Compass Rose; 5320 Ferry Terminal Drive; (360) 293-6600; varied lunch menu

Courtyard Bistro; 419 Commercial Avenue; (360) 299-2923; European fine dining

GERE-A-DELI; 502 Commercial Avenue; (360) 293-7383; deli/pasta/pastries

La Petite; 3401 Commercial Avenue; (360) 293-4644; European/fine dining

Slocum's Restaurant; 2201 Skyline Way; (360) 293-0644; innovative seafood

ASHFORD
Alexander's Country Inn; 37515 State Route 706 East; (206) 569-2300; Continental

Rainier Overland; 31811 SR 706 East;

BELLEVUE
Angelos; 1830 130th NE; (206) 883-2777; Italian

Eques; NE Eighth and Bellevue Way, Hyatt Regency Hotel; (206) 451-3012; west coast/fine dining

The New Jake O'Shaughnessey's; 401 Bellevue Square, NE Sixth and Bellevue Way; (206) 455-5559; peachwood broiled poultry/meats/seafood

Nicks; 2285 140th NE; (206) 747-1333; Greek & Italian

Yankee Dinner; 13856 Bellevue-Redmond Road; (206) 643-1558; traditional American

BELLINGHAM
The Black Cat; 1200 Harris, The Marketplace; (206) 733-6136; French

il Fiasco; 1309 Commercial Street; (206) 676-9136; Italian

Pacific Cafe; 100 North Commercial; (206) 647-0800; Asian/northwest

BOW
The Oyster Bar; 240 Chuckanut Drive; (360) 766-6185; northwest seafood

Oyster Creek Inn; 190 Chuckanut Drive; (360) 766-6179; oysters/seafood

The Rhododendron; 553 Chuckanut Drive; (360) 766-6667; country fare with a flair

DINING HIGHLIGHTS - WASHINGTON

FRIDAY HARBOR

The Bistro; 35 First Street; (360) 378-3076; Italian/pizza/salads

Duck Soup Inn; 3090 Roche Harbor Road; (360) 378-4878; fresh local seafood

Roberto's; First and A Streets; (206) 378-6333; Italian

Springtree Eating Establishment and Farm; 310 Spring Street; (360) 378-4848; varied

GIG HARBOR

Marcos Ristorante; 7707 Pioneer Way; (206) 585-2899

North by Northwest; 9916 Peacock Hill Road; (206) 851-3134; pasta & seafood

Somewhere in Time; 7716 Pioneer Way; (206) 851-8199; tea room

Tides Tavern; 2925 Harbor View Drive; (206) 858-3982; pub

GLACIER

Innisfree Restaurant; 9393 Mt Baker Highway; (360) 599-2373; organic vegetables/chicken/seafood

Milano's Market & Deli; 9990 Mount Baker Highway; (360) 599-2863; Italian

HOQUIAM

Levee Street Restaurant; 709 Levee Street; (360) 532-1959; imaginative seafood plus

Marios's; 716 Simpson Street; (360) 533-1401; Italian

ISSAQUAH

IL Monello Ristorante; 38 Front Street; (206) 557-8794; Sicilian

La Costa; 240 NW Gilman Boulevard; (206) 392-8980; Mexican

Lombardi's Cucina; 719 NW Gilman Boulevard; (206) 391-9097; garlic specialties

Nicolinos Ristorante Italiano; 317 NW Gilman Boulevard #30-A; (206) 391-8077; family oriented

O'Char Thai Cuisine; 1025 NW Gilman Boulevard #E-5; (206) 392-2100; Thai

The Roost; 120 NW Gilman Boulevard; (206) 392-5550; American upscale

Street Light Cafe; 205 NW Gilman Boulevard; (206) 392-0508; lunches

LA CONNER

Calico Cupboard; 720 South First Street; (360) 466-4451; bakery items/sandwiches/soups/desserts/all from scratch

China Pearl; 505 South First Street; (360) 466-1000; oriental

Palmer's; 205 East Second at Washington Street; (360) 466-4261; Continental/pacific northwest

MERCER ISLAND

Thai on Mercer; 7691 27th Street SE; (206) 236-9990

DINING HIGHLIGHTS - WASHINGTON

MOUNT VERNON
Wildflowers; 2001 East College Way; (360) 424-9724; Skagit Valley/northwest

PORT TOWNSEND
Silverwater Cafe; 126 Quincy; (360) 385-6448; Continental

PUYALLUP
Applebee's Neighborhood Grill and Bar; South Hill Mall; (206) 840-4000

REDMOND
The British Pantry; 8125 161st Avenue NE; (206) 883-7511; English

RENTON
Armondos Cafe Italiano; 919 South 3rd St; (206) 228-0759

SEATTLE
Cafe Flora; 2901 East Madison; (206) 325-9100; vegetarian

Campagne; 86 Pine Street, Inn at the Market; (206) 728-2800; country French/Italian/northwest

Chandler's Crabhouse & Fresh Fish Market; 901 Fairview Avenue North; (206) 223-2722; extensive seafood menu/view dining

Coastal Kitchen; 429 Fifteenth Avenue East; (206) 322-1145; fresh

Fuller's; 1400 Sixth Avenue, Sheraton Seattle Hotel; (206) 447-5544; northwest/seafood/fine dining

Hiram's-At-The Locks Restaurant; 5300 34th NW; (206) 784-1733; seafood

Il Bistro; 93A Pike Street, Pike Place Market; (206) 682-3049; country French/Italian/seafood

Ivar's Acres of Clams; 1000 Alaskan Way at Pier 54 between Madison & Spring; (206) 624-6852; casual seafood

Jack's Bistro; 405 Fifteenth Avenue East; (206) 324-9625

Kamon on Lake Union; 1171 Fairview Avenue North; (206) 622-4665; Asian

Le Gourmand; 425 NW Market Street; (206) 784-3463; upscale northwest

Pailin; 2223 California Avenue SW, West Seattle; (206) 937-8807; Thai

Pasta Bella; 1530 Queen Anne Avenue North; (206) 284-9827

Phoenecia at Alki; 2716 Alki Avenue, West Seattle; (206) 935-6550; Mediterranean

Ray's Boathouse; 6049 Seaview Avenue NW; (206) 789-6309; seafood

Rover's; 2808 East Madison Street; (206) 325-7442; French/northwest

Salty's on Alki; 1936 Harbor Avenue SW, West Seattle; (206) 937-1600; casual seafood

Santa Fe Cafe; 5910 Phinney Avenue North; (206) 783-9755; southwest

Shuckers; 411 University; (206) 621-1984; seafood/oysters

Siam on Broadway; 616 Broadway East; (206) 324-0892; Thai

Wild Ginger; 1400 Western Avenue; (206) 623-4450; Asian/satay bar

Zula; 916 East John; (206) 322-0852; East African

DINING HIGHLIGHTS - WASHINGTON

SNOQUALMIE
Honey Farm Inn Restaurant; 8910 384th Avenue SE; (206) 888-9399; northwest

SPOKANE
C.I. Shenanigan's; 322 North Spokane Falls Court; (509) 455-5072; seafood/steak

Clinkerdagger; West 621 Mallon (Flour Mill); (509) 328-5965; seafood/steak/chicken

Milford's Fish House and Oyster Bar; North 719 Monroe Street; (509) 326-7251

The Onion; North 7522 Division; (509) 482-6100; soups/salads/burgers/dinners

TACOMA
C.I. Shenanigan's; 3017 North Ruston Way; (206) 752-8811; seafood/steak

El Toro; 5723 North 26th and Pearl; (206) 759-7889; Mexican

Harbor Lights; 2761 North Ruston Way; (206) 752-8600; seafood/steak

The Lobster Shop; 4013 North Ruston Way; (206) 759-2165; lobster/seafood/fine waterfront dining

The Old House Cafe; 2717 North Proctor Street; (206) 759-7336; versatile menu for lunch/tea/dinner served in elegant yet homey setting

Stanley and Seaforts Steak, Chop, and Fish House; 115 East 34th Street; (206) 473-7300

Zeppo; 100 South Ninth Street; (206) 627-1009; Italian

VASHON ISLAND
Back Bay Inn; 24007 Vashon Highway SW, Burton; (206) 463-5355

Fork in the Road; near north end ferry; (206) 567-5800

Turtle Island; 9924 SW Bank Road, Vashon; (206) 463-2125

Certainly, travel is more than the seeing of sights; it is a change that goes on, deep and permanent, in the ideas of living.

--Miriam Beard

For my part, I travel not to go anywhere, but to go. I travel for travel's sake. The great affair is to move.

--Robert Louis Stevenson

BRITISH COLUMBIA

British Columbia
Prince George
16
97
20
5
TWEEDSMUIR PROVINCIAL PARK
WELLS GRAY PROV PARK
Kinbasket Lake
YOHO NATL PARK
COAST MOUNTAINS
Revelstoke
Invermere
Port Hardy
STRAIT
VANCOUVER
19
99
1
Kamloops
Vernon
23
31
95
6
OF
GARIBALDI PROVINCIAL PARK
STRATHCONA PROV PARK
97c
Kelowna
Kootenay Bay
PACIFIC
VANCOUVER
Hope
5A
Penticton
3
Nelson
4
GEORGIA
Nanaimo
ISLAND
14
Victoria
See Detail Below

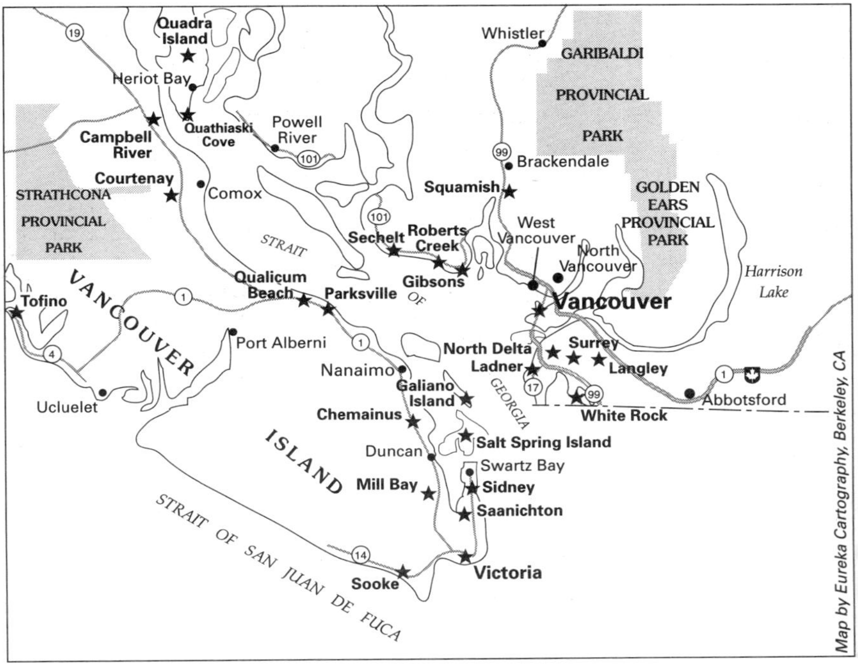
19
Quadra Island
Whistler
Heriot Bay
GARIBALDI PROVINCIAL PARK
Campbell River
Quathiaski Cove
Powell River
101
99
Brackendale
Courtenay
Comox
Squamish
STRATHCONA PROVINCIAL PARK
GOLDEN EARS PROVINCIAL PARK
STRAIT
Sechelt
Roberts Creek
West Vancouver
North Vancouver
Harrison Lake
Gibsons
Qualicum Beach
Parksville
OF
Tofino
VANCOUVER
Vancouver
1
Port Alberni
North Delta
Surrey
Ladner
Langley
Nanaimo
4
Galiano Island
17
GEORGIA
Abbotsford
Ucluelet
Chemainus
White Rock
ISLAND
Salt Spring Island
Duncan
Swartz Bay
Mill Bay
Sidney
Saanichton
STRAIT OF SAN JUAN DE FUCA
Victoria
Sooke
Map by Eureka Cartography, Berkeley, CA

ABOUT BRITISH COLUMBIA

British Columbia, the westernmost Canadian Province, stretches from the Pacific Ocean to the Rocky Mountains. The province shares a southern border with Washington, Idaho, and Montana; a western border with Alaska; a northern border with the Yukon and Northwest Territories; and an eastern border with the province of Alberta. Over twice the size of California, British Columbia is huge and magnificent. Whatever your interests or vacation desires, winter or summer, BC offers rugged natural beauty and outdoor adventures in close proximity to urban elegance and sophistication. This section provides some insights into the geography of the province with some travel suggestions for your visit.

Vancouver Island is the most western part of the province, lying about 30 miles off the mainland, west of the city of Vancouver. Victoria, the capital of British Columbia, is located on the very southern tip of the island. Vancouver Island and Victoria are accessible from many directions, but only by plane or boat. Several ferry companies serve the island with a variety of ship types and vehicle and passenger accommodations. From Seattle to Victoria there is a hydrofoil passenger ferry, and during the summer a large liner that takes passengers and cars. From Anacortes, the Washington State Ferry winds through the San Juan Islands to the town of Sidney (20 miles north of Victoria). From Port Angeles, on the northern tip of the Olympic Peninsula, the Black Ball Ferry (passengers and vehicles) goes right to downtown Victoria. From Vancouver, the BC Ferries have frequent service to the Gulf Islands, Victoria, and Nanaimo, a city of 60,000 residents, 70 miles up-island from Victoria. Schedules change with the seasons and reservations are mandatory on some carriers and not available on others. Good maps usually have basic ferry information on the map borders. Call the ferry company, your B&B host, or Tourism Victoria for help in planning your ferry connections.

Victoria is a must for first time visitors to BC. It also serves as a starting point for trips to the rest of Vancouver Island. The peaceful city is a tourist's delight, with everything easily accessible: the Empress Hotel, the intriguing Royal Provincial Museum, Parliament Buildings, and the charming inner harbour. All are easy and fun to explore on foot. An enjoyable 27-mile drive west will take you to the quaint village of Sooke, with excellent salmon fishing and many walking and hiking trails. Victoria and vicinity can also be toured if you stay in Sidney, Saanichton, Mill Bay, or Chemainus, known for its murals.

North of Victoria is the picturesque Saanich peninsula, home of the famous Butchart Gardens. From Swartz Bay at the tip of the peninsula, near Sidney, you can embark on a ferry to visit Salt Spring Island or Galiano Island, two of the fabulous Gulf Islands. These picturesque, tree-covered islands are located between Vancouver Island and the mainland in the calm waters of the Strait of Georgia. Similar to, but quieter than the San Juan Islands northwest of Seattle, they offer tranquility, breathtaking views, water sports, and hiking. The secluded lifestyle has drawn a variety of artists and crafts people, resulting in a growing reputation as a center of artists' creations and endeavors.

Traveling north from Victoria on Highway 1, the east coast of Vancouver Island stretches 300+ miles. Nanaimo, known for its chocolaty Nanaimo bars, is a growing city, offering a variety of water and other recreational activities. Twenty miles further at Parksville, you may want to turn west and cross the island through some of BC's most spectacular forest to the Pacific Rim National Park and the fishing and resort village of Tofino. The village is at the end of Highway 4, right on the open Pacific Ocean. Miles of beaches are available for exploration, beachcombing, and whale-watching.

Back on the east coast, Parksville and nearby Qualicum Beach offer wonderful protected sandy beaches and scenic rivers surging into the strait. North of Parksville, Courtenay and the Comox Valley have an unbelievable selection of things to do in any season – swimming, hiking, skiing, relaxing. From Comox, you may travel by ferry to Powell River and the well-named Sunshine Coast on the mainland, north of Vancouver.

Continuing north, the next major town is Campbell River, famous for its salmon fishing and salt water pier. Quadra Island, at the north end of the Strait of Georgia, is a ten minute ferry ride from Campbell River. On Quadra there is boating, fishing, and scenic coastal hiking trails. A magnificent panoramic view can be seen at the end of the hike up Chinese Mountain. Shortly after leaving Campbell River, Highway 19 drifts from the coast and weaves through forest and logging towns to Port Hardy and the ferry, north through the inside passage to Prince Rupert .

Relaxing and enjoying the Sunshine Coast north of Vancouver City, your B&B hosts in the Sechelt-Gibsons-Roberts Creek area can help plan a circle trip around the peninsula or advise you on the best way to get to Vancouver, or to Squamish, Brackendale, and Whistler areas near Garibaldi Provincial Park.

The cosmopolitan city of Vancouver boasts a Mediterranean climate and spectacular setting. It is easily accessible by ferry from Vancouver Island (Victoria or Nanaimo) or by good freeway from eastern BC or Seattle to the south. The Vancouver metropolitan area has complete visitor facilities: parks, golf courses, museums, indoor and outdoor theaters, domed stadium, fine stores, and myriad restaurants that offer a world of choice cuisines. Granville Island, set in the heart of the False Creek inlet south of downtown Victoria, has a superb Public Marketplace, a great place to enjoy a succulent seafood dinner or collect supplies for a picnic in Stanley Park, the northwest tip of the downtown peninsula. In Vancouver, you can sunbathe on the splendid city beaches, take a leisurely stroll along the seawall surrounding lush Stanley Park, skim the Pacific in a kayak, canoe or powerboat, or ski the groomed slopes of Grouse and Seymour Mountains.

If you would like to stay nearby but outside Vancouver, the cities of Ladner, Langley, Delta, and White Rock, are close and convenient just south of Vancouver. All offer slower-paced accommodations in a more suburban and rural area. Nearby Fort Langley is a good spot to start your visit to Vancouver and the fertile Fraser Valley. Once the capital of British Columbia, the fort is open to the public, and the quaint town is full of antique stores and good restaurants.

Driving east from Vancouver, at Hope, on the Fraser River, you have three highway choices to head inland. Each route offers unforgettable scenery. An entire holiday could be spent taking a number of circle trips, or you can select a thorough route continuing on to the Rockies and Banff, returning to the States from further east. The oldest and original route out of Hope, Highway 1, heads north, following the canyon of the mighty Fraser River. This route travels through the Cariboo and Chilcotin areas, then turns east after Ashcroft, continuing across Canada. Newer Highway 5, the Coquihala Highway, is a quicker route to Kamloops, where it connects with Highway 1. Highway 97C, a connector highway off Coquihala Highway, is a direct route to the Okanagan Lake area and city of Kelowna.

Okanagan means "place of water." A valley of fruit trees — cherries, apricots, peaches, plums, apples, pears, and grapes — provides summer fare amidst sage brush, ponderosa pine, and glistening lakes. The three major Okanagan cities, Penticton, Kelowna, and Vernon, have art galleries, museums, stores, and restaurants. There is an abundance of recreational activities at beaches, parks, golf courses, summer festivals, and winter resorts. Vineyards with wine tasting abound in the region. Lush hills and farms are everywhere, with fresh fruit and juices for sale.

The third route out of Hope, Highway 3, is known as the Crow's Nest Highway. It stays close to the US border, offering a constantly changing topography. East of Hope is the 67,000 hectare Manning Provincial Park, which connects with the North Cascades National Park in Washington. Manning Park has skiing in winter, nature programs, swimming, and boating in mountain lakes. Continuing east, there are miles of verdant hills and pleasant touring until the large section of southeast BC, known as the Kootenays, is reached. Forests, lakes, fertile valleys, and mountains beckon visitors to this area. Nelson, on the west side of Kootenay Lake and settled in the 1880s, is full of heritage homes and is now a mecca to artists and artisans.

Twelve miles east of Nelson, a ferry crosses Kootenay Lake to Kootenay Bay, with views of the beautiful Kokanee Glacier across the lake. Hot springs, water sports, and hiking are some of the activities available in this area. Continuing east along Highway 3 to Highway 95, one drives through beautiful valleys surrounded by snowcapped mountains. Turning north on Highway 95, you reach the head of the Columbia River and the lovely town of Invermere on Lake Windemere. Bird-watching around the head of the lake is excellent. Nearby, the famous Radium Hotsprings and Fairmont Hotsprings offer relaxation and therapy.

North of Invermere, at Golden on Highway 95, a decision must be made either to turn east toward the Rockies, Banff, and Calgary, or loop back west toward Revelstoke, the Okanagan, and the coast.

British Columbia is a big province with cosmopolitan cities, historic towns, islands, ocean vistas, beaches, farmland, mountains, glaciers, rivers, and lakes. The tours described here are just a few of the many exciting and wonderful travel opportunities that can be found. The maps on the preceding page will get you started. When planning your trip, include stops at the many fine B&B homes that are listed on the following pages. Their rates are very reasonable and the hosts are happy to assist in getting to know the special people and places of British Columbia.

For further general visitor information:

Ministry of Tourism
Parliament Building
Victoria, BC, Canada V8V 1X4
(800) 663-6000

For recreation information:

Extension and Information Branch
Ministry of Parks
4000 Seymour Place, 3rd Floor
Victoria, BC, Canada V8V 1X5
(800) 663-6000

BC Ferries
1112 Fort Street
Victoria, BC, Canada V8V 4V2
Reservations: (604)* 386-3431   Recorded schedule (604)* 656-0757

Black Ball Ferry, Port Angeles to Victoria, (604)* 386-2202

Washington State Ferries, Anacortes to Sidney, (604)* 381-1551

Victoria Clipper passenger ferry, Seattle to Victoria,
(800) 888-2535

Victoria Line passenger and vehicle ferry, Seattle to Victoria, information recording (800) 668-1167

*Area code **250** effective October, 1996. You will see this note throughout the BC section. The area code for BC outside the Lower Mainland, Sunshine Coast, and Whistler area will change from 604 to 250 in October of 1996. A phase-in period will extend into 1997.*

CAMPBELL RIVER

Pier House Bed & Breakfast (604)* 287-2943
Hosts: Peter Dwillies and Patricia Young
670 Island Highway, Downtown, Campbell River, BC V9W 2C3
In the heart of Campbell River facing the ocean and harbor.

Pier House, circa 1924, is distinguished as the oldest house in town and the home of its first provincial policeman. Furnished with antiques of the period, it is an utterly charming combination of old curiosity shop, museum, and "Grandma's house." The allure of the library is most immediate: There are floor-to-ceiling bookshelves packed with vintage hardbacks, a dictionary on a stand, a globe, an old short-wave radio, and myriad other relics that beg to be examined. It's a place to settle in for a good read or a visit. Guest rooms, too, are long on character. Mementos, art, and reading matter create the sense that the residents of yesteryear have just stepped out for a bit. Tunes from the old Victrola may accompany breakfast set with bone china and unique serving pieces now found mostly in antique shops. Pleasant surprises and touches of whimsy abound in the easy going warmth of the Pier House. Peter and Patricia suggest that when you are out and about in Campbell River, explore the commercial fishing boat harbor and pier, or take a tour of near by forests and the excellent free guided tour of the paper mill.

No pets or children; smoking outside only; full breakfast; restaurants, pubs, shops, harbor, fishing pier, and Quadra Island ferry nearby; off-street parking; credit cards (V,MC,AMEX).

ROOM	BED	BATH	ENTRANCE	FLOOR	DAILY RATES S	D	EP+
Bombay	1Q	Pvt	Main	1	$60	$75	
Alert Bay	1Q	Shd	Main	2	$60	$75	
Nova Scotia	1D	Shd	Main	2	$50	$65	
Nanaimo	2T	Pvt	Main	2	$60	$80	

Rates stated in Canadian funds   *Area code **250** effective October, 1996*

British Columbia

CHEMAINUS

Bird Song Cottage Bed & Breakfast (604)* 246-9910
Hosts: Larry and Virginia Blatchford   FAX: (604)* 246-2909
Box 1432, Chemainus, BC V0R 1K0
9909 Maple Road in Chemainus.

The lovely seaside village of Chemainus is famous for its murals and dinner theater. Virginia and Larry Blatchford are becoming equally famous for their graciousness and hospitality. They've successfully followed many dreams, from homesteading to raising Angora goats to playing in rock and Top 40 bands, and can often be heard in local rhythm and blues bands, too. Entering the attractive house, songs of canaries and splendids illustrate the inspiration for Bird Song's name. Feel free to admire the incredible hat collection and many touches of Victorian whimsy. The beautiful outside garden is brought inside with Virginia's stenciled flowers on the walls in the living and dining rooms. And her breakfasts? They're the talk of the bed and breakfast circuit. The magic continues to the three "nests", all with private baths. Main-floor *Nightingale* has a queen bed, single bed, and separate back-garden entrance. Spacious *Bluebird* has a queen and a twin, and *Hummingbird* has a twin and a double, plus a great ocean view. Larry and Virginia suggest Bird Song as a base for exploring Chemainus and nearby Island attractions.

Cat and birds in residence; no animals; smoking outside only; children welcome; full breakfast; TV; fireplace; guest living room; grand piano; patio; credit cards (MC,V).

ROOM	BED	BATH	ENTRANCE	FLOOR	DAILY RATES S	D	EP+
Nightingale	1Q & 1T	Pvt	Main	1	$65	$75	$20
Bluebird	1Q & 1T	Pvt	Main	2	$65	$75	$20
Hummingbird	1D & 1T	Pvt	Main	2	$65	$75	$20

Rates stated in Canadian funds   *Area code **250** effective October, 1996*

COURTENAY

The Beach House   (604)* 338-8990
Hosts: Anke Burkhardt   FAX (604)* 338-5651
RR#6, Site 688, C28, Courtenay, BC V9N 8H9
3614 South Island Highway, two kilometers past Royston light.

    Beach House is a hub of activity on the water. Surrounded by a lovely split-rail fence, this large 1986 cedar house has an old-fashioned, homelike feeling. You're welcome to play pool, but you'd better be good to beat the hostess! The darts and piano in the rustic living room hint at many congenial evenings around the woodstove. You can sit peacefully on the deck overlooking the water, and even beach comb right from the front door. Anke runs Beach House with her young son, and they welcome children over ten. Three modestly-priced rooms have shared baths; one has a private bath and separate entrance. Full, healthy breakfasts await you in the morning. Anke speaks both English and German, gathering folks from around the world to her B & B. Knowing the area well, Anke enjoys helping with plans to hike nearby Strathcona Park. In the winter, Beach House attracts skiers from Mt. Washington and Forbidden Plateau. Anke suggests the Strathcona hike, year-round golfing and fishing, and dinner at the Old House Restaurant.

    Cats and chickens; no pets; smoking outside only; children over ten welcome; full breakfast; TV in each room; pool table; barbecue; outdoor patio over water; credit cards (MC,V); German spoken.

ROOM	BED	BATH	ENTRANCE	FLOOR	DAILY RATES S	D	EP
Green Room	1D	Shd	Main	2	$35	$45	
Blue Room	1D	Shd	Main	2	$35	$45	$10
TW Room	3T	Shd	Main	2	$35	$45	$10
Private Room	1Q	Pvt	Sep	1	$55	$65	

Rates stated in Canadian funds   **Area code 250** *effective October, 1996*

COURTENAY

Greystone Manor (604)* 338-1422
Hosts: Mike and Mo Shipton
RR#6, S-684, C-2, Courtenay, BC V9N 8H9
On Comox Bay, East Vancouver Island.

You can reach the Comox Valley, a year round recreation destination, via the Sunshine Coast, highway from Victoria and Nanaimo, or Port Hardy. Built in 1918, Greystone Manor is one of the oldest homes in the Valley. The waterfront house is set on 1 1/2 acres, surrounded by huge firs, maples, and beautiful English flower gardens. Hanging baskets and planters adorn the front porch and deck. The gardens and flowers are tended by avid gardeners Mike and Mo who emigrated from Bath, England in 1990. In the five years they have operated Greystone Manor they have created some of the most spectacular private gardens you'll find. With views across Comox Bay to the mainland mountains this is the perfect place to relax or use as a base for the many region's many activities including skiing, hiking and beach combing. The Comox Valley has a good selection of restaurants, galleries, shops, and golf courses. Watch eagles, seals and sea birds from the house or take a stroll through the gardens to the beach. For longer walks, Mike and Mo have a good knowledge of local walks and hikes and can suggest many excursions.

No pets or smoking; adult oriented; full breakfast; guest sitting room with fireplace; off-street parking; credit cards (MC,V).

ROOM	BED	BATH	ENTRANCE	FLOOR	DAILY RATES		
					S	D	EP
A	1Q	Pvt	Main	2	$55	$70	
B	1D	Pvt	Main	2	$55	$70	
C	2T	Pvt	Main	2	$55	$70	$20

Rates stated in Canadian funds   *Area code 250 effective October, 1996*

GALIANO ISLAND

The Bellhouse Inn   **(800) 970-RING (7464)**
Hosts: Andrea Porter and David Birchall   FAX: **(604)* 539-5316**
29 Farmhouse Road, Galiano Island, BC V0N 1P0
One kilometer from the ferry dock at Sturdies Bay.

Approaching Sturdies Bay by ferry from Victoria or Vancouver, the eye is drawn to the protected beach and beyond, to an alluring turn-of-the century farmhouse inn, owned and run by the Bellhouse family from 1910 until 1965. Thirty years later, Andrea and David renovated and reopened the Bellhouse Inn, furnishing it mainly with English antiques. Spacious verandahs and grounds invite a peaceful interlude, perhaps counting the eagles; strolling the orchard; or swimming at the Bellhouse beach. You can be met at the ferry, or a chartered float plane can deliver you to the Bellhouse beach. Your hosts will help you plan activities that can include fishing, golfing, hiking, cycling, and kayaking. *Kingfisher* has an ensuite jacuzzi, four-poster queen bed, and a private balcony with spectacular views. *Eagle* has an ensuite bath, brass double bed, and private ocean-view balcony. *Heron*, the largest room, features an 1860's brass bed, plus a single bed and sitting area. And there's also a self-contained 2-bedroom cottage rented on a weekly basis. Full English breakfasts are served. Galiano Island is known for good beaches, pleasant hiking, interesting restaurants, artists' studios, and tranquility (only 900 residents). Andrea and David suggest fishing off Bellhouse Point, counting eagles and killer whales, reading, or just relaxing.

Dog and cat in residence; no pets; smoking outside only; Children welcome in cottage; full breakfast; three fireplaces; large decks. Weekly rate for *The Cottage* - $650.

ROOM	BED	BATH	ENTRANCE	FLOOR	DAILY RATES S	D	EP
Kingfisher	1Q	Pvt	Main	2	$140	$150	
Heron	1D & 1T	Pvt	Main	2	$115	$125	
Eagle	1D	Pvt	Main	2	$115	$125	
The Cottage	2D	Pvt		1		$125	

Rates stated in Canadian funds   **Area code **250** effective October, 1996*

GALIANO ISLAND

Moonshadows Guest House   **(604)* 539-5544**
Hosts: Pat Goodwin and Dave Muir   FAX: **(604)* 539-5544**
RR#1, S-16, C-16, Galiano Island, BC V0N 1P0
771 Georgeson Bay Road, three km from the Sturdies Bay Ferry.

Architect-designed as a B & B, this wood, glass, and stone house blends comfort with spaciousness. The cozy fireplace may conjure a wistfulness for the rare Galiano Island rain; it invites you to curl up with a book from the large library, or look out the picture windows into the fields where horses graze. Wandering about the house, one is impressed by the art work on the walls featuring the work of local artists. Upstairs, the two rooms are separated by a second reading/writing area. Downstairs is the *Special Occasion Suite* with private entrance, covered patio, shower, and large jacuzzi. Pat or Dave will make reservations for cycle rentals, kayaks, fishing golf, or a special dinner. Hot-tubbing above the pond and gardens on a moonlit night reveals the origin of the name "Moonshadows." Your hosts suggest watching the ferries at Bluff Park, sunset at Montague Harbour, or the peaceful pursuits of birding or beach combing. Whatever your pleasure, both do their best to ensure you find it.

Dogs in residence; no pets; smoking outside only; children 12 years or older welcome; TV/VCR; robes provided; outdoor hot tub; large fireplaces (living room & dining room); wood stove in entry. Off season rates.

ROOM	BED	BATH	ENTRANCE	FLOOR	S	D	EP
Quilt	1D & 1Q	Pvt	Main	2	$90	$100	$20
Wicker	1Q	Pvt	Main	2	$90	$100	$20
Special Occasion Suite	1Q	Pvt	Sep	1		$125	

Rates stated in Canadian funds   **Area code 250 effective October, 1996*

GALIANO ISLAND

Orca View   (604)* 539-3051
Hosts: Brian and Trish Cowperthwaite
RR 2, 20675 Porlier Pass Road, Galiano Island, BC V0N 1P0
24 kilometers north of the ferry on the main island road.

    The day begins. Breakfast is brought to one of your two private decks overlooking the Tincomali Channel at the north end of sparsely populated Galiano Island. Trish and Brian have rendered this secluded third-floor retreat very near perfection with: windows all around, queen bed with view of the water, microwave, fridge, pool table, hot tub, and barbecue for your use on the ground floor deck. *Little Orca* (available only when booked with *Orca*) has a twin bed separate from the master bedroom, and a crib is available. (This B & B is suitable only for non-mobile infants and children six and over.) The continental breakfast includes fruit, homemade breads and muffins, and when available, smoked salmon. Though it's tempting to simply read, paint, or watch the orcas swimming in the bay, other Galiano activities beckon: kayaking, biking/hiking, golfing; Trish will even make you a picnic to take to Coon Bay beach, if you like. She and Brian also suggest walking the Bodega Trail, visiting Dionisio Pt. Provincial Park, catamaran trips, and diving excursions. Hurry home for the spectacular sunsets!

    Dog and cats in residence; no pets; smoking outside only; children age six or over and non-mobile infants welcome; crib available; full breakfast; hot tub; pool table; kitchenette with microwave; barbecue; picnic table. Call hosts for ferry schedule. Little Orca is only rented with Orca. *Open May through October.*

ROOM	BED	BATH	ENTRANCE	FLOOR	DAILY RATES S	D	EP
Orca	1Q	Pvt	Sep	3		$95	
Little Orca		1T	Pvt	Sep	3		$30

Rates stated in Canadian funds   *Area code **250** effective October, 1996*

British Columbia

GIBSONS

Bonniebrook Lodge   **(604) 886-2887**
Hosts: Karen and Philippe Lacoste
RR#4, S-10, C-34, Gibsons, BC V0N 1V0
1532 Ocean Beach Esplanade, Gower Point.

This 1920s oceanside lodge has been brought up to present-day standards and redecorated throughout by Karen and Philippe Lacoste. The upper floor is comprised of four guest rooms; one has a private bath and the others share two baths. Bedrooms are beautifully appointed with bordered wall coverings, floral valances and bedspreads, velvety carpeting, soothing artwork, fresh flowers, and plants. A large front sun deck is a relaxing vantage point from which to watch crashing waves and passing ships. For breakfast or dinner, simply descend the stairs into Chez Philippe, a dining room with considerable charm, excellent service, and divine French/West Coast cuisine. Take an after-dinner moonlit walk along the shore or retire to your comfortable room on the floor above. Bonniebrook Lodge is a romantic seaside getaway where you'll find everything you need right where you are. Karen and Philippe suggest you come see the salmon spawn in their creek during late October.

Cat in residence; no pets; no smoking in bedrooms; full breakfast in Chez Philippe; sofa bed extra in *Green Room*; extra-long bed in *Rose Room*; beach, salmon spawning creek, Chaster Park, and Molly's Lane Craft Market nearby; off-street parking; French spoken; credit cards (V,MC); outside staircase to second-floor rooms.

ROOM	BED	BATH	ENTRANCE	FLOOR	S	D	EP+
Blue Room	1Q	Shd	Main	2		$75	
Green Room	1D	Shd	Main	2		$85	$25
Yellow Room	1Q	Shd	Main	2		$85	
Rose Room	1D	Pvt	Main	2		$95	

Rates stated in Canadian funds

GIBSONS

Ocean View Cottage (604) 886-7943
Hosts: Dianne and Bert Verzyl
RR#2, S-46, C-10, Gibsons, BC V0N 1V0
On the Sunshine Coast.

When Bert and Dianne Verzyl designed their home and guest cottage on three rural acres, the view took top priority—and rightfully so. The cliff side setting looks out across the Strait of Georgia with Vancouver Island in the background. There are two neat guest rooms with private baths in the main house; they're at the opposite end from the hosts' quarters, and one has a great view. Set well away from the main house, the contemporary wood cottage is generously proportioned and completely self-contained. It has a full kitchen, a bedroom, a sofa bed, a futon, cable television, skylights, plenty of comfortable seating, a deck with table and chairs, and expansive windows to bring in the mesmerizing panorama. A few days at Ocean View Cottage should prove peaceful, restful, and utterly undemanding. Visit the reopened Molly Beach Restaurant, made famous during the 19 year run of the series "The Beachcombers".

No pets or smoking; full breakfast; shopping, dining, golfing, hiking, cross country skiing, fishing, scenic cruises, and sandy beaches nearby; off-street parking; Dutch and French spoken; airport pickup (Tyee at Sechelt); *Note: extra adult $25, extra child $10.*

ROOM	BED	BATH	ENTRANCE	FLOOR	DAILY RATES S	D	EP
A	1Q	Pvt	Main	1	$55	$65	
B	2T	Pvt	Main	1	$45	$65	
C	1D	Pvt	Sep	1		$95	$25*

Rates stated in Canadian funds

INVERMERE

Delphine Lodge Country Inn Bed & Breakfast
Hosts: Anne and David Joy (604)* 342-6851
Box 2797, Invermere, BC V0A 1K0
Hwy. 93/95, Invermere exit, right to Wilmer, on Main St., Wilmer.

Near Invermere you'll find the head waters of the Columbia River. Whether you are driving from Calgary and the Rockies, or from the coast or the south, time spent at historic Delphine Lodge is refreshing and rejuvenating. Built in the 1890's as the local hotel (and named for the builder's wife), it's just twelve kilometers from Panorama Ski Resort and five kilometers from Windermere Lake, relished for its warm swimming. Radium Hot Springs and Fairmont Hot Springs are an easy drive and golf courses abound. The Tamarack wood floors of the lodge are highlighted with custom hooked rugs; early Canadian antiques are found throughout. The rooms have handmade quilts lovingly collected from back east. Four poster beds and antique dressers complete the decor. Anne and David have a baby grand piano and a huge stone fireplace in the dining room, another large fireplace in the cozy lounge. This east Kootenay area is full of wetlands, hills, and mountains with excellent hiking and skiing. Anne and David suggest hiking in the Purcell Mountains or cross country skiing from the lodge door.

Dog in residence; no pets; smoking outside only; children by prior arrangement; full breakfast; TV/VCR in living room; two fireplaces; ski rack; credit cards (V); childrens rate $10; off season rates.

ROOM	BED	BATH	ENTRANCE	FLOOR	S	D	EP
A	1D	Shd	Main	2	$45	$60	$20
B	1D	Shd	Main	2	$45	$60	$20
C	2T	Shd	Main	2	$45	$60	$20
D	1D	Shd	Main	2	$45	$60	$20
E	1T & 1D	Shd	Main	2	$45	$60	$20
F	1Q	Pvt	Main	2	$45	$75	$20

Rates stated in Canadian funds   *Area code **250** effective October, 1996*

KELOWNA

Chateau Christian Laurenn Bed & Breakfast   (604)* 768-5273
Hosts: Christian and Wayne Kelly
3542 Ranch Road, Westbank, Kelowna, BC V4T 1A1
Three kilometers south of Westbank off Highway 97.

At Chateau Christian Laurenn, you can enjoy your privacy yet know Wayne and Christian are nearby, willing to help plan a memorable holiday. Christian has anticipated every wish; each richly decorated room has an ensuite bathroom, and for families or two couples traveling together, a living/dining area with fireplace and a panoramic view of the city, Lake Okanagan, and mountains. Private entrance and garden patio complete the accommodations. Wayne and Christian's welcoming spirit extends to the breakfast table, where Christian serves a beautiful meal in the dining room or on the patio with Lake Okanagan as a backdrop. Each season offers a range of activities: skiing, hiking, golfing, and all water sports are nearby. Kelowna is an easy day's drive from Vancouver, and a good stopping place on the way East. The Kellys, who offer off-season rates and a special-occasion weekend package, are understandably proud of their triple-diamond CAA-AAA rating, and are open year-round. They suggest touring Mission Hill Winery (their favorite) and dinner at Gasthaus on the lake.

No pets; smoking outside only; children accepted with entire suite; full breakfast; TV in each room; guest refrigerator; patio; credit cards (V); off season rates.

ROOM	BED	BATH	ENTRANCE	FLOOR	DAILY RATES S	D	EP
A	1D & 1T	Pvt	Sep	1	$60	$75	$15
B	1D	Pvt	Sep	1	$60	$75	$15

Rates stated in Canadian funds   **Area code **250** effective October, 1996*

KELOWNA

The Grapevine Bed & Breakfast (604)* 860-5580
Hosts: Andy Szita and Marilyn Rae FAX (604)* 860-5586
2621 Longhill Road, Kelowna, BC V1V 2G5
North on Highway 97, left at Dilworth Mountain Drive, right at Longhill.

Centrally located in the beautiful Okanagan Valley, The Grapevine Bed & Breakfast is open year-round. In the Valley there is something for everyone: 14 excellent golf courses, 3 superb ski hills, all water sports, hiking or cycling the Kettle Valley Railway bed, and many award winning wineries. The Grapevine itself offers four charming bedrooms as well as a cozy living room with fireplace and plenty of books. A welcoming country atmosphere encourages relaxing on the covered patio or in the garden where many wild birds come to feed. Andy and Marilyn enjoy people and love sharing their knowledge of the many local attractions. The tasty, creative breakfast features home baked goods accompanied with Okanagan jams, homemade sausages, fresh herbs. local fruit, and strawberries from their garden. At 9 p.m. evening refreshments are served—a good opportunity to share the day's experiences with Marilyn and Andy. They especially suggest their golf and ski packages, and local wine tours.

No pets; smoking outside only; children over 10 welcome; full breakfast; AC; laundry facilities; king beds convert to extra long twins; picnic lunches; credit cards (MC,V). Special golf and ski packages.

ROOM	BED	BATH	ENTRANCE	FLOOR	S	D	EP
Chardonnay	1K or 2T	Shd	Main	2	$55	$65	
Pinot	1T & 1Q	Shd	Main	2	$55	$65	$15
Cabernet	1Q	Pvt	Main	2	$60	$70	
Chablis	1K or 2T	Pvt	Main	2	$65	$75	$15

Rates stated in Canadian funds   *Area code **250** effective October, 1996*

KOOTENAY BAY

Tara Shanti Retreat Bed & Breakfast (800) 811-3888
Hosts: John and Marie Wells FAX: (604)* 227-9617
PO Box 77, Kootenay Bay, BC V0B 1X0
134 Riondel Road, 80 kilometers north of Creston on Highway 3A.

The view of the Kokanee Glacier across Kootenay Lake from the large decks of Tara Shanti Retreat Bed & Breakfast is truly breathtaking. Located northeast of Nelson at the foot of the Purcell Mountains, the large wood and brick home was built for European vacationers on 5 acres of woods and native gardens. It's since been expanded and adapted to fit the needs of travelers who are looking for a respite from the everyday rush and has rooms to accommodate small or large parties. Guests can enjoy the spectacular setting while sitting under an umbrella on the deck or relax in the cozy fireside den, living room, or in the upstairs reading lounge. A wood fired, dry sauna and hot tub are also available. Three comfortable bedrooms are in a new wing and have lovely views, pine furniture, and separate heat thermostats. A full breakfast of free-range egg dishes, fresh fruit, and home baked bread is served. With advance notice, they will also provide other meals. John and Marie suggest taking Canada's longest FREE ferry ride to visit Kaslo and the Ainsworth Hot Springs.

Dog in residence; smoking outside only; children welcome; full breakfast; hot tub; wood fired sauna; library; credit cards (MC,V); children 6-10 years $10, under 6 free; open all year; off season rates.

ROOM	BED	BATH	ENTRANCE	FLOOR	DAILY RATES S	D	EP+
21	2T & 1D	Shd	Sep	2	$55	$75	$20
22	1D	Shd	Sep	2	$50	$70	$20
23	1D	Shd	Sep	2	$45	$65	$20
24	1K or 2T	Pvt	Sep	2	$80	$100	$20
25	1K or 2T	Pvt	Sep	2	$70	$90	$20
26	1K or 2T	Pvt	Sep	2	$70	$90	$20

Rates stated in Canadian funds   *Area code **250** effective October, 1996*

LADNER

River Run Cottages   **(604) 946-7778**
Hosts: Bill and Janice Harkley   FAX: **(604) 940-1970**
4451 River Road West, Ladner, BC V4K 1R9
Off Highway 99.

Ladner is on the Fraser River Delta, twenty minutes south of downtown Vancouver and ten minutes from the Victoria and Gulf Island ferries. A stay at River Run Cottages makes every day a very special occasion. The cottages are truly unique: There's *Waterlily*, a fantasy floating cottage beautifully finished with teak, maple, mahogany, and cedar. With a woodstove and private deck, it gently rises and falls with the tides. Then there's *Net Loft*, formerly an artist's studio and fisherman's workshop. Now it has a spiral staircase to the delightful loft bedroom, a fireplace and pullout queen bed downstairs. Its French doors open onto the deck and river and outdoor Japanese soaking tub. The *Farmer's Cottage,* built out from the banks of the river is perfect for up to four people. It has a complete kitchen and jacuzzi tub. Lie in bed and enjoy the river view. Breakfast is delivered to your cottage. The originality and exquisite detail Bill and Janice have put into these cottages will make you want to return until you have stayed in all three. They suggest biking or boating to explore the Riefel Waterfowl Refuge and beautiful Delta farmland.

Pets considered, smoking outside only; children welcome; full breakfast delivered to cottages; TV/VCR; bicycles; kayak; wood burning fireplaces; barbecue; gift certificates; credit cards (MC,V); 2 night rate $125/night; 3 night rate $115/night.

ROOM	BED	BATH	ENTRANCE	FLOOR	DAILY RATES S / D / EP+
Waterlily	1Q	Pvt	Sep	1	$150
Farmer's Cottage	1Q	Pvt	Sep	1	$150
Net Loft	1Q	Pvt	Sep	2	$150

Rates stated in Canadian funds

LANGLEY

Cedaridge Country Estate Bed & Breakfast **(604) 882-8570**
Host: Lucille Johnstone   FAX: **(604) 888-7872**
9260 222 Street, Langley, BC V1M 3T7
Off Highway 1, east of Vancouver.

Located near Fort Langley, Cedaridge is an hour from Vancouver or the Victoria ferry and a convenient stop if you're driving from Seattle or the Interior. Lucille Johnstone, a natural hostess, enjoys sharing her spectacular home and 50 acre grounds with her bed and breakfast guests. Many extras come with this Cedaridge; beautiful fields and meadows stretching to the banks of the Salmon River, a large indoor swimming pool, a day or night tennis court, sauna, game room and library are here for your pleasure. If you need more, the Equestrian Centre often has activities and three golf courses are within five minutes of Cedaridge. In addition, wonderful shopping and restaurants await you in historic Fort Langley, British Columbia's original capital. *Serenity* has a sunken tub, covered balcony, fireplace, and king bed. *Mountainview* has a queen bed, sun deck, patio, and 70 mile view. *Meadowview* is a two-room suite with twin beds plus a pull-out bed in the sitting room. All rooms have private baths. Lucille suggests making Cedaridge your base for exploring Vancouver and the Fraser Valley.

Horses on premises; pets with prior arrangement; smoking outside only; children over twelve welcome; full breakfast; TV/VCR; sauna; tennis court; billiard table; shuffleboard; library; equestrian centre; laundry facilities; credit card (V).

ROOM	BED	BATH	ENTRANCE	FLOOR	DAILY RATES S	D	EP
Serenity	1K	Pvt	Main	2		$75	$12
Mountainview	1Q	Pvt	Main	2		$60	$12
Meadowview	2T	Pvt	Main	2		$60	$12

Rates stated in Canadian funds

MILL BAY

Maple Tree Lane Bed & Breakfast   (604)* 743-3940
Hosts: Dot and Jim Garbet
440 Goulet Road, RR #2, Mill Bay, BC V0R 2P0
From Island Highway, east on Hutchinson towards Arbutus Ridge.

   The countryside, waterfront, and South Cowichan Valley area are ideal for a splendid holiday. The large wooden home known as Maple Tree bed and breakfast is nestled among beautiful gardens and trees overlooking Saanich Inlet. Just a half-hour north of Victoria, Maple Tree is ideally situated for visiting Victoria, Duncan, Chemainus, or beginning your journey up-Island. Boating and beach combing are at your door; kayaking, canoeing (Jim and Dot can loan you the canoe), and perhaps fishing, with Jim as captain, are further options. Or you can just sit back and enjoy the gazebo, seasonal swimming pool, lovely fruit trees and patios, and the large, sweeping deck. A "from scratch" breakfast is served in the country kitchen or on the deck, where you can enjoy spectacular sunrises. *Hearts and Flowers* is richly decorated with a queen bed, family TV room with fireplace, patio, and private entrance. It's also wheelchair-accessible, with a hide-a-way bed and special rate for children. Whimsical *Buttons and Bows* has two twin beds, ensuite bathroom, and complete privacy. Jim and Dot suggest a visit to Whippletree Junction or the art galleries in Shawnigan Lake.
   Cats in residence; pets with prior approval; smoking outside; children welcome; full breakfast; fireplace; swimming pool; wheelchair accessible; canoe and paddles; playpen; crib; cot; special children rates.

ROOM	BED	BATH	ENTRANCE	FLOOR	S	D	EP
Buttons 'n Bows	2T	Pvt	Main	1	$45	$65	
Hearts 'n Flowers	1Q	Pvt	Sep	LL	$50	$70	$20

*Rates stated in Canadian funds   *Area code **250** effective October, 1996*

NELSON

Emory House   **Voice/Fax: (604)* 352-7007**
Hosts: Janeen Mather and Mark Giffin
811 Vernon Street, Nelson, BC V1L 4G6
One street north of Baker Street, the main street in Nelson.

Three hours from Spokane or eight hours from Vancouver or Calgary, the trip to Nelson is a scenic delight with good roads; beautiful tree covered mountains; lakes; and green, green valleys. The Emory House is centrally located in downtown historic Nelson. The 1926 English cottage-style home beckons you inside to sunny rooms with oak floors, fireplace, comfortable guest living room, and views of Kootenay Lake. Local art works grace the walls showing off some of Nelson's many talented artisans. The four rooms are named after local spots of interest. The *Balfour* and *New Denver* rooms are on the main floor and are ideal for a party of four or five traveling together since they share a bathroom. The *Ainsworth Room* and *Silverton Suite* are upstairs and have private ensuite bathrooms. All the rooms are tastefully decorated with antiques. An aquatic center, arena, restaurants, and shopping are all within walking distance. Mark, a professional chef, serves a delicious breakfast in the dining room overlooking the lake. Janeen and Mark suggest the Slocan Circle day trip by car or visiting Ainsworth Hotsprings, and the Artwalk which runs from June-September.

Cat in residence; no pets; smoking outside only; children over twelve welcome; full breakfast; TV/VCR; off street parking; credit cards (MC,V); ski and golf packages.

ROOM	BED	BATH	ENTRANCE	FLOOR	S	D	EP
Balfour Room	1Q	Shd	Main	1	$60	$65	
New Denver Room	1D & 1T	Shd	Main	1	$60	$65	$15
Ainsworth Room	1Q	Pvt	Main	2	$70	$75	
Silverton Room	1D & 1Q	Pvt	Main	2	$80	$85	$15

Rates stated in Canadian funds   **Area code 250 effective October, 1996*

NELSON

Inn the Garden   **(604)* 352-3226**
Hosts: Lynda Stevens and Jerry VanVeen   FAX: **(604)* 352-3284**
408 Victoria Street, Nelson, BC   V1L 4K5
Downtown, 1 block south of Baker between Stanley & Ward Streets.

Nelson is a vibrant heritage city nestled in the heart of the Selkirk Mountains of southeastern British Columbia. The area is known for its world class skiing, fishing, hiking, and golfing. Within an hour's drive, you'll find hot springs, caves, a restored paddle wheeler, old mining towns, and Kokanee Glacier Park to explore. Upon arrival at Inn the Garden you feel a sense of well-being and know you will be well treated. Lynda and Jerry have renovated the large, 1900 heritage home into an exceptionally comfortable bed and breakfast. The terraced gardens, the riot of colors in the flower pots on the porch, and plants throughout the house attest to the owners' passion for gardening. The lounge is filled with magazines and is a good place to meet fellow guests and exchange travel suggestions. The six rooms offer a variety of accommodations including a two room suite on the third floor. Guests' needs are anticipated with such extras as bathrobes, toiletries, complimentary tea & coffee and a guest fridge. Lynda and Jerry suggest the Heritage walking tours, arts and crafts shopping on historic Baker Street, and the many fine restaurants.

No pets; smoking outside only; children over fifteen welcome; full breakfast; bathrobes; guest lounge; fridge; patios; terraced gardens; Dutch spoken; bicycle and ski storage; credit cards (MC, V, AMEX); off season and corporate rates; golf and ski packages.

ROOM	BED	BATH	ENTRANCE	FLOOR	DAILY RATES S	D	EP
Fir	1D	Pvt	Main	2	$65	$70	
Spruce	1Q	Shd	Main	2	$60	$65	
Pine	2D	Shd	Main	2	$65	$70	$15
Cedar	1Q	Pvt	Main	2	$75	$85	
Aspen	1Q	Pvt	Main	2	$75	$85	
Tamarack	1D & 2Q	Pvt	Sep	3	$95	$105	$25

Rates stated in Canadian funds   **Area code **250** effective October, 1996*

NORTH DELTA

Sunshine Hills Bed & Breakfast   **(604) 596-6496**
Hosts: Putzi and Wim Honing   FAX: **(604) 596-2560**
11200 Bond Boulevard, North Delta, BC V4E 1M7
In the Vancouver area, twenty minutes north of the U.S.- Canadian border.

   Putzi and Wim Honing are seasoned travelers and experienced tour guides who are especially attuned to the individual needs of their guests. They are also knowledgeable about the area's unique attractions and the logistics of getting to them. In the quiet surroundings of a well-established neighborhood, the Honings' Sunshine Hills Bed & Breakfast has a welcoming spirit and the extra privacy of guest quarters with a separate entrance on the ground floor. There are two comfortable bedrooms, a bathroom, kitchenette, and an enclosed backyard garden. Full European-style breakfasts are served in the main floor dining room. People desiring reasonably priced lodgings in a location that is central to the border, the airport, ferries, the beach at White Rock, and the Skytrain to Vancouver will find Sunshine Hills just the ticket. Bring your clubs because you will find good golfing at the many courses in the area.

   Cat in residence; no pets; smoking outside only; full breakfast; TV, radio, and fireplace on guest floor; golf; park with tennis courts across street; off-street parking; German, Dutch, some French spoken; two-night minimum.

ROOM	BED	BATH	ENTRANCE	FLOOR	DAILY RATES S	D	EP
Mexican Room	2T	Shd	Sep	1G	$55	$60	$15
Dutch Room	1D	Shd	Sep	1G	$55	$60	$15

Rates stated in Canadian funds

PARKSVILLE

Marina View Bed & Breakfast (604)* 248-9308
Hosts: Dea and Art Kern
895 Glenhale Crescent, Parksville, BC V9P 1Z7
Between Parksville and Qualicum Beach.

In a spectacular waterfront setting overlooking the Strait of Georgia, the islands, and the mountains beyond is Marina View Bed & Breakfast. It's a home full of modern luxuries where the main floor is almost entirely turned over to guests. From one guest room, from the large deck, and from the expansive solarium, you might catch the unforgettable sight of Alaskan cruise ships sailing past the marina into showy sunsets. Use the handy binoculars to spot eagles, shorebirds, seals, otters, and the occasional whale. A comfortable guest lounge offers TV, games, and bumper pool. Bedrooms feature bay windows with cushioned window seats. There is handy direct access from the house to the shoreline where serious beach combing can ensue and host Dea Kern has worked out many intriguing day trips for people keen to explore. She can even charter you a fishing expedition and send you off with a delicious breakfast to enjoy on the boat. At Marina View, the oceanfront setting and the personalized service stand out.

No pets or small children; smoking outside only; full breakfast; rollaway bed available; off-street parking; credit cards (V,MC); airport pickup (Qualicum); *closed mid-October to mid-March.*

ROOM	BED	BATH	ENTRANCE	FLOOR	DAILY RATES S	D	EP
1	1Q	Pvt	Main	1	$60	$75	$20
2	1D	Shd	Main	1	$60	$70	
3	2T	Shd	Main	1	$60	$70	

Rates stated in Canadian funds   *Area code **250** effective October, 1996*

QUADRA ISLAND

Bonnie Belle Bed & Breakfast (604)* 285-3578
Hosts: John and Trudy Parkyn
Mail address: Box 331, Campbell River, BC V9W 5B6
Located on Quadra Island, two and one-half miles from ferry dock.

When John and Trudy Parkyn designed the country home of their dreams, respect for the natural setting was their prime concern. Situated on seven acres, this B&B is set in the leafy privacy of alder and fir overlooking Gowlland Harbor, where loons and seals may be sighted. In every aspect, the ambiance is simple and pure, clean and uncluttered. The traditionally-styled home combines country freshness with handcrafted construction. The living and dining area has an open-beamed ceiling and high windows all around. White walls, a brick hearth, and an array of fine woodwork are enhanced by a few well-chosen antiques and heirlooms. Second-floor guest quarters with tree and water views consist of two wonderful bedrooms, a large, old-fashioned bathroom, a reading nook, and an enclosed porch. If you choose, you may charter the Heritage West Coast Vessel Bonnie Belle, skippered by John, a Master Mariner and lifelong resident. If boating isn't for you, John & Trudy suggest visiting museum potters or art studios and can suggest a variety of hiking trails. After a tranquil night's sleep, arise to an ample breakfast prepared by Trudy on the wood-fired cook stove; it can be plain or fancy, depending on your appetite. I suggest you let Trudy use her imagination—you won't be sorry.

Dog in residence; smoking on porch; full breakfast.

ROOM	BED	BATH	ENTRANCE	FLOOR	DAILY RATES S	D	EP
A	2T	Shd	Main	2	$35	$55	
B	1D	Shd	Main	2	$35	$55	

Rates stated in Canadian funds   **Area code 250** *effective October, 1996*

QUADRA ISLAND

Joha's Eagleview (604)* 285-2247
Hosts: Joyce and Harold Johnson
Box 668, Quathiaski Cove, Quadra Island, BC V0P 1N0
Less than one mile from ferry dock.

Beautiful coastal holidays on Quadra Island inspired Joyce and Harold Johnson's early retirement, and B&B hosting became a way of sharing the joy of island living. Their unbridled enthusiasm is justified, as any visitor quickly learns. The contemporary wood home is oriented toward a breathtaking view of Quathiaski Cove, tiny Grouse Island, and the Inside Passage. Watch occasional cruise ships and regular ferries, or spot eagles and herons. Accommodations at Joha's Eagleview include a self-contained, private garden suite and two B&B rooms on the upper level. Bedrooms are full of country charm with attractive quilts providing the color schemes. The living/dining area features custom-designed stained-glass windows and a fireplace of smooth local stones with hand-hewn yellow cedar trim. It's a splendid setting for enjoying a tasty breakfast in full view of nature's glory. With the Johnsons' help, discover the many joys of Quadra Island. One of those is the Kwagiulth Native Museum with its potlatch collection. Also canoes and kayaks can be rented nearby.

No pets; children welcome in suite; smoking permitted on deck; full breakfast; robes provided; woodstove and sofa bed in suite; dock for guest boats; good collection of literature on hiking, whale-watching trips (July-September), and other local activities; fishing charters arranged; off-street parking; ferry pickup for walkers; three-night minimum in suite; weekly rates available.

ROOM	BED	BATH	ENTRANCE	FLOOR	S	D	EP
A	1D	Shd	Main	2	$45	$55	
B	1Q	Shd	Main	2	$55	$65	
C	1Q & 1D	Pvt	Sep	LL		$80	$15

Rates stated in Canadian funds   *Area code **250** effective October, 1996*

QUALICUM BEACH

Blue Willow Bed & Breakfast   (604)* 752-9052
Hosts: Arlene and John England   FAX: (604)* 752-9039
524 Quatna Road, Qualicum Beach, BC V9K 1B4
South end of town, just before golf course.

The fame of the Blue Willow's breakfasts—bountiful English fare packed with homemade goodness—is well deserved, but its other assets are equally notable. A world of country luxury resides at the Tudor-style home nestled in a cottage garden bursting with foliage and blossoms. The interior has a hint of French country flavor, with dark ceiling beams against white, accented by brass, copper, and lace. There is a guest lounge with a clubby atmosphere, beautifully tailored guest rooms with various bed and bath choices, and a dining room that is a vision of old pine and Blue Willow china. As often as possible, breakfast is served at white wicker tables on the garden patio. Separate accommodation for a family or two couples is available in the lovely *Garden Suite*, consisting of a bed/sitting room, a full bath, and a bedroom. Arlene and John England are the superb hosts of this truly exceptional B&B. A special event suggested by the Englands is the Brant Wildlife Festival, a nature celebration held the first weekend in April during the migration of the small talkative sea geese to the Arctic.

Dog in residence; children welcome in Garden Suite; smoking outside only; your choice of English or continental breakfast; robes provided; TV/VCR in guest lounge/library; village, golf courses, beaches, bird sanctuaries, and waterfalls nearby; off-street parking; French and German spoken; credit cards; airport (Qualicum Beach) and train pickup; off-season rates.

ROOM	BED	BATH	ENTRANCE	FLOOR	DAILY RATES S	D	EP
Rose Room	1K or 2T	Pvt	Main	1G	$70	$85	
Blue Room	1Q	Pvt	Main	1G	$70	$85	
Garden Suite	1Q & 3T	Pvt	Sep	2		$95	$25

Rates stated in Canadian funds   *Area code 250 effective October, 1996*

QUALICUM BEACH

Grauer's Getaway, Destination Bed & Breakfast
Hosts: Steven and Brenda Grauer (604)* 752-5851
395 Burnham Road, Qualicum Beach, BC V9K 1G5
Overlooking Strait of Georgia. FAX: (604)* 752-5860

A rare discovery indeed is this English-style cottage built in the twenties on a bluff overlooking the sea with a pathway down to the beach. Grauer's Getaway has evolved into a bed and breakfast resort, boasting a tennis court with a ball machine, a swimming pool with a slide, and a spa—all with a knockout view of the ocean and distant mountains of the mainland. There are rose gardens and patios where guests may linger or picnic. Rooms are particularly spacious, including the breakfast room where couples can savor the view at their own table for two. B&B rooms offer the extra privacy of ensuite baths and a separate entrance. All three romantic creations are light and airy, with pretty wall coverings and linens, luxurious carpeting, and tastefully chosen antiques and artwork. Steven and Brenda go to great lengths to make theirs the perfect getaway—and it is. Grauer's offers an early spring getaway special featuring steelhead fishing in one of three local rivers one day, and a round of golf the next day, offered from March 1st to mid April.

Dog and cat in residence; no pets; smoking outside only; tennis court with ball machine; pool; spa; central to four golf courses; weekly, off-season, and family rates; two-night minimum for long holiday weekends. Also available by the week in summer is a self-contained, one-bedroom cottage on property with loft, kitchen, and cots and cribs (as needed).

ROOM	BED	BATH	ENTRANCE	FLOOR	DAILY RATES S	D	EP
Hardie Room	2T	Pvt	Sep	1	$90	$95	$15
Windsor Room	1Q	Pvt	Sep	1	$90	$95	$15
Courtyard Room	1Q & 1T	Pvt	Sep	1	$90	$95	$15

Rates stated in Canadian funds *Area code **250** effective October, 1996*

QUALICUM BEACH

Quatna Manor   **(604)* 752-6685**
Hosts: Betty and Bill Ross
512 Quatna Road, Qualicum Beach, BC V9K 1B4
South end of town, just before golf course.

Set on one gorgeous acre, the English Tudor-style home of Bill and Betty Ross is surrounded by lush grounds with a fish pond, a patio, a grape arbor, flower gardens, and benches. Quatna Manor's multiple dormers and bay windows enhance the home's considerable character, and the interior has an elegant, old-world ambiance. Crystal chandeliers collected abroad, beautiful wall coverings, borders, and linens blend well with a marvelous array of antiques—Betty rescues wonderful old pieces of furniture and revives them to their original glory. Second-floor accommodations include a guest lounge and four bedrooms, offering a variety of bed sizes, private and shared baths, and the option of a two-bedroom suite. Breakfast in the dining room amid antiques and fine silver is a civilized affair; pretty mornings find guests enjoying a meal on the patio under the arbor. For luxurious lodgings, fine hospitality, and great value, Quatna Manor is a find.

Dog in residence; no pets; no small children; smoking outside only; English or continental breakfast; TV and fireplace in guest lounge; village, four local golf courses, beaches, bird sanctuaries, and waterfalls nearby; off-street parking; credit cards (V); airport (Qualicum Beach), train, and bus pickup; off-season and family rates.

ROOM	BED	BATH	ENTRANCE	FLOOR	DAILY RATES S	D	EP
A	1K	Pvt	Main	2	$65	$80	
B	1Q	Shd	Main	2	$55	$65	
C	2T	Shd	Main	2	$55	$65	
D	1Q	Shd	Main	2	$55	$65	

Rates stated in Canadian funds   **Area code 250 effective October, 1996*

ROBERTS CREEK

Bed & Breakfast at Roberts Creek   **(604) 885-5444**
Hosts: Ian and Barb Cattanach
RR#5, S-18, C-7, Gibsons, BC V0N 1V0
Off Highway 101 at 1756 Hanbury Road in Roberts Creek.

Walls of huge logs imbue the interior of the Cattanachs' home on five wooded acres with golden warmth. Trees on the property were felled to build this rustic dwelling where the feeling of domestic security is almost tangible. On the main floor, there's an antique wood cookstove, a floor-to-ceiling natural stone hearth and wood-burning stove, and a view of grazing horses from the dining room. Upstairs, guests have their own sitting room, a bathroom off the hallway, and two bedrooms full of cozy charm. A crib can be provided, and there are books, games, and a television. Families find the arrangement particularly comfortable, but most anyone would take pleasure in the snug country ambiance of Bed & Breakfast at Roberts Creek. The Sunshine Coast has many walking and hiking trails suitable for every age and fitness level.

No pets or smoking; full breakfast; golfing, dining, horseback riding, picnicking, and good beaches nearby; off-street parking.

ROOM	BED	BATH	ENTRANCE	FLOOR	S	D	EP
Deanna's Room	1Q	Shd	Main	2	$40	$50	$10
Heather's Room	2T	Shd	Main	2	$40	$50	$10

Rates stated in Canadian funds

ROBERTS CREEK

Country Cottage Bed & Breakfast (604) 885-7448
Hosts: Philip and Loragene Gaulin
General Delivery, Roberts Creek, BC V0N 2W0
On the Sunshine Coast, off Highway 101 just north of Gibsons.

In the tiny hamlet of Roberts Creek, Loragene and Philip Gaulin's Country Cottage is a small, butterscotch-colored farmhouse with flower gardens flanking the walkway. The interior is a vision of rich woodwork, hand loomed rugs, nostalgic collectibles, and family heirlooms, recalling the simple pleasures of an earlier time. Loragene's legendary breakfasts, prepared on a wood-burning cook stove, are served with care in the old-fashioned country kitchen. Incurable romantics like to escape to their own sweet little cottage, just to the right of the farmhouse. It has an antique Canadiana iron bed, a full kitchen, a wood stove, colorful rugs, and decor in blues and reds. *Cedar Lodge*, is set on its own forested acre overlooking the sheep pasture. It sleeps up to six, has a river rock fireplace, full kitchen, and resembles an Adirondack trout fishing lodge. The decor includes lots of fly fishing memorabilia, wooden skis, antique Arts and Crafts furniture, Navajo rugs, and rich Indian colors. The Gaulins suggest outdoor activities for any time of year: fly fishing for trout, cutthroat, and steelhead in streams and lakes, back country skiing October to May, mountain biking forest service roads, ocean kayaking, and day boat cruises.

Dog and cat in main house; no pets or smoking; adults only; full breakfast; afternoon tea and scones; short walk to beach and restaurant; French spoken.

ROOM	BED	BATH	ENTRANCE	FLOOR	DAILY RATES S	D	EP
The Cottage	1D	Pvt	Sep	1	$85	$95	
Cedar Lodge	3Q	Pvt	Sep	1 & 2	$99	$115	$50

Rates stated in Canadian funds

ROBERTS CREEK

The Willows Inn   **(604) 885-2452**
Hosts: John and Donna Gibson
Box 1036, Sechelt, BC V0N 3A0
On Beach Avenue, off Highway 101 at Roberts Creek.

Imagine getting away to a meticulously handcrafted little cottage in the woods with its own yard enclosed by a rose-clad split-rail fence. The 500-square-foot dollhouse has beautiful hardwood floors and cabinetry, skylights, ceiling fans, a full tiled bath with a host of little luxuries, a table for two by a picture window, a glass-front woodstove, and a small kitchen area where coffee, tea, and goodies are kept. Peachy-pink walls cast a warm glow on an interior accented by evergreen, white, and brass. After a restful night in a bed of exceptional comfort, a home-cooked breakfast is delivered to your doorstep at the time of your choosing from the Gibson's luxurious log home at the front of the property. They have created this heartwarming haven in the forest where their guests are pampered in countless ways. The Willows Inn is a place to make some romantic dreams come true.

No pets; no smoking; full breakfast; color TV; sink and small fridge; fine dining, salmon fishing (information available), beaches, shops, and galleries nearby; guest parking beside cottage; golf holiday packages available; airport pickup (Tyee at Sechelt).

ROOM	BED	BATH	ENTRANCE	FLOOR	DAILY RATES S	D	EP
A	1Q	Pvt	Sep	1	$75	$85	$15

Rates stated in Canadian funds

SAANICHTON

Wintercott Country House   (604)* 652-2117
Hosts: Peter and Diana Caleb   FAX: (604)* 652-8884
1950 Nicholas Road, Saanichton, BC V8M 1X8
Off Highway 17.

You approach Wintercott, just 15 minutes from Victoria, through idyllic scenes of sheep and horses, colorful vegetables, and flower farm roadside markets. The bed and breakfast is like an elegant English manor house with Laura Ashley fabrics, antiques, and collectibles from Peter and Diana's years of living in Europe and Asia. The Calebs are delightful hosts who work together to see their guests feel wanted and special. Peter is the enthusiastic chef. Breakfast is a special occasion served on fine china in a most gracious dining room. Diana, in charge of the extensive English country gardens, is willing to share her knowledge of horticulture. The rooms and indoor hot tub are built with quiet and privacy in mind and connect to the main house with a sunny atrium. All rooms have ensuite baths and are wheelchair-accessible. Three rooms have queen four-poster beds; *Pineapple Room* has twin four-posters; there's also a drawing room. Room names reflect either the flower drapes in the room or the style of the bed. Butchart Gardens is nearby. Peter and Diana suggest taking the quaint Brentwood-Mill Bay ferry for a day of sightseeing up-Island.

Cat in residence; pets permitted; smoking outside; children welcome; full breakfast; TV in each room; hot tub; atrium; drawing room with fireplace; wheelchair accessible; crib available; camper and boat parking; credit cards (V,DS); open year round; seasonal rates on request.

ROOM	BED	BATH	ENTRANCE	FLOOR	DAILY RATES S	D	EP
Lily of the Valley	1Q	Pvt	Sep	1	$60	$95	$15
Pineapple Room	2T	Pvt	Sep	1	$60	$95	$15
Sweet Pea	1Q	Pvt	Sep	1	$60	$95	$15
Shaker Room	1Q	Pvt	Sep	1	$60	$95	$15

Rates stated in Canadian funds   *Area code 250 effective October, 1996*

British Columbia

SALT SPRING ISLAND

Kitchener House   **(604)* 537-9879**
Host: Olive Layard
166 Booth Road, Salt Spring Island, BC V8K 2M8
Waterfront on Booth Canal, five kilometers from Ganges.

    Everyone on Salt Spring Island seems to know Olive Layard and Kitchener House and for good reason. Olive has lived on the Island for 45 years and is a respected artist, gardener, travel agent, and fun bed and breakfast host. People are forever visiting to seek her gardening advice and always leave with cuttings, slips, and ideas. Kitchener House is the epitome of west coast comfort—life centers around the country kitchen full of books, flowers, and watercolors in progress. The wood burning stove takes the chill off the mornings and breakfast is healthy and fresh from the garden; Olive is still serving raspberries in October! A huge deck overlooks the gardens, Booth Canal (which has warm water for swimming in summer) and out to the ocean. The two rooms on the main floor share a bath and garden views while the double room downstairs has a patio overlooking the canal. The *Cottage*, built in 1994 from wood milled on the eight acre property, is completely separate and self contained with large decks overlooking the canal. Olive suggests the island artist studio tours to view the variety of artwork originating on Salt Spring or take advantage of the many good hiking trails, kayaking, and outdoor activities found here.
    No pets; smoking outside only; children welcome; full breakfast; TV; fireplace in living room; barbecue at cottage; patios; rowboat; *Cottage* weekly rate $850.

ROOM	BED	BATH	ENTRANCE	FLOOR	DAILY RATES S	D	EP
A	1D	Pvt	Sep	LL		$80	
B	2T	Shd	Main	1		$70	
C	1T	Shd	Main	1	$50		
Cottage	1Q	Pvt	Sep	1		$130	

Rates stated in Canadian funds   *Area code **250** effective October, 1996*

SALT SPRING ISLAND

Summerhill Guest House   (604)* 537-2727
Hosts: Michael McLandress and Paul Eastman
209 Chu-An Drive, Salt Spring Island, BC V8K 1H9
Near Vesuvius Bay, seven kilometers from Ganges.

    Salt Spring is the largest of the Gulf Islands and enjoys warm, dry summers and mild green winters. It's a tranquil oasis for reading and relaxing, yet it also has a thriving arts community and offers numerous diversions for nature lovers. Salt Spring is easily accessible by ferry from Victoria, Vancouver, Seattle, and Crofton (near Nanaimo). Summerhill is a special bed and breakfast that evokes peace and serenity. Tasteful and understated, the three rooms overlook either magnificent Sansum Narrows or pastoral meadows. All have private baths, cozy duvets, and excellent reading lamps by the beds. A wonderful oceanside sitting room with a fireplace and CD player is available for guest's use. Tantalizing full breakfasts are served overlooking the water. A pub, restaurant, and general store are all within walking distance. The village of Ganges has many shops and galleries. A recent Summerhill guest summed up their visit: "Perfection. I wouldn't change a thing—except to stay longer."

    No pets; smoking outside; adult oriented; CD player; fireplace; fridge; in room snacks; arrival refreshments; early morning coffee; credit cards (MC,V).

ROOM	BED	BATH	ENTRANCE	FLOOR	DAILY RATES S	D	EP
Edgewater Room	1Q	Pvt	Sep	2	$100	$105	
Rockcliff Room	1Q	Pvt	Sep	2	$90	$95	
Hillcrest Room	1K or 2T	Pvt	Main	2	$80	$85	

Rates stated in Canadian funds   *Area code **250** effective October, 1996*

British Columbia

SECHELT

Four Winds Bed & Breakfast　　　　　**(604) 885-3144**
Hosts: David Fedor and Brenda Wilkinson　FAX: **(604) 885-3182**
5482 Hill Road, RR #1 Blacks Site, C-33, Sechelt, BC V0N 3A0
5 kilometers from Sechelt.

Just twenty feet from the water, Four Winds is exciting any time of year. Each ocean view bedroom has a cozy window seat, perfect to curl up in while listening to the waves breaking on the rocks below. You can enjoy one of the many private patios amidst arbutus trees and hummingbirds. David prides himself on fresh, creative breakfasts in a dining room framed with spectacular water views. The living room, surrounded by the sea on three sides, is where you'll find afternoon tea and scones, and chances are you'll also catch a glimpse of sea birds, seals, and herons. Brenda is a registered massage therapist; hot tub and towels await you after a swim, tour, or massage. Care shows in the rooms and guest areas: view and comfort are of prime importance. Five dollars a night from one of the rooms is donated to the World Wildlife Fund. Brenda and David suggest hiking to Skookumchuk Narrows, and fishing, hiking, and kayaking.

Dog and cat in residence; no pets; no children (3 year old and 6 year old in residence); full breakfast; hot tub; robes provided; facilities for small weddings; reservations required; credit cards (MC,V).

ROOM	BED	BATH	ENTRANCE	FLOOR	DAILY RATES S	D	EP
A	2T	Shd	Main	1	$80	$95	$20
B	1Q	Pvt	Main	1	$90	$105	$20

Rates stated in Canadian funds

SIDNEY

Orchard House Bed & Breakfast (604)* 656-9194
Host: Gerry Martin
9646 Sixth Street, Sidney, BC V8L 2W2
Central Sidney.

Lovely gardens and old trees punctuate this orchard land of yesteryear that once extended to water's edge. The Craftsman-style heritage home was built in 1914 by the son of the town's founder. Its friendly appearance hints at the welcoming spirit within and welcoming coffee to be sipped on the front porch, surrounded by the English country gardens. Inside, handsome interior features include ample woodwork, leaded and stained glass, built-in cabinetry, and a quaint fireplace of small beach stones and shells. On the main floor are the spacious *Rose Room* and the *Duck Room*, which has its own sink and toilet, so it shares only the shower of the bathroom down the hall. Charming upstairs quarters are all wood, angles, and sloped ceilings. The *Lace Room* and the *Tree Room* share a hallway bath and a cozy wood stove in the common area. Breakfasts are large, healthy, and homemade. Gerry suggests visiting during Sidney Days, the first weekend in July. The main street is filled with crafts and music. Fireworks cap off the evening.

No pets; no children under twelve; smoking outside only; full breakfast; walk to parks, tennis courts, shops, restaurants, and Anacortes ferry terminal; short drive to Swartz Bay ferries, airport, and Butchart Gardens; under half an hour from Victoria; off-street parking; credit cards (MC).

ROOM	BED	BATH	ENTRANCE	FLOOR	S	D	EP
Rose Room	1Q	Shd	Main	1	$59	$69	$15
Duck Room	1Q	Shd	Main	1	$59	$69	$15
Lace Room	1D	Shd	Main	2	$49	$59	$15
Tree Room	1D	Shd	Main	2	$49	$59	$15

Rates stated in Canadian funds   *Area code **250** effective October, 1996*

SOOKE

Hartmann House Bed & Breakfast   (604)* 642-3761
Hosts: Ray and Ann Hartmann   FAX: (604)* 642-7561
5262 Sooke Road, RR 1, Sooke, BC V0S 1N0
Highway 14 toward Sooke, two kilometers past 17-Mile Pub.

Overlooking Sooke Harbour and the Olympic Mountains, the romantic English country cottage home of Ray and Ann Hartmann is surrounded by flower, herb, and vegetable gardens. Just 30 minutes from Victoria, Hartmann House successfully combines exquisite taste and comfort, with privacy. Ray enjoys working with red cedar and there are wonderful pieces of his work in every room. Beds, armoires, benches, chairs and tables offer warmth and stability to the bed and breakfast. Guests are invited to enjoy reading and conversation in the living room/library which boasts a large Count Rumford fireplace. Brick patios and wicker furniture beckon you outdoors to rest among the gardens and fish ponds. Breakfast is served in the country kitchen which is the heart of this delightful home. Dried flowers and herbs hang from the beams and the Hartmanns are proud to have been featured in *Better Homes & Gardens*. The two bedrooms have canopied four-poster beds with feather comforters. Ray and Ann are building a large honeymoon suite to add to the bed and breakfast accommodations in the future. They spoil their guests with champagne, fruit, cheese and chocolates. For activities, they suggest their guests enjoy miles of ocean beaches near Sooke or take advantage of the best fishing on the West Coast.

No pets; smoking outside only; adult oriented; full breakfast; TV/VCR; fireplace; library; robes provided; off-street parking; parking for large vehicles; German spoken; credit cards (V).

ROOM	BED	BATH	ENTRANCE	FLOOR	DAILY RATES S	D	EP
Garden	1D	Pvt	Main	1	$100	$100	
Bay	1K or 2T	Pvt	Sep	1	$120	$120	

Rates stated in Canadian funds   **Area code 250** *effective October, 1996*

SOOKE

Peace & Plenty Bed & Breakfast　　　　　(604)* 642-4091
Hosts: Roy and Cindy Talbot
2016 Gillespie Road, Sooke, BC V0S 1N0
Highway 14 toward Sooke, left on Gillespie Road.

Peace & Plenty Bed and Breakfast is what a traditional bed and breakfast should be—a home away from home with hosts who truly enjoy meeting people. The large Tudor country home is just 35 minutes from Victoria and is surrounded by gardens and woods. You are near the unspoiled West Coast beaches of Vancouver Island and East Sooke Park for hiking, picnicking, and rock climbing. Just minutes from Peace & Plenty is the recently completed Galloping Goose Trail, 60 kilometers of walking, cycling, or horseback riding. After "doing" the trail, relax in the hot tub before setting out to the historic English 17-Mile Pub serving pub fare and fresh seafood. Fine dining is nearby at the Sooke Harbour House. Plan to spend extra days at Peace & Plenty as you can easily tour Victoria from here. The two bedrooms each have a queen bed, TV, private bath (*Laura* has a half-bath), and are tastefully decorated with a touch of yesteryear. The rooms overlook the gardens and woods. A full breakfast is served in the dining room which also overlooks the gardens. Enjoy afternoon tea upon your arrival.

Cat in residence; no pets; smoking outside only; children over twelve welcome; full breakfast; fireplace; hot tub; robes provided; cot available; credit cards (V); special holiday packages.

ROOM	BED	BATH	ENTRANCE	FLOOR	DAILY RATES S	D	EP
Laura	1Q	Pvt	Main	2	$65	$75	$15
Victoria	1Q	Pvt	Main	2	$75	$85	15

Rates stated in Canadian funds　　　**Area code 250 effective October, 1996*

British Columbia

SQUAMISH (BRACKENDALE)

Glacier Valley Farm   **(604) 898-2810**
Hosts: Sue, Marty and Jessica Vanderhoef   Msg: **(604) 892-7533**
Box 30 Mile 16 1/2 Upper Squamish, Brackendale, BC V0N 1H0
20 minutes from Brackendale, 45 minutes to Whistler.

"Glacier Valley Farm" says it all: peaceful farm and valley charm, spectacular glacial views! It's easy to see why it was chosen for the filming of White Fang II, and yet, Glacier Valley Farm is just an hour-and-a-half from Vancouver and 45 minutes from the ski hills of Whistler. Three comfy rooms on the second floor share two baths. Downstairs guests can relax on the patio, gazing at the fields, sheep, and horses, or settle in by the impressive fieldstone fireplace. Wandering around the farm, you'll find a short walk takes you to the river. The Vanderhoefs and their daughter Jessica, a first-rate area guide, offer tours and riding lessons, and will gladly arrange rafting or kayaking for you with Rivers and Oceans Expeditions. Sue serves a full farm breakfast, and additional meals as requested. The Vanderhoefs know the area well and have plenty of ideas for a memorable holiday. They suggest hiking, biking, river rafting, eagle watching, glacier air tours, photography. Winter visitors will join the nearly 4,000 bald eagles which winter in nearby Brackendale from November to March. Summer or winter, Glacier Valley Farm is a great destination.

Pets with prior approval; smoking outside only; children welcome (free under 6 years old); full breakfast; VCR; trails through the property; credit cards (V).

ROOM	BED	BATH	ENTRANCE	FLOOR	S	D	EP
1	2T & 1D	Shd	Main	2	$60	$75	$15
2	1Q	Shd	Main	2	$60	$75	$15
3	2T & 1D	Shd	Main	2	$60	$75	$15

Rates stated in Canadian funds

SURREY

White Heather Guest House   (604) 581-9797
Hosts: Glad and Chuck Bury
12571 - 98 Avenue, Surrey, BC V3V 2K6
Twenty minutes from U.S.-Canada border at Blaine.

A sincere welcome awaits you at White Heather Guest House, home of Glad and Chuck Bury. The quiet southeast suburb of Vancouver offers good bus service, as well as a fun and easy trip downtown by Skytrain. At afternoon tea time, you may wish to enlist the help of your seasoned hosts in planning your stay. They consistently search out cream-of-the-crop experiences to share with guests. Whether you're looking for the perfect restaurant—ethnic, family, or special occasion— or for attractions that are most worth visiting, the Burys offer sound advice. They did disclose some advance ideas to consider including the mountain gondola ride to the lookout, the museum, art gallery, beaches, and Stanley Park. Full English breakfasts, cooked to perfection by Chuck, are served in a sunny, garden-like room with a dramatic view of snow-capped mountains. Spend leisure moments relaxing or visiting on the patio overlooking the back garden. All this, plus a good night's sleep, makes White Heather Guest House a most hospitable place to stay.

No pets; family accommodation by arrangement; no smoking; no RV parking; full breakfast; fireplace and TV available; game room with toys and piano; licensed chauffeur available; off-street parking; pickup from airport or cruise ships; inquire about EP rates.

ROOM	BED	BATH	ENTRANCE	FLOOR	DAILY RATES S	D	EP+
Matheson Room	1Q	Pvt 1/2	Main	1	$50	$55	
Angus Room	1D	Shd	Main	1	$45	$50	

Rates stated in Canadian funds

TOFINO

Netty's Bed & Breakfast **Voice/Fax: (604)* 725-3451**
Host: Netty Cullion
1284 Lynn Road, Box 506, Chesterman Beach,
Tofino, BC V0R 2Z0
Left off Pacific Rim Highway near Orca Lodge.

Tofino, a fishing village on the west coast of Vancouver Island, is one of the special places on this earth. The tranquil atmosphere of Netty's leaves your energy free for walks on miles of sandy beach, bird watching, whale watching, wilderness hikes in the rain forest, or trips to nearby hot spring. Families are welcomed at Netty's attractive west coast cedar home located a short walk from the beach. The rooms are inviting. One room has twin beds, plus a loft that sleeps four. Tea and coffee are available in the open living room where you can relax before setting out again for more explorations. Netty's warm smile and welcoming manner help you unwind from the minute you arrive. Remember, reservations are a must in Tofino during the summer and the long scenic drive (four and a half hours from Victoria) makes you want to stay 2 or 3 nights. Netty suggests sampling the many fine Tofino restaurants, enjoying the whale-watching tours, and boating to the hot springs.

Pets outside only; smoking on porches only; children welcome; full breakfast; TV in each room; fireplace; outdoor deck; private outside shower; open year round; off season rates.

ROOM	BED	BATH	ENTRANCE	FLOOR	DAILY RATES		
					S	D	EP
A	1Q	Pvt	Main	2	$65	$75	
B	2T	Shd	Main	2	$60	$75	$15
C	1Q	Shd	Main	1	$60	$70	$15

Rates stated in Canadian funds   **Area code 250 effective October, 1996*

TOFINO

The Tide's Inn on Duffin Cove (604)* 725-3765
Hosts: Valerie and James Sloman FAX: (604)* 725-3325
P.O. Box 325, Tofino, BC V0R 2Z0
160 Arnet Road, steps from the shore of Duffin Cove.

The tranquil beauty of Duffin Cove is ever-present from the guest quarters of Val and James Sloman's comfortable home. Savor the dramatic, close-up view of the forest, sea, and mountains of Clayoquot Sound from the spacious bedrooms, decks, or hot tub; or, from the shoreline itself. Explore the tide pools or take a short stroll to sandy Tonquin Beach. The *Loon Room* features a picture window with views of Duffin Cove, Duffin Passage, Mearse Island and Clayoquot Sound. The en-suite bath has a jacuzzi tub for 2. *Chinook Room* has a beautiful view of the shoreline and forest on Lonecone Mountain on Mearse Island. *Lonecone Suite* has two bedrooms and large living room with the comfort of a brick fireplace. It is named after Lonecone Mountain which is the featured view and is a good choice for groups.

No pets or smoking; children over ten welcome; full homemade breakfast; TV and robes in *Lonecone Suite*; coffee bar and fridge in rooms; deck; hot tub; off-street parking; Pacific Rim National Park, year-round golf course, fishing, boating, kayaking, whale watching, and beach combing nearby; open year round; off-season rates; discount for stays of 2 nights or longer.

ROOM	BED	BATH	ENTRANCE	FLOOR	DAILY RATES S	D	EP
Loon Room	1Q	Pvt	Sep	1G	$85	$95	$20
Chinook Room	1Q	Pvt	Sep	1	$80	$90	
Lonecone Suite	1Q or 2T	Pvt	Sep	1G		$95	$25

Rates stated in Canadian funds   **Area code 250 effective October, 1996*

TOFINO

Wilp Gybuu (604)* 725-2330
Hosts: Wendy and Ralph Burgess
PO Box 396, Tofino, BC V0R 2Z0
311 Leighton Way, overlooking Duffin Passage.

Wilp Gybuu, meaning Wolf House, derives from Ralph's native heritage. Since he and Wendy moved to Tofino, he has honed his skills as a fine craftsman in silver and gold native design jewelry and his work is featured in better BC galleries. Their natural cedar home is exceptionally quiet and immaculate, with a mesmerizing view of water, mountains, mist, and sky from the main floor and outdoor deck. Flattering peachy pink walls add to the warm atmosphere. Guests are accommodated on the entry level which also contains a small "coffee room" where complimentary beverages and cookies can be found. A refrigerator is provided for guest use. Relax in comfort and peruse the wealth of information provided on the wonders of the wild yet fragile environment that makes Tofino so special. The *Cedar Room* features prints by Emily Carr. The *Alder Room* features prints by Canada's Group of Seven and America's Edward Hopper. Both rooms have ensuite baths. Join Ralph and Wendy upstairs for breakfast and engaging conversation. They appreciate having guests from a variety of life styles. There is fantastic winter storm watching!

Cat in residence; no pets or children under 12; smoking outside only; early coffee/tea delivered; full breakfast; TV/VCR in living room; deck; Pacific Rim National Park, year-round golf course, fishing, boating, kayaking, whale watching, and beach combing nearby; off-street parking; bus & airport pickup; open year round; off-season rates October-April; discount for 2 night and longer stays.

ROOM	BED	BATH	ENTRANCE	FLOOR	DAILY RATES S	D	EP
Cedar Room	1Q	Pvt	Main	1G	$70	$75	
Alder Room	2T	Pvt	Main	1G	$70	$80	

Rates stated in Canadian funds   *Area code **250** effective October, 1996*

VANCOUVER

Beachside Bed & Breakfast (604) 922-7773
Hosts: Gordon and Joan Gibbs (800) 563-3311
4208 Evergreen Avenue, FAX: (604) 926-8073
West Vancouver, BC V7V 1H1
Four miles west of Lion's Gate Bridge, just south of Marine Drive.

It would be difficult to top this Vancouver location: Just steps from the door you're on a sandy beach sniffing the salt air, watching gulls circle overhead, and feeling buoyant. The contemporary waterfront home offers fantastic views from the dining room where breakfast is served, from the outdoor whirlpool spa and deck, and from the deluxe suite at the rear of the ground-level guest floor. Soothing pastel colors blend with the seaside setting, and fresh fruit and flowers, delightful artwork, and comfortable furnishings enhance the accommodations. Gordon and Joan want you to enjoy the quiet, relaxing ambiance of their home as well as the interesting local activities and day trips that they thoughtfully describe in the literature placed in each room. A couple of trip ideas they did share were the rain forests at Lighthouse Park (within a mile of Beachside Bed & Breakfast) and the salmon barbecue and festival in September during the spawning season. The Gibbs promise "a warm, friendly Canadian welcome." Believe me, that's only the beginning.

Dog in residence; no pets; no children under eight; no smoking; TV and coffee maker in each room; jacuzzi tub in *Oceanfront Room*; full breakfast; off-street parking; credit cards (V,MC). Save with off-season discounted rates (Oct. 31 - April 30, except holidays).

ROOM	BED	BATH	ENTRANCE	FLOOR	DAILY RATES S D EP+
Oceanfront Room	1Q	Pvt	Sep	1G	$180
Seaside Suite	1Q	Pvt	Sep	1G	$150
Diane's Room	1Q	Pvt	Sep	1G	$110
Karen's Room	1Q	Pvt	Sep	1G	$110

Rates stated in Canadian funds

VANCOUVER

Jane's Gourmet Bed & Breakfast   **(604) 929-6083**
Hosts: Jane and Lorne Rae
4187 Fairway Place, North Vancouver, BC V7G 1Y8
Deep Cove, twenty-five minutes from downtown Vancouver.

Jane Rae's culinary skills figure heavily in the rave reviews from her B&B guests, but they also appreciate having an entire ground-floor apartment all to themselves. Fresh flowers and family heirlooms add to the luxurious warmth of the guest quarters, consisting of a beautiful bedroom with a queen bed; kitchenette behind folding doors; a bathroom with a wonderful spa bathtub; a utility area with washer and dryer; a commodious living room with a double sofa bed, large stone fireplace; dining area; and garden patio with table and chairs. From Jane's, a fascinating day of exploration might include a circular route to the major attractions of Vancouver, hiking at nearby Mount Seymour, or strolling around the seaside village of Deep Cove. Theater, golf, tennis, cycling, swimming, diving, canoeing, and kayaking are all within minutes of Jane's. A couple of extra special events she mentioned were the live theater at Deep Cove Theater and the concerts on the beach at Panorama Park in Deep Cove. At Jane's, you'll find the best aspects of a quiet, posh, country resort and home sweet home, all rolled into one!

No pets; smoking outside only; full breakfast; TV/VCR; bicycle, diving gear, canoe, and kayak rentals nearby; express bus to downtown; off-street parking; wheelchair access; EP rates vary according to age; cot available. *Open March 1 to October 31*.

ROOM	BED	BATH	ENTRANCE	FLOOR	DAILY RATES S	D	EP
Two Room Suite	1Q & 1D	Pvt	Sep	1G		$110	$20

Rates stated in Canadian funds

VANCOUVER

The Johnson House   **(604) 266-4175**
Hosts: Sandy and Ron Johnson
2278 West 34th Avenue, Vancouver, BC V6M 1G6
Central to UBC, Van Duesen Gardens, and Queen Elizabeth Park.

Rock-solid is an apt description of The Johnson House, from the neighborhood, to the front stone and flower garden, to the home's construction. A lovingly thorough restoration has left this 1920s Craftsman-style beauty standing tall, proud, and oh, so welcoming. Very large rooms with wood floors and extensive moldings are full of homey charm and comfort. Unique brass and iron beds are joined by Canadian wooden antiques and the hosts' impressive collection of carousel animals, coffee grinders, Victrolas, and more. Nostalgia reigns in every aspect of this marvelous home. The two guest rooms and the deluxe suite have distinct personalities of their own, and a couple have mountain views. Everywhere there is something to make you smile. Indeed, staying at The Johnson House is a joy through and through. The Johnsons suggest seeing the Bard on the Beach Shakespeare Festival and enjoying the Granville Island's four live theaters. There is good hiking on the Baden Powell Trail.

No pets; children over twelve welcome; smoking outside only; full breakfast; TV/VCR and fireplace in living room; front covered porch; back sun porch; handy to downtown and many attractions; quiet neighborhood, good for walking; near bus line; off-street and street parking; off-season rates.

ROOM	BED	BATH	ENTRANCE	FLOOR	DAILY RATES S	D	EP
Mountain Room	1Q & 1T	Shd	Main	2		$85	
Sunshine Room	1Q	Shd	Main	2		$75	
Carousel Suite	1K & 1T	Pvt	Main	2		$135	

Rates stated in Canadian funds

VANCOUVER

Jolie Maison Bed & Breakfast   (604) 730-8010
Hosts: Dimka and Louis Gheyle   FAX: (604) 730-8045
1888 West 3rd Avenue, Vancouver, BC V6J 1K8
Burrard to 3rd Avenue, west on 3rd Avenue.

Jolie Maison, located in Kitsilano—one of the safest and most desirable neighborhoods in Vancouver—is a heritage home recently restored to its former beauty. A pleasant walk takes you to the beach, shops, restaurants, and not-to-be-missed Granville Market. Downtown Vancouver and Stanley Park are close by. The originality of the room names chosen by Dimka and Louis is indicative of the hosts' creative flair. The bright, cheerful rooms are filled with quilts made by Dimka and antiques from Europe and the Gheyles' native Belgium. *Thelma and Louise* has a king bed which can be converted to two twins, ensuite bathroom, jacuzzi, and walk-in shower. *Sophie's Choice* is decorated in shades of green. *Esmeralda's Hideaway*, on the third floor, has wonderful mountain views and is great for three people traveling together; its private bath is on the second floor. The sitting room is inviting with a fireplace, TV, and games. Dimka and Louis are very knowledgeable about the local scene and enjoy helping you select the perfect restaurant. They suggest a visit to Granville Island and to view the totem poles at the Museum of Anthropology at the University of British Columbia.

Cat in residence; no pets; smoking outside only; children over eight welcome; full breakfast; TV/VCR; French, Dutch, and German spoken; credit cards (V); extended occupancy rates on request.

ROOM	BED	BATH	ENTRANCE	FLOOR	DAILY RATES S	D	EP
Thelma and Louise	1K or 2T	Pvt	Main	2	$115	$125	
Sophie's Choice	1Q	Shd	Main	2	$70	$85	
Esmeralda's Hideaway	Q & 1T	Shd	Main	3	$70	$85	$25
Babette's Feast	1Q	Pvt	Main	LL	$80	$95	

Rates stated in Canadian funds

VANCOUVER

The Penny Farthing Inn　　　　　　　**(604) 739-9002**
Host: Lyn Hainstock　　　　　　　　　FAX: **(604) 739-9004**
2855 West Sixth Avenue, Vancouver, BC　V6K 1X2
email: farthing@uniserve.com
Six blocks from Kitsilano Beach.

It's cheering just to look at this 1912 character home painted in vivid colors with its pretty English country garden. The warmth of the welcome matches that of the bright, bold shades used tastefully throughout the house. Lyn Hainstock has combined lovely antiques brought from England with Victorian lace. The home's stained glass windows and inlaid oak floors add to an ambiance rich in warmth and comfort. Among the choice accommodations is *Bettina's Boudoir*, with a queen-sized pine four-poster bed, en suite bath, a porch facing the rear garden with partial mountain views, and a sitting room with TV/VCR and sofa bed. *Abigail's Attic* is a deluxe suite with a queen brass bed; en suite bath with skylight; and a sitting room with mountain and water views, TV/VCR, and sofa bed. Breakfast in the rear garden among flowers and herbs is a sensory delight. But then, everything about Penny Farthing is a delight, including its super location. Lyn suggests attending the childrens festival in late May and early June or the film festival in late September and October.

Cats in residence; no pets; teens welcome; smoking on porches only; full breakfast; guest sitting room with TV/VCR and video tape library; guest fridge; easy walk to beach, shops, and restaurants; 6 to 8 minutes downtown; near bus stop; ample street parking; some French spoken; off-season and long-term rates.

ROOM	BED	BATH	ENTRANCE	FLOOR	DAILY RATES S	D	EP
Bettina's Boudoir	1Q & 1D	Pvt	Main	2	$125	$150	$20
Sophie's	1D	Shd	Main	2	$75	$95	
Lucinda's	1K or 2T	Shd	Main	2	$75	$95	
Abigail's Attic	1Q & 1D	Pvt	Main	3	$140	$165	$20

Rates stated in Canadian funds

British Columbia

VANCOUVER

Treehouse Bed and Breakfast Voice/Fax: **(604) 266-2962**
Hosts: Bob and Barb Selvage
2490 West 49th Avenue, Vancouver, BC V6M 2V3
From Granville Street, west on 49th Avenue.

Treehouse Bed & Breakfast was originally built with aplomb and style to be Barb and Bob's home. They later decided to share the large contemporary home in the heart of the lovely Kerrisdale area of Vancouver with guests and started the bed and breakfast. The home is ideal for the traveler who desires a calm and peaceful atmosphere while visiting one of the most exciting and cosmopolitan cities on the west coast. There are two self-enclosed suites where privacy and serenity are paramount. The *Treetop Suite* encompasses the entire third floor, has a skylit bathroom with two person jacuzzi tub, private sundeck and queen four-poster bed. *Pacific West Suite* has a queen bed, large sitting room with hide-a-bed, bath with jacuzzi tub, and secluded patio. The *School Room* (named for the educational poster on the wall featuring host/teacher Barb) has a queen bed and looks out on Japanese gardens. Breakfast is served in the elegant dining room. An adjoining guest living room has a marble fireplace. Carefully selected art and sculpture is found throughout the house. Barb and Bob know their bed and breakfast is a "rather unique experience" and want you to discover why their guests return year after year.

No pets; smoking outside only; children ten and over welcome; full breakfast; TV/VCR; jacuzzi; fireplace; covered decks; robes provided; guest telephone; open year round.

ROOM	BED	BATH	ENTRANCE	FLOOR	DAILY RATES S	D	EP
School Room	1Q	Pvt	Main	1	$80	$85	
Pacific West Suite	1Q	Pvt	Main	1	$105	$115	$20
Treetop Suite	1Q	Pvt	Main	3	$115	$125	$20

Rates stated in Canadian funds

VERNON

Castle on the Mountain (604)* 542-4593
Hosts: Eskil and Sharon Larson
8227 Silver Star Rd., S 10, C 12, RR 8, Vernon, BC V1T 8L6
Upper Okanagan Valley.

This large Tudor-style home is located on the southern exposure of Silver Star Mountain, seven miles from city center. The elevation not only allows a sweeping view of valley, lakes, and the lights of Vernon, but gives you a head start in getting to the ski slopes at Silver Star (seven miles away). In this choice setting, Castle on the Mountain offers a unique lodging experience. Sharon and Eskil are artists/crafts people; they have an ever-changing collection in their in-home gallery studio where people enjoy browsing. The entire ground floor is for guests. There's a living room with places to relax by the fire; a kitchen area for light meals. *Green Garden Room* is a huge turret-shaped and multi windowed room, with private bath and phenomenal views. It can be combined with the *Blue Garden Room* into a private suite. The third floor has the luxury suite, *Stargazer's Tower*, with fireplace, jacuzzi, wet bar, and two balconies. Castle Apartment is separate, two-story family apartment with outdoor hot tub. Enjoy the luxury of the Castle while touring the excellent Okanagan area wineries.

Smoking outside only; allergy-free environment; full breakfast; TV; phone; outdoor spa; picnic area; summer hiking, beaches, and fruit-picking; winter skiing (Alpine and Nordic) and snowmobiling; off-street parking; wheelchair access; credit cards (V,MC,AMEX).

ROOM	BED	BATH	ENTRANCE	FLOOR	DAILY RATES S	D	EP
Green Garden Room	1Q	Pvt	Sep	1G	$75	$85	
Blue Garden Room	1Q	Pvt	Sep	1G	$60	$70	
Rose Garden Room	1Q	Pvt	Sep	1G	$75	$85	
Castle Apartment	1K & 3T	Pvt	Sep	1G & 2	$75	$85	$30
Stargazer's Tower	1K	Pvt	Main	3		$145	

Rates stated in Canadian funds   **Area code 250** *effective October, 1996*

VERNON

Harbourlight Bed & Breakfast   (604)* 549-5117
Hosts: Helga and Peter Neckel   FAX: (604)* 549-5162
RR#4, S-11, C-50, 135 Joharon Road, Vernon, BC V1T 6L7
Near downtown Vernon, overlooking Okanagan Lake.

Harbourlight Bed & Breakfast, convenient to downtown Vernon and Silver Star Resort, is situated on two quiet acres with panoramic lake and mountain views. The newer modern home of Helga and Peter Neckel has spacious, immaculate rooms offering great comfort and privacy. Plenty of windows, shiny wood floors covered with beautiful rugs, and the three-piece en suite baths add to the luxurious ambiance of the Neckels' home. Featured in their generous full breakfasts are homemade jams and breads. Just moments away are beaches, public boat launching, fishing, golf courses, and hiking trails. Each season brings its own pleasures in the Okanagan, and Harbourlight beckons guests to discover them all year round.

No pets, children, or smoking; full breakfast; AC; deck; wineries and varied outdoor recreation nearby; German spoken.

ROOM	BED	BATH	ENTRANCE	FLOOR	DAILY RATES S	D	EP
2	1Q	Pvt	Main	1	$45	$55	
3	1Q	Pvt	Main	1G	$45	$65	
4	1Q	Pvt	Main	1G	$45	$55	

Rates stated in Canadian funds   **Area code 250 effective October, 1996*

VERNON

The Maria Rose Bed & Breakfast   (800) 662-7977
Hosts: Ruth-Maria Cushing and Peter Filas   (604)* 549-4773
RR #3, Site 11, Comp 156, Vernon, BC V1T 6L6
8083 Aspen Road, off Silver Star Road.

Seven acres of peace halfway up Silver Star Mountain, with fabulous views overlooking Kalamalka and Okanagan lakes and surrounding mountains is the setting for Maria Rose Bed & Breakfast. The newly-built Royal Coach House, adjacent to the main dwelling, has four comfortable private rooms—great for groups and families as well as individuals. All rooms have private entrances and sitting rooms. *Prince* and *Princess* can be rented separately or as a suite. A European ski lodge flavor is everywhere, and Ruth-Maria has bought many precious antiques and collectibles from abroad for the main house, where breakfast is served. World-famous Silver Star Mountain is "a yodel away" and offers spectacular skiing, winter sports, summer hiking, and horseback riding. The many Okanagan lakes offer all water sports. There's a ski storage area and a sauna for relaxation after a day on the slopes. Ruth-Maria and Peter suggest ski and golf packages, winery tours, and bird watching on their grounds.

Pets by arrangement; smoking outside only; children welcome; full breakfast; TV/VCR; sauna; barbecue; ski storage; German spoken; Slavic languages understood; credit cards (V); open year round.

ROOM	BED	BATH	ENTRANCE	FLOOR	S	D	EP
King	1K	Pvt	Sep	1	$60	$75	$20
Queen	1Q	Pvt	Sep	1	$50	$70	
Prince	2T	Shd	Sep	1	$40	$65	$20
Princess	1D	Shd	Sep	1	$40	$60	

Rates stated in Canadian funds   **Area code 250 effective October, 1996*

British Columbia

VICTORIA

Ambleside Bed & Breakfast (604)* 383-9948
Hosts: Marilyn Jessen and Gordon Banta FAX: (604)* 383-9317
1121 Faithful Street, Victoria, BC V8V 2R5
email: mjessen@pinc.com
Bordering Beacon Hill Park and a block from the waterfront.

Ambleside is an inviting home located on a quiet street in Fairfield, one of Victoria's most scenic and walkable heritage neighborhoods. A fine Craftsman home built in 1920, it is decorated with assured restraint that's in perfect keeping with the style and scale of the house. A striking palette of rose, blue, and ivory set off the exquisite vintage woodwork, gleaming hardwood floors, and the dark, handsome colors of the furnishings. On the main floor, guests feel immediately at home in the comfortable, attractive living room and the delightful dining room where sumptuous multi-course breakfasts are beautifully served. There's a fresh, clean feeling throughout the house. Choice antiques, floral and botanical motifs, Oriental and braided rugs, and custom bed coverings and valances enhance the guest rooms. The wonderful location of this gracious home and the relaxed, helpful hospitality of Marilyn and Gordon make staying at Ambleside the perfect treat while visiting Victoria. For a special Victoria experience, they recommend you comb the shops on nearby Antique Row and enjoy the color and excitement of the twice-weekly estate auctions.

No pets or smoking; children over fifteen welcome; full breakfast; robes provided; fireplace and piano in living room; 15 - 20 minute stroll downtown through Beacon Hill Park, or 8 minutes by bus; near oceanside pathways and popular neighborhood eateries; off-street and street parking; credit cards (V,MC); off-season rates.

ROOM	BED	BATH	ENTRANCE	FLOOR	S	D	EP+
Mountain Ash	1Q	Pvt	Main	1	$85	$95	
Silver Birch	1K or 2T	Shd	Main	2	$75	$85	
Grindelwald	1D	Shd	Main	2	$65	$75	

Rates stated in Canadian funds   *Area code 250 effective October, 1996*

VICTORIA

Bender's Bed & Breakfast (604)* 472-8993
Host: Glenda Bender   FAX: (604)* 472-8995
4254 Thornhill Crescent, Victoria, BC V8N 3G7
One mile from the University, five miles from downtown.

Bender's suburban location is near University of Victoria, Mount Douglas Park, Cordova Bay, and shopping centers, yet only five miles from the heart of town. The clean, comfortable accommodations here are easy on the budget and offer variety and flexibility—very helpful for families or larger groups. Guests in the bedrooms on the lower level of the house may enjoy a large sitting room with a stone fireplace and a TV. Upstairs, guests tend to gather in the living room. The neighborhood is safe, quiet, and good for walking. Mrs. Bender has a lot of regular guests who appreciate her easy, come-and-go-as-you-please manner and the all-around good value she offers.

No pets or smoking; full breakfast; TV in Rooms A and E; off-street and street parking.

ROOM	BED	BATH	ENTRANCE	FLOOR	DAILY RATES S	D	EP+
A	1D	Pvt	Main	1		$55	
B	1D	Shd	Main	1		$50	
C	1D	Shd	Main	1		$50	
D	1D & 1T	Shd	Main	LL		$45	$20
E	1D & 1T	Pvt	Main	LL		$55	$20
F	1Q	Shd	Main	LL		$50	

*Rates stated in Canadian funds   *Area code **250** effective October, 1996*

British Columbia

VICTORIA

Carriage Stop Bed & Breakfast   Voice/Fax: **(604)* 383-6240**
Host: Jane McAllister
117 Menzies Street, Victoria, BC   V8V 2G4
Short walk from beach and downtown.

Close proximity to the heart of Victoria is just one of the assets of Carriage Stop Bed & Breakfast. Jane McAllister's blue heritage home has a gabled roof, interesting angles, and lots of character. The charm of its age comes through, while renovations have given the interior a clean, new feeling of light and openness. With this background, the well-chosen artwork shows up to good advantage. One of the guest rooms is on the first floor; two rooms and a bath on the second floor make ideal quarters for several people traveling together. Besides the convenient location and agreeable atmosphere, you'll get expert advice on picking that special restaurant to suit your mood, your palate, and your purse. Jane suggests taking a harbour boat to Pt. Ellis for tea. At Carriage Stop, the best of old and new come together in an ambiance of casual comfort.

Two cats in residence; no pets; children by arrangement; smoking outside only; full breakfast; robes and hair dryers provided; common room with fireplace and TV; patio in summer; credit cards (MC,AMEX); good public transportation and airport connections.

ROOM	BED	BATH	ENTRANCE	FLOOR	DAILY RATES S	D	EP
Sorrel	1Q	Pvt	Main	1	$65	$75	
Jasmine	1D	Shd	Main	2	$65	$75	
Juniper	1D & 1T	Shd	Main	2	$65	$75	$15

Rates stated in Canadian funds   **Area code 250 effective October, 1996*

VICTORIA

The Crow's Nest   (604)* 383-4492
Hosts: Kit and Dene Mainguy   FAX: (604)* 383-3140
71 Linden Avenue, Victoria, BC V8V 4C9
Just east of Beacon Hill Park and a half-block from waterfront.

This 1911 heritage home was designed by Samuel Maclure, a leading architect of the time, in his American Chalet style. It has large, sunny rooms, an abundance of impressive woodwork, beveled and stained glass, and polished fir floors covered with Oriental rugs. Original light fixtures lend an Arthurian charm. Furnishings are largely English and Flemish antiques. A second-floor guest room at the front of the house uses the original bathroom off the hallway, and another at the back has an en suite shower. Kit and Dene Mainguy are superb hosts. Kit has honed his skills as a former hotelier down to a smaller, more personal scale. He serves a most savory English breakfast in the formal dining room. He and Dene intuit guests' needs very well and accommodate them in every way possible. They suggest attending the free "Symphony Splash" at the inner harbour in August.

Dog and cats in residence; no pets; infants and children over eight welcome; no smoking; full breakfast; special diets accommodated; robes provided; rollaway beds available; Dallas Road waterfront, shops, bistros, and tearooms nearby; 25-minute walk to town, or 10 minutes by bus; ample street parking; French spoken; off-season rates.

ROOM	BED	BATH	ENTRANCE	FLOOR	DAILY RATES S	D	EP
Blue Room	1Q	Shd	Main	2	$70	$85	$15
Victory Room	1T	Shd	Main	2	$70		
Rose Room	1K or 2T	Pvt	Main	2	$75	$90	$15

Rates stated in Canadian funds   *Area code **250** effective October, 1996*

British Columbia

VICTORIA

Eagles Rest Bed & Breakfast (604)* 478-5996
Host: Marg Mercer
3307 B Metchosin Road, Victoria, BC   V9C 2A4
Off Highway 1A between Victoria and Sooke.

When Marg Mercer decided to turn her neat and clean contemporary home into a B&B, she chose a name that reflects her fondness for eagles. Many are on display throughout the house. The upper floor is just for guests, and the names of the comfortable bedrooms—*Lilac*, *Rose*, and *Fern*—indicate their color schemes. *Lilac* has an ensuite bath, while the other two share a bath off the hallway. Marg invites guests to enjoy her friendly kitchen, where she serves full country breakfasts. Hiking is superb in nearby East Sooke Park, while some may prefer golfing or salmon fishing. At Eagles Rest, you'll be well-situated to explore the fascinating Sooke region and enjoy the charming city of Victoria as well. Springtime is especially nice for golfing and enjoying the spring blooms in Butchart Gardens.

No pets; children over eight welcome; smoking outside only; full breakfast; TV in some rooms; bus stop nearby; off-street parking; credit cards (V).

ROOM	BED	BATH	ENTRANCE	FLOOR	DAILY RATES S	D	EP
Lilac	1D	Pvt	Main	2		$65	$5
Rose	2T	Shd	Main	2		$55	
Fern	1T	Shd	Main	2		$45	

Rates stated in Canadian funds   **Area code 250 effective October, 1996*

VICTORIA

The Inn on St. Andrews (604)* 384-8613
Host: Joan Peggs (800) 668-5993
231 St. Andrews Street, Victoria, BC V8V 2N1
James Bay area, near Beacon Hill Park. FAX: (604)* 384-6063

The glorious gardens surrounding this heritage property do justice to its stature and grace. Built in 1913 by Edith Carr, eldest sister of the famous Canadian artist and author Emily Carr, the grand home is lovingly tended by proud owner Joan Peggs. Starting with its innate fine craftsmanship, elegant woodwork, stained and beveled glass, and gracious proportions, she has used ivory, pale green, peach, and pink in fashioning an interior that is at once light, welcoming, and soothing. Common areas—living room, delightful sun room, formal dining room, and TV room—seem truly meant to be enjoyed as one's own. Large, bright bedrooms are located off the central second-floor landing. At Joan's beautifully preserved inn, guests usually reach such a level of at-homeness that they return whenever possible to its familiar embrace. She wants you to know the Butchart Gardens Christmas Light display is very impressive and First Night celebration on New Years provides great family fun.

Smoking outside only; full breakfast; walk to heart of town, ocean front, and Beacon Hill Park; near bus route; ample street parking; credit cards (MC, en route); *Room A also available with shared bath.

ROOM	BED	BATH	ENTRANCE	FLOOR	S	D	EP+
A	1Q	Pvt*	Main	2	$70	$85	$15
B	1Q	Shd	Main	2	$55	$70	$15
C	2T	Shd	Main	2	$55	$70	$15

*Rates stated in Canadian funds   *Area code 250 effective October, 1996*

British Columbia

VICTORIA

Laird House 　　　　　　　　　　**Voice/Fax: (604)* 384-3177**
Host: Ruth Laird 　　　　　　　　　　　　**(800) 845-0586**
134 St. Andrews Street, Victoria, BC V8V 2M5
A short walk to town, one half block to Beacon Hill Park.

   An exceptional place to stay in the quiet and lovely James Bay section of Victoria is the inviting 1912 heritage home of Ruth Laird. It has been restored and decorated with the utmost attention to detail. In fact, one gets the feeling that every square inch of Laird House was fashioned to offer visual delight and comfort to its inhabitants. On the main floor, a guest lounge/library exudes quality; coffered ceilings and impressive woodwork are enhanced by beautiful floral motifs in burgundy, green, and cream. Tea and sherry are available to sip as soft music soothes the senses. On the second floor, two most attractive bedrooms (one with a fireplace and balcony) are full of special touches including fresh flowers and fruit. The private bathrooms are stocked with amenities while a galley contains a guest refrigerator, sink, coffee, tea, and cookies. Guests are invited to make use of the adjacent sitting rooms with its array of books, games, and puzzles. Wholesome three-course breakfasts are served in the elegant dining room—a sterling way to start your glorious day in Victoria!

   Three cats in residence; no pets, young children, or smoking; full breakfast (Heart Smart menu on request); robes and hair dryers provided; walk to heart of town, ocean front, and Beacon Hill Park; half a block to bus route; good public transportation and airport connections; off-street parking; credit cards (V,MC,AMEX).

ROOM	BED	BATH	ENTRANCE	FLOOR	DAILY RATES S	D	EP
A	1Q	Pvt	Main	2	$65	$85	
B	1Q	Pvt	Main	2	$65	$85	

Rates stated in Canadian funds　　　**Area code **250** effective October, 1996*

VICTORIA

Olive House   (604)* 381-4239
Hosts: Don and Elizabeth Chambers
179 Olive Street, Victoria, BC V8S 3H4
Between Beacon Hill Park and Ross Bay.

As you approach the large old-fashioned verandah of Olive House, you begin to feel what life was like at the turn of the century. Elizabeth and Don have done a good job of restoring and updating their 1913 Edwardian home; Don is a cabinetmaker and his pride in workmanship is evident. Persian rugs, stained glass windows, fine hand-crafted furniture and gleaming hardwood floors complement the cheerful rooms. Olive Street is quiet and close to Juan de Fuca Strait, Beacon Hill Park, the public bus, and downtown Victoria. Don or Elizabeth will pick you up downtown by prior arrangement and will help with ideas for outings, restaurants and entertainment. The two upstairs bedrooms are attractive and colorful with local art on the walls; a soak in the claw-foot tub is a treat (there is also a shower). Don and Elizabeth suggest you bring comfortable apparel for early morning walks along the sea cliff and for working up an appetite for their famous Belgian waffles.

Dog and cat in residence; no pets; smoking outside only; children over twelve welcome; full breakfast; fireplace; verandah; transportation from downtown by arrangement.

ROOM	BED	BATH	ENTRANCE	FLOOR	DAILY RATES S	D	EP
Browning	2T	Shd	Main	2	$60	$65	
Burns	1D	Shd	Main	2	$60	$65	

Rates stated in Canadian funds   *Area code 250 effective October, 1996*

VICTORIA

Scholefield House
Hosts: Tana and George
email: scholhouse@cyberstore.ca
731 Vancouver Street, Victoria, BC V8V 3V4
Four blocks East of the Empress Hotel.

(604)* 385-2025
(800) 661-1623
FAX: (604)* 383-3036

Step back in time to the warmth of a Heritage House, built in 1892 for Ethelbert Olaf Stuart Scholefield, one of B.C.'s earliest historians. On a quiet tree-lined street in downtown Victoria, Scholefield House now offers to guests from around the world, the refinement and splendor of a bygone era. A glass of sherry or a cup of tea in the Library awaits you after checking in or on your return from a day of sight seeing. Guest rooms in this authentically restored Victorian home are individually decorated with antiques, beautiful quilts and lace, and each has its own private bath with a choice of clawfoot tub or shower. A full and scrumptious breakfast featuring herbs and flowers from the garden, fresh fruit, and home made jams, is served in the front Dining Room. And it's just a short stroll to the Inner Harbor, Empress Hotel, Beacon Hill Park, Old Town, Antique Row and much more. Tana and George remind you that Victoria is the only Canadian city that stays green and has flowers growing all year long. Discover gracious comfort, refined relaxation and helpful hospitality at Scholefield House.

Cats and Teddy Bears in residence; no pets; smoking in the garden only; children twelve and over accepted; full breakfast; ensuite baths; robes provided; on bus route; off-street and street parking; credit cards (V,MC). **KNIGHTTIME PUBLICATIONS SPECIAL: 10% discount with this book.

ROOM	BED	BATH	ENTRANCE	FLOOR	DAILY RATES S	D	EP+
King Suite	1K	Pvt	Sep	2	$90	$100	$20
Oak Room	1Q	Pvt	Sep	2	$75	$85	
Walnut Room	1Q	Pvt	Sep	2	$75	$85	

Rates stated in U.S. funds   *Area code **250** effective October, 1996*

VICTORIA

Seaview Bed & Breakfast   (604)* 383-7098
Hosts: Alec and Pat Gordon   FAX: (604)* 383-3524
1144 Dallas Road, Victoria, BC V8V 1C1
email: seaview@visual.net
On the sea front near Beacon Hill Park.

Think back to your most satisfying bed and breakfast experience in England—or imagine what it would be like. In other words, think of the very *essence* of bed and breakfast: warm, lively hosts, a comfortable bed, and a hearty breakfast. Add to this a breathtaking view of the Olympic Mountains and lights of Port Angeles across the Strait of San Juan de Fuca. From Pat and Alec Gordon's seaside home, stroll along the waterfront, explore adjacent Beacon Hill Park, or make the five minute drive to the city center (many people walk). They suggest the jazz festivals in April and July, the May "Swiftsure" and Victoria to Maui yacht races as exciting times to visit the city. These words from a former guest of the Gordons appeared in the *San Francisco Examiner:* "The hosts...provide comfortable beds and a superb breakfast, with congeniality, a rare sense of humor, and an unusual willingness to help out a tired or frustrated tourist." I couldn't have said it better myself.

No pets or smoking; full English breakfast; TV in each room; Pick up at the harbour and bus depot. Hosts also operate a B&B reservation service listing homes in the same price range as Seaview.

ROOM	BED	BATH	ENTRANCE	FLOOR	DAILY RATES S	D	EP+
View Room	1Q	Pvt	Main	1	$60	$95	$20
Balcony Room	1Q	Pvt	Main	2	$60	$85	$20
Garden Room	1Q	Pvt	Main	2	$60	$75	$20

Rates stated in Canadian funds   *Area code **250** effective October, 1996*

British Columbia

VICTORIA

Top O'Triangle Mountain   (604)* 478-7853
Hosts: Henry and Pat Hansen   FAX: (604)* 478-2245
3442 Karger Terrace, Victoria, BC V9C 3K5
Between Victoria and Sooke.

Staying out of the city has its advantages—peace and quiet, a slower pace, ease of parking—but this B&B offers much more. Top O'Triangle Mountain is just twenty-two minutes out of Victoria, but the view from this elevation is wondrous: the city and inner harbour, Port Angeles, the Olympic Mountains, and a spectacular light show at night. The house is built of interlocking cedar logs, and the warm look of wood permeates the interior. There are plenty of windows, decks all around, and a solarium where ample breakfasts are served. The three guest accommodations include a room on the main floor (3); a mini-suite (1); and suite (2) with a TV/sitting room on the ground floor. Comfort and silence ensure a sound sleep. Henry and Pat Hansen encourage unrestricted relaxation and sincerely want guests to think of their B&B as home. For activities, they suggest close by hiking trails or parks, visiting nearby Equimalt Lagoon (bird sanctuary) or Fort Rodd Hill, and enjoying Juan de Fuca Recreation Centre as well as many nearby golf courses.

No pets; families welcome (children under twelve, $5); no smoking in rooms or dining area; full breakfast; off-street and street parking; credit cards (V,MC). (3) has a water and mountain view, a sliding glass door to the deck, TV, and ensuite bath; it is available May 15-October 15 only; otherwise, another room on the main floor is used.

ROOM	BED	BATH	ENTRANCE	FLOOR	DAILY RATES S	D	EP
(1)	1Q	Pvt	Main	1G		$65	
(2)	1Q	Pvt	Main	1G		$75	$20
(3)	1Q	Pvt	Main	2		$85	

Rates stated in Canadian funds   **Area code **250** effective October, 1996*

VICTORIA

The Vacationer (604)* 382-9469
Hosts: Anne and Henry DeVries FAX: (604)* 384-6553
1143 Leonard Street, Victoria, BC V8V 2S3
Two blocks from waterfront, bordering Beacon Hill Park.

One glance at this B&B and you feel the promise of something good inside. Pass the manicured front lawn and flower beds, enter the front door, and you'll receive the heartiest of welcomes from Anne and Henry DeVries. They raised their family here and now keep their home in top shape for B&B guests. The spacious living room with a fireplace of stone is so comfortable that you might feel like inviting friends in for a visit—and you are welcome to do so. The adjacent dining area is the scene of beautifully presented, four-course breakfasts. Anne prides herself on coming up with a different specialty each morning, no matter how long you stay. Three pretty bedrooms with excellent mattresses and color televisions, along with two bathrooms, occupy the second floor. The DeVries offer the use of their secluded back yard, bicycles, and a separate phone line. They have a wealth of budget-stretching tips that should help to maximize your resources while visiting lovely Victoria.

No pets, children, or smoking; full breakfast; robes provided; tennis courts nearby; walking distance from downtown; off-street parking; Dutch and German spoken; credit cards (V,MC); free pickup from downtown ferries and bus depot; off-season rates. The DeVries also operate a B&B reservation service offering a variety of other accommodations.

ROOM	BED	BATH	ENTRANCE	FLOOR	S	D	EP
A	1Q	Shd	Main	2	$45	$65	$20
B	1Q	Shd	Main	2	$45	$65	
C	2T	Shd	Main	2	$45	$65	

Rates stated in Canadian funds   *Area code 250 effective October, 1996*

VICTORIA

Wellington Bed & Breakfast Voice/Fax: **(604)* 383-5976**
Host: Inge Ranzinger
66 Wellington Street, Victoria, BC V8V 4H5
Just east of Beacon Hill Park and a half-block from waterfront.

With her marvelous talent for design, Inge Ranzinger has coaxed every charming nuance out of her Fairfield character home. Its interior is fresh, artistic, and classy. In the main-floor common areas, tones of mauve, pink, and aquamarine contrast with lots of white—a splendid setting for pretty patterned rugs, myriad collectibles and art objects, and very homey furnishings. Equal flair marks the upstairs guest quarters. The *White Room* is a vision of palest lilac, white, fresh and dried flowers, and lovely works of glass. The *Hearth Room* has colonial blue wallpaper, lace curtains, and a fireplace; The *Antique Room* is a bit smaller and more traditional. Inge offers hospitality to match the inspired design of Wellington Bed & Breakfast.

No pets or smoking; children twelve and over welcome; full breakfast; ensuite bath in *White Room*; bath across hall from *Hearth Room*; bath on first floor for *Antique Room*; Dallas Road waterfront, shops, bistros, and tearooms nearby; 20-minute walk to town, or 10 minutes by bus; off-street and street parking; credit cards (MC); German spoken; off-season and weekly rates.

ROOM	BED	BATH	ENTRANCE	FLOOR	S	D	EP+
Antique Room	1Q	Pvt	Main	2	$45	$80	
White Room	1K	Pvt	Main	2	$55	$90	
Hearth Room	1Q & 1T	Pvt	Main	2	$60	$95	$25

Rates stated in Canadian funds   *Area code **250** effective October, 1996*

VICTORIA

Wooded Acres Bed & Breakfast   (604)* 478-8172 *or* **474-8959**
Hosts: Elva and Skip Kennedy
RR#2, 4907 Rocky Point Road, Victoria, BC   V9B 5B4
Between Victoria and Sooke.

    This cozy bed and breakfast is nestled on an acreage where "made-from-scratch" finds full expression. In a majestic forest setting, Elva and Skip Kennedy's home was built with logs from their property, and the mellow beauty of cedar, oak, and fir has tremendous appeal. Honeymooners delight! Relax in your own private hot tub and surround yourself with pleasures and relics of bygone times. Country antiques and intriguing displays of artifacts add to the many welcoming touches. Breakfast is a feast of home-baked specialties. Elva serves jams, jellies, scones, muffins, breads, cereals, old fashioned slab bacon, and fresh, from-the-henhouse eggs. Served with lace and fine china which provide the finishing touch of elegance to the pleasure of an old fashion breakfast. Metchosin, Victoria's countryside, has the rural flavor of small farms combined with beaches, breathtaking scenery, wilderness parks, bird watching, and trails for hiking and mountain bikes. Here too are golf courses for those who pursue this less "rustic" activity. Metchosin also has become a center for organic farms, arts and crafts. Combine the rural feeling with real convenience to downtown Victoria and the Sooke area. The Kennedy's suggest fishing, whale watching, and horseback riding as activities that are easy to take advantage of in the area.

    No pets; adult-oriented; full breakfast at guests' convenience; special diets accommodated.

ROOM	BED	BATH	ENTRANCE	FLOOR	DAILY RATES S	D	EP+
A	1Q	Pvt	Main	2		$95	
A	1Q	Pvt	Main	1		$95	

Rates stated in Canadian funds   **Area code **250** effective October, 1996*

British Columbia

WHITE ROCK

Dorrington Bed & Breakfast   **(604) 535-4408**
Hosts: Pat and Helen Gray   FAX: **(604) 535-4409**
13851 19A Avenue, White Rock, BC V4A 9M2
In White Rock, north of the US-Canadian border, off Hwy 99A.

Dorrington is full of surprises and delights and the comfortable rooms, patios, and tennis court make it difficult to leave. White Rock offers a good starting place for touring the lower mainland areas (40 minutes from Vancouver; 30 minutes from the Victoria ferry). You'll find golfing, restaurants, wonderful shopping and sandy beaches. In the market you can fill your basket (the basket's provided) with goodies for a picnic later in Vancouver's Stanley Park or at the beach. After a day of touring, you can play tennis, or be soothed in the hot tub. Pat and Helen have spent 20 years between them in the hospitality field, and they're expert in pampering without pestering. The *St. Andrews* room, with plaid golf wallpaper and golf memorabilia, features a hand-hewn maple branch bed and ensuite jacuzzi. The *Victorian Room's* four-poster bed and floral chintz is warm and cozy. For a special occasion, the 700 square foot *Windsor Room* has a canopied brass bed with fireplace and sitting room. Pat delights in making cappuccinos, and breakfast is served in the 'Hunt room' or on the patio overlooking the garden and the tennis court. Helen and Pat suggest a picnic in Vancouver's Stanley Park and a stroll on the beach at White Rock.

Miniature daschunds in residence; no pets, no smoking; adult oriented; full breakfast; hot tub; patio; tennis court with ball machine; picnic baskets; robes and slippers; small weddings; private parties; credit cards (MC,V). Open year round, off season discount.

ROOM	BED	BATH	ENTRANCE	FLOOR	DAILY RATES S	D	EP
Victorian	1D	Pvt	Main	2	$80	$90	
Saint Andrews	1Q	Pvt	Main	2	$65	$75	
Windsor	1Q	Pvt	Main	2		$185	

Rates stated in Canadian funds

DINING HIGHLIGHTS - BRITISH COLUMBIA

Please read "About Dining Highlights" on page ix.

CAMPBELL RIVER

Gourmet-by-the-Sea; 4378 South Island Highway, Oyster Bay; (604)* 923-5234; fresh seafood/creative Continental

Le Chateau Briand; 1170 Island Highway; (604)* 287-4143; Continental

Panache; 1090 Shoppers Row, Campbell River; (604)* 830-0025

The Royal Coachman Inn; 84 Dogwood Street; (604)* 286-0231; Continental

The Willows Neighbourhood Pub; 521 Rockland Road; (604)* 923-8311

COMOX

Gaff Rig Restaurant; 1984 Buena Vista Avenue; (604)* 339-7181; local seafood/steaks/European specialties

COURTENAY

La Cremaillere Restaurant; 975 Comox Road; (604)* 338-8131; French

DELTA

Greek Village; 7953 - 120 Street; (604) 597-1515

Portofino; 9493 - 120 Street; (604) 581-7555; steak/prime rib/Greek

Wimaan Thai Restaurant; 8665 - 120 Street; (604) 594-6524

GIBSONS

Chez Philippe at Bonniebrook Lodge; 1532 Ocean Beach Esplanade, Gower Point; (604) 886-2887; French/west coast

PARKSVILLE

Creek House Restaurant; 1025 Lee Road, #1; (604)* 248-3214; Italian/Greek/fresh seafood/more

Kalvas Restaurant; 180 Molliet; (604)* 248-6933; seafood/European

PORT HARDY

Brigg Seafood House; Market and Granville Streets; (604)* 949-6532

Sportsman's Steak & Seafood House; Market Street; (604)* 949-7811

QUALICUM BEACH

G. Willies; 710 Memorial in the village; (604)* 752-1050; deli/cafe with varied menu for all appetites/kids menu

Kalvas Restaurant; 180 North Moillet, Parksville; (604)* 248-6933; seafood with a European touch

Sand Pebbles Inn; 2767 West Island Highway; (604)* 752-6974; fabulous views

Tudor House Restaurant; 3336 West Island Highway; (604)* 752-6053; British and Continental

ROBERTS CREEK

The Creekhouse; Roberts Creek Road and Beach Avenue; (604) 885-9321; Continental

*Area code *250* effective October, 1996

DINING HIGHLIGHTS - BRITISH COLUMBIA

SECHELT
Blue Heron Inn; East Porpoise Bay Road; (604) 885-3847; waterfront fine dining

Keepers Restaurant; Porpoise Bay; (604) 885-4994

SIDNEY
Blue Peter Pub & Restaurant; 2270 Harbour Road; (604)* 656-4551; waterfront seafood

Cafe Mozart; 2470 Beacon Avenue; (604)* 655-1554; fine dining

Deep Cove Chalet; 11190 Chalet Road, Deep Cove; (604)* 656-3541; Continental with a light touch/fine dining

The Latch; 2328 Harbour Road; (604)* 656-6622; Continental/seafood in elegant historic waterfront home

Marg's Bleue Moon Cafe; 9535 Canora Road; (604)* 655-4450; pub-style restaurant

Newport House; 9853 Seaport Place; (604)* 656-3320; waterfront pasta/seafood/lunch/dinner

Odyssia Steak House; 9785 5th Street; (604)* 656-5596; pasta/steaks/pizza

Pelicano's Cafe and Bakery; 9851 Seaport Place; (604)* 655-4116; coffee/muffins/lunch on waterfront

The Stonehouse Pub; 2215 Canoe Cove; (604)* 656-3498; pub fare in old English character house

SOOKE
The Breakers; West Coast Road, Jordan River; (604)* 646-2079; varied seafood

Good Life, A Bookstore Cafe; 2113 Otter Point Road; (604)* 642-6821; fresh local specialties

Margison House; 6605 Sooke Road; (604)* 642-3620; lunch and afternoon tea

Mom's Cafe; 2036 Shields Road; (604)* 642-3314; hearty house-made dishes

Sooke Harbour House; 1528 Whiffen Spit Road; (604)* 642-3421; pacific northwest/fresh local seafood/fine dining

TOFINO
Orca Lodge Restaurant; 1200 block of Pacific Rim Highway; (604)* 725-2323; northwest coastal

VANCOUVER
Anton's Pasta Bar; 4260 East Hastings Street, North Burnaby; (604) 299-6636

Athene's Restaurant; 3618 West Broadway; (604) 731-4135; Greek

Avenue Grill; 2114 West 41st Avenue; (604) 266-8183; west coast/good salmon

Area code 250 effective October, 1996

DINING HIGHLIGHTS - BRITISH COLUMBIA

VANCOUVER (continued)

Beans Brothers; 2179 West 41st Avenue; (604) 266-2185; deli style/good deserts

Bishop's; 2183 West 4th Avenue; (604) 738-2025; contemporary home cooking

Bon Japanese; 53 West Broadway; (604) 872-0088; Japanese

Bridges; 1696 Duranlean, Granville Island; (604) 687-4400; fresh seafood

Cafe Norte; 3108 Edgemont Boulevard, North Vancouver; (604) 255-1188; Mexican

Cafe Roma; 60 Semisch Street North at Esplanade, North Vancouver; (604) 984-0274; Italian

The Cannery; 2205 Commissioner Street; (604) 254-9606; fine seafood dining on waterfront

Capers; 2285 West 4th Avenue; (604) 739-6685; cafe/deli/market emphasizing organic, vegetarian dishes

Chesa Restaurant; 1734 Marine Drive, West Vancouver; (604) 922-2411; Continental/west coast

Cincin; 1154 Robson Street; (604) 688-7338; Mediterranean

Daisy Garden Restaurant; 2163 East Hastings Street; (604) 255-6783; authentic Chinese cooking

Isadora's; 1540 Old Bridge Street, Granville Island; (604) 681-8816; seafood/meats/vegetarian/child-friendly

Kettle of Fish; 900 Pacific Street; (604) 682-6661; fresh seafood

La Cucina; 1509 Marine Drive, North Vancouver; (604) 986-1334; northern Italian

La Toque Blanche; 4368 Marine Drive, West Vancouver; (604) 926-1006; Continental

Le Crocodile; 909 Burrard Street; (604) 669-4298; fine dining/French

Maria's Taverna; 2324 West 4th Avenue; (604) 731-4722; Greek

The Naam; 2724 West 4th Avenue; (604) 738-7151; vegetarian

Nyala Ethiopian Restaurant; 2930 West 4th Avenue; (604) 731-7899

Pasparos Taverna; 132 West 3rd Street, North Vancouver; (604) 980-0331; Greek

Raga; 1177 Broadway; (604) 733-1127; Indian

Raintree; 1630 Alberni Street; (604) 688-5570; northwest coast

Red Onion; 2028 West 41st Avenue; (604) 263-8033; burgers/salads

Salmon House on the Hill; 2229 Folkestone Way, West Vancouver; (604) 926-3212

The Savoury Restaurant; 4390 Gallant Ave, #107C, Deep Cove; (604) 929-2373

Sawasdee; 4250 Main Street; (604) 876-4030; Thai

*Area code **250** effective October, 1996*

DINING HIGHLIGHTS - BRITISH COLUMBIA

VANCOUVER (continued)

Scoozi's; 808 West Hastings Street; (604) 684-1009; French cafe/great soups

Shijo; 1926 West 4th Avenue; (604) 732-4676; Japanese

Sophie's Cosmic Cafe; 2095 West 4th Avenue; (604) 732-6810; eclectic menu

Star* Anise; 1485 West 12th Avenue; (604) 737-1485; local ingredients with a French flair

Szechuan Chongqing Restaurant; 1668 West Broadway; (604) 734-1668

Tojo's; #202-777 West Broadway; (604) 872-8050; Japanese specialties by master sushi chef

Tomato Fresh Food Cafe; 3305 Cambie Street; (604) 874-6020; healthful, tasty, homemade dishes in one of city's oldest diners

Top of Vancouver Revolving Restaurant; Harbour Center, 555 West Hastings Street; (604) 669-2220; international

Vong's Kitchen; 4298 Fraser Street at 26th; (604) 879-4298; Chinese

Water Street Cafe; 300 Water Street; (604) 689-2832; west coast

Zeppos; 1967 West Broadway; (604) 737-7444; Italian

VICTORIA

Adrienne's Tea Garden Restaurant; 5325 Cordova Bay Road; (604)* 658-1535; Continental

Banana Belt Cafe; 281 Menzies Street; (604)* 385-9616

The Bird of Paradise Pub; 4291A Glanford Avenue; (604)* 727-2568; Mediterranean/pub fare

Blethering Place; 206-2250 Oak Bay Avenue; (604)* 598-1413; British

Camille's Fine Westcoast Dining; 45 Bastion Square; (604)* 381-3433; west coast contemporary

Chantecler Restaurant; 4509 West Saanich Road; (604)* 727-3344; Continental

The Clubhouse at Cordova Bay Golf Course; 5333 Cordova Bay Road; (604)* 658-4075; casual dining for breakfast/lunch/dinner

Columbo's Restaurant; 7855 East Saanich Road, Saanichton; (604)* 652-3936; Greek pasta dishes/more

Colwood Corners Pub; 1889 Island Highway; (604)* 478-1311

Country Rose Pub; 592 Ledsham Street; (604)* 478-4200; English pub

Da Tandoor Restaurant; 1010 Fort Street; (604)* 384-6333; Indian

Four Mile House Tea Room & Restaurant; 199 Island Highway; (604)* 479-2514; tea room/pub/restaurant in historic roadhouse

Green Cuisine; 5-560 Johnson; (604)* 385-1809; vegetarian

Harbour House Restaurant; 607 Oswego Street; (604)* 386-1244; seafood/steaks

Herald Street Caffe; 546 Herald Street; (604)* 381-1441; Italian/Continental

Area code 250 effective October, 1996

DINING HIGHLIGHTS - BRITISH COLUMBIA

VICTORIA (continued)

Il Terrazzo; 555 Johnson Street; (604)* 361-0028; Italian

James Bay Tea Room; 332 Menzies Street; (604)* 382-8282; British

John's Place; 723 Pandora Avenue; (604)* 389-0711; house-made fresh and innovative breakfast/lunch/dinnerKaz Japanese; 100-1619 Store Street; (604)* 386-9121

Le Valentine; 739 Pandora Avenue; (604)* 385-2233; northern French/creperie

My-Chosen Cafe; 4480 Happy Valley Road; (604)* 474-2333; west coast casual

Oak Bay Beach Hotel; 1175 Beach Road; (604)* 598-4556; afternoon tea/pub fare in the snug

Olde England Inn; 429 Lampson Street; (604)* 388-4353; English/prime rib

The Oxford Arms Pub & Restaurant; 301 Cook Street; (604)* 382-3301; international/pub fare

Pablo's Dining Lounge; 225 Quebec Street; (604)* 388-4255; French Continental

The Parsonage Cafe; 1115 North Park; (604)* 383-5999; country-style Scottish home cooking

Periklis Greek Restaurant; 531 Yates Street;p(604)* 386-3313

Princess Mary; 358 Harbor; (604)* 386-3456; vessel restaurant

Re-bar; 50 Bastion Square; (604)* 361-9223; vegetarian

Rebecca's; 1127 Wharf Street; (604)* 380-6999; view dining

Romeo's Place; 760 Johnson, downtown; (604)* 383-2121; pizza

Romeo's Place; 122-2945 Jacklin, Langford; (604)* 474-2121; pizza

Romeo's Place; 1581 Hillside, Victoria East; (604)* 595-0212; pizza

Romeo's Place; 777 Royal Oak Drive, Broadmead; (604)* 744-1177; pizza

Sam's Deli; 805 Government Street; (604)* 382-8424; soups/sandwiches

Soho Village Bistro; 1311 Gladstone Avenue; (604)* 384-3344; eclectic menu

Spinnakers Brew Pub; 308 Catherine Street; (604)* 386-2739; brew pub/lunch/snacks/dinner

Swan's Pub; 506 Pandora Avenue; (604)* 361-3310; pub fare

The Swiss Restaurant; 1280 Fairfield Road; (604)* 384-6446; Swiss/European

Thai Siam; 1314 Government Street; (604)* 383-9911; Thai

*Area code **250** effective October, 1996*

*I journeyed fur,
I journeyed fas';
I glad I foun' de place at las'!*

--Joel Chandler Harris,
<u>Nights with Uncle Remus</u>

INDEX OF CITIES AND TOWNS

BRITISH COLUMBIA

Brackendale, see Squamish . . 214
Campbell River 179
Chemainus. 180
Courtenay 181–182
Galiano Island 183–185
Gibsons. 186–187
Invermere 188
Kelowna 189–190
Kootenay Bay 191
Ladner 192
Langley. 193
Mill Bay 194
Nelson 195–196
North Delta 197
Parksville 198
Quadra Island 199–200
Qualicum Beach. 201–203
Quathiaski Cove, see
   Quadra Island 200
Roberts Creek 204–206
Saanichton. 207
Salt Spring Island 208–209
Sechelt 210
Sidney 211
Sooke 212–213
Squamish. 214
Surrey. 215
Tofino 216–218
Vancouver. 219–224
Vernon 225–227
Victoria 228–241
White Rock 242

CALIFORNIA

Ahwahnee 18–19
Albion 20
Arroyo Grande. 21
Bishop 22
Bolinas 23
Brentwood. 24
Cambria 25–27
Carmichael, see
   Sacramento Area 52

CALIFORNIA (continued)

Chico. 28
Clearlake 29–30
Crescent City 31
Davenport. 32
El Cerrito, see
   San Francisco - East Bay . . 63
Eureka. 33
Gilroy 34
Half Moon Bay 35
Idyllwild. 36
Inverness 37
Ione. 38
Los Angeles 39–40
Mariposa 41–42
Mendocino 43
Montara, see
   Half Moon Bay 35
Muir Beach. 44
Novato. 45
Orland 46
Pasadena 47
Point Reyes Station 48
Red Bluff 49
Redding 50
Sacramento. 51
Sacramento Area 52
San Anselmo. 53
San Diego. 54–57
San Francisco 58–62
San Francisco - East Bay 63
Santa Barbara 64
Santa Clara 65
Sonora 66
Springville 67
St. Helena 68
Tahoe City 69
Tahoe Paradise 70
Three Rivers. 71–72
Watsonville. 73–74
Westport 75
Whittier 76
Yosemite West, see
   Yosemite National Park. . . 77

INDEX OF CITIES AND TOWNS

OREGON

Ashland 97
Astoria 98
Beaverton 99
Bend 100
Brookings 101
Coos Bay 102
Corvallis 103
Eugene 104–105
Garibaldi 106
Gold Beach 107
Government Camp, see
    Mount Hood Area 114
Grants Pass 108
Hood River 109
Jacksonville 110
Lafayette 111
Lincoln City 112
McMinnville 113
Mount Hood Area 114
Newberg 115–116
Newport 117–118
Oakland 119
Port Orford 120
Portland 121–123
Roseburg 124
Salem 125
Seaside 126
Sisters 127
Tillamook 128
Westfir 129

WASHINGTON

Aberdeen 139
Anacortes 140–141
Ashford 142
Bellevue 143–144
Friday Harbor 158
Gig Harbor 145
Issaquah 146
La Conner 147
Leavenworth 148
Maple Falls 149
Maple Valley 150
Mercer Island 151–152
Morton 153
Port Townsend 154
Puyallup 155
Redmond 156
Renton 157
San Juan Island -
    Friday Harbor 158
Seattle 159–163
Spokane 164
Tacoma 165–166
Vashon Island 167

INDEX OF B&Bs BY NAME

BRITISH COLUMBIA

Ambleside B&B 228	Jolie Maison B&B 222
Beach House, The 181	Kitchener House 208
Beachside B&B 219	Laird House 234
Bellhouse Inn, The 183	Maple Tree Lane B&B 194
Bender's B&B 229	Maria Rose B&B, The 227
Bird Song Cottage B&B 180	Marina View B&B 198
Blue Willow B&B 201	Moonshadows Guest House . . 184
Bonnie Belle B&B 199	Netty's B&B 216
Bonniebrook Lodge 186	Ocean View Cottage 187
Carriage Stop B&B 230	Olive House 235
Castle on the Mountain 225	Orca View 185
Cedaridge Country Estate B&B 193	Orchard House B&B 211
Chateau Christian Laurenn B&B 189	Peace & Plenty B&B 213
	Penny Farthing Inn, The 223
Country Cottage B&B 205	Pier House B&B 179
Crow's Nest, The 231	Quatna Manor 203
Delphine Lodge Country Inn B&B 188	River Run Cottages 192
	Roberts Creek, B&B at 204
Dorrington B&B 242	Scholefield House 236
Eagles Rest B&B 232	Seaview B&B 237
Emory House 195	Summerhill Guest House . . . 209
Four Winds B&B 210	Sunshine Hills B&B 197
Glacier Valley Farm 214	Tara Shanti Retreat B&B . . . 191
Grapevine B&B, The 190	Tide's Inn on Duffin Cove, The 217
Grauer's Getaway Destination B&B 202	Top O'Triangle Mountain . . . 238
Greystone Manor 182	Treehouse B&B 224
Harbourlight B&B 226	Vacationer, The 239
Hartmann House B&B 212	Wellington B&B 240
Inn on St. Andrews, The 233	White Heather Guest House . 215
Inn on the Garden 196	Willows Inn, The 206
Jane's Gourmet B&B 220	Wilp Gybuu 218
Joha's Eagleview 200	Wintercott Country House . . 207
Johnson House, The 221	Wooded Acres B&B 241

251

INDEX OF B&Bs BY NAME

CALIFORNIA

Abigail's 51	Judy's B&B 68
Annie's B&B. 67	Knighttime B&B. 74
Argonaut House. 65	Lamorte, Mario & Suellen . . . 53
Artists' Inn, The 47	Lavender Hill B&B 66
Bears at the Beach B&B 54	Marina Gardens 61
Big Canyon B&B. 29	Matlick House, The. 22
Blom House B&B 55	Mendocino Farmhouse. 43
Carole's B&B 56	Moffatt House 62
Casa Arguello 58	Muir Beach B&B 44
Casa Mia B&B 45	Muktip Manor 30
Casabel 63	New Davenport B&B. 32
Chalet A-Capella 70	Norja B&B Inn. 39
Chaney House. 69	Ocean View House 64
Coleen's California Casa 76	Old Town B&B Inn. 33
Cort Cottage 71	Palisades Paradise B&B. 50
Country Rose Inn B&B. 34	Pebble Beach B&B 31
Diablo Vista 24	Pelennor B&B, The. 42
Elsbree House B&B 57	PineStone B&B By The Sea . . 25
Esplanade B&B, The 28	Salisbury House 40
Faulkner House, The 49	Seaview Through the Pines. . . 26
Finch Haven B&B 41	Silver Spur B&B. 18
Garden Room, The 72	Terri's Homestay 37
Garden Studio, The 59	Thirty-nine Cypress. 48
Goose & Turrets B&B, The . . 35	Thomas' White House Inn . . . 23
Guest House, The 21	Villa Carota 73
Heirloom B&B, The. 38	Waldschloss B&B 77
Herb'n Inn, The 60	Whispering Pines 27
Howard Creek Ranch 75	Wilkum Inn 36
Inn at Shallow Creek Farm . . . 46	Wool Loft, The 20
Johnson's Studio,	Yosemite's Apple
Mary and Bruce. 52	Blossom Inn B&B 19

INDEX OF B&Bs BY NAME

OREGON

Abed and Breakfast. 103
Alderstreet B&B. 113
Beckley House B&B, The . . . 119
Blue Haven Inn 128
Brey House Ocean
  View B&B, The 112
Cascade Avenue B&B. 109
Cascade Country Inn. 127
Clinkerbrick House, The. . . . 121
Cottonwood Cottage B&B . . . 125
Country House, The 104
Endicott Gardens 107
Falcon's Crest Inn 114
Flery Manor B&B 108
Georgian House B&B 122
HOME by the SEA. 120
House in the Woods, The . . . 105
House of Hunter. 124
Inn-Chanted B&B, The 98
Kelty Estate. 111
Oar House B&B. 117
Oceancrest House. 101
Pelican's Perch B&B 106
Portland Guest House 123
Reames House 1868 110
Sather House, The 100
Secluded B&B 115
Spring Creek Llama
  Ranch and B&B 116
Summer House. 126
Tyee Lodge 118
Upper Room Chalet 102
Westfir Lodge,
  A B&B Inn 129
Woods House
  B&B Inn, The 97
Yankee Tinker B&B, The 99

WASHINGTON

Albatross B&B 140
Angels of the Sea. 167
Bacon Mansion, The 159
Bosch Garten B&B 148
Capitol Hill House B&B. . . . 160
Cascade View B&B, A. 143
Channel House 141
Commencement Bay B&B. . . 165
Cooney Mansion B&B 139
Cottage Creek Inn B&B 156
Dibble House 161
Duck-In B&B 151
Hart's Tayberry House. 155
Holly Hedge House-
  A Private Retreat 157
Holly Hill House 154
Maple Valley B&B 150
Marianna Stoltz House 164
Mildred's B&B 162
Mole House B&B 152
Mountain Meadows Inn 142
Mountains and Planes B&B. . 146
Peacock Hill Guest House. . . 145
Petersen B&B 144
Prince of Wales. 163
St. Helens Manorhouse. 153
Tower House B&B 158
Villa, The. 166
White Swan Guest
  House, The. 147
Yodeler Inn 149

253

APPLICATION TO LIST YOUR B&B IN
BED & BREAKFAST HOMES -
BEST OF THE WEST COAST

Host Name(s) _____

B&B Name _____

Mailing address _____

City/State/Zip _____
City/Province/Postal Code

Telephone _____

Best time to phone you _____

Brief description of your home and room(s) available: _____

_____

_____

_____

_____

_____

_____

_____

CUT HERE

There is a two-year listing fee which is equal to two times your average double occupancy rate for one night's lodging. Example: If your average room rate is $75, the listing fee is $150. Hosts must maintain clean, comfortable accommodations, a hospitable manner toward guests, and guarantee rates for the first year of the listing. Fee is payable upon author's visit. Normal deadline is mid-summer of odd number years for the next year's edition

Signature _____

Date _____

From

```
FIRST
CLASS
POSTAGE
```

George Winsley
Knighttime Publications
PO Box 128
Jacksonville, OR 97530

---------------- FOLD HERE ---------------

CUT HERE

STAPLE OR TAPE

B&B TRAVELERS REPORT

Knighttime Publications would like to receive any comments you may have about your experiences while using this directory. Please report any comment, suggestion, compliment or criticism as indicated:

Name and location of B&B _____

Date of visit _____

Length of stay _____

Comments _____

_____

_____

_____

_____

_____

_____

_____

_____

_____

_____

_____

_____

Your name _____

Address _____

City/State/Zip_____
City/Province/Postal Code

Telephone (optional) _____

CUT HERE

From

```
FIRST
CLASS
POSTAGE
```

George Winsley
Knighttime Publications
PO Box 128
Jacksonville, OR 97530

-------------------- FOLD HERE -----------------

CUT HERE

STAPLE OR TAPE

B&B TRAVELERS REPORT

Knighttime Publications would like to receive any comments you may have about your experiences while using this directory. Please report any comment, suggestion, compliment or criticism as indicated:

Name and location of B&B _____

Date of visit _____

Length of stay _____

Comments _____

_____

_____

_____

_____

_____

_____

_____

_____

_____

_____

_____

_____

_____

Your name _____

Address _____

City/State/Zip_____
City/Province/Postal Code

Telephone _____

CUT HERE

From

FIRST
CLASS
POSTAGE

George Winsley
Knighttime Publications
PO Box 128
Jacksonville, OR 97530

---------------- FOLD HERE ---------------

CUT HERE

STAPLE OR TAPE

ORDERING ADDITIONAL BOOKS

Please send me: (I enclose payment with order)

_____additional copies of *BED & BREAKFAST HOMES - BEST OF THE WEST COAST* (9th edition) at **$14.95** each. For shipping via book rate enclose **$2.00** postage and handling for first copy, plus **$1.00** for each additional copy to the same address. For 1st Class postage send $3.00 per copy.

Canadian residents, please send payment in U.S. funds or current equivalent in Canadian fund using the above pricing.

Name _____

Address _____

City/State/Zip_____
City/Province/Postal Code

Send as a gift to: (Use extra paper for additional gifts)

Name _____

Address _____

City/State/Zip_____
City/Province/Postal Code

Gift card should read: _____

Mail this form with payment to:

KNIGHTTIME PUBLICATIONS
PO Box 128
Jacksonville, OR 97530

CUT HERE

From

FIRST
CLASS
POSTAGE

George Winsley
Knighttime Publications
PO Box 128
Jacksonville, OR 97530

---------------- FOLD HERE ----------------

CUT HERE

ORDERING ADDITIONAL BOOKS

Please send me: (I enclose payment with order)

_____additional copies of *BED & BREAKFAST HOMES - BEST OF THE WEST COAST* (9th edition) at **$14.95** each. For shipping via book rate enclose **$2.00** postage and handling for first copy, plus **$1.00** for each additional copy to the same address. For 1st Class postage send $3.00 per copy.

Canadian residents, please send payment in U.S. funds or current equivalent in Canadian fund using the above pricing.

Name _____

Address _____

City/State/Zip_____
City/Province/Postal Code

Send as a gift to: (Use extra paper for additional gifts)

Name _____

Address _____

City/State/Zip_____
City/Province/Postal Code

Gift card should read:_____

Mail this form with payment to:

KNIGHTTIME PUBLICATIONS
PO Box 128
Jacksonville, OR 97530

CUT HERE

From

```
         FIRST
         CLASS
         POSTAGE
```

George Winsley
Knighttime Publications
PO Box 128
Jacksonville, OR 97530

---------------- FOLD HERE ----------------

CUT HERE